Refining the Elixir

練
丹

Refining the Elixir

練 丹

*The Internal Alchemy Teachings of
Taoist Immortal Zhang Sanfeng*

Translation and Commentary
by Stuart Alve Olson

Valley Spirit Arts
Phoenix, Arizona

This work is part of the **Daoist Immortal Three Peaks Zhang Series**, presenting translations on the teachings of the great immortal Zhang Sanfeng. The first volume, *Tai Ji Quan Treatise: Attributed to the Song Dynasty Daoist Priest Zhang Sanfeng* by Stuart Alve Olson, was published in 2011.

Note: The preferred Pinyin spellings of Chinese terms is used throughout the book except in the spellings of *Tao, Taoist,* and *Taoism.* Spelling Tao with a "T" instead of a "D" is more common and recognizable in English.

Copyright © 2016 by Stuart Alve Olson.

All rights reserved. No part of this book may be reproduced or used in any form or by any means, electronic or mechanical, including photocopying, recording, or by any information storage and retrieval system, without prior written permission from Stuart Alve Olson and Valley Spirit Arts.

Library of Congress Control Number: 2016934381
ISBN-13: 978-1-5302-2055-7
ISBN-10: 1-5302-2055-6

Valley Spirit Arts, LLC
www.valleyspiritarts.com
contact@valleyspiritarts.com

Frontispiece image of Immortal Zhang Sanfeng. Early Qing dynasty. Taken from *The Complete Book of Zhang Sanfeng* (張三豐全書, *Zhang Sanfeng Quan Shi*) by Li Xiyue (李西月), 1844. Original source of artwork unknown.

Dedication

*To the two great men who turned my life upside down
so I could hopefully become right side up,
Chan Master Hsuan Hua
and Taijiquan Master T.T. Liang.*

Acknowledgments

To Master T.T. Liang for opening the door to this incredible world of internal alchemy.

Many thanks and much appreciation to those individuals who so kindly lent their support to the publication of this work: Joseph Greer, Wayne Gaige, and Knut Gollenbeck.

Much appreciation to Patrick Gross for his typesetting and editing skills in making this an actual book.

To all my students, past and present, for all their questions, support, and encouragement on this path and science of inner discovery. As Master Liang often pointed out, "Teaching is the best teacher." I bow in deepest gratitude to all.

Contents

Preface 1
Timeline of Zhang Sanfeng's Life 7
Introduction 11
The Great Process 41
   Important Terms in Internal Alchemy 44
      Dan (Elixir) 45
      Tian (Field) 47
      Ming Men (Life Gate) 49
      Sheng Men (Mortality Gate) 49
      Jing Men (Essence Gate) 49
      San Bao (Three Treasures) 52
      Dumai and Renmai (Control and Function) Meridians 53
The Fire and Water Processes 55
   The Four Stages of Internal Alchemy Practice 58
   Water (Shui)—Reverting Jing 67
      Blood 69
      Saliva 70
      Tears 76
      Sweat 77
      Sexual Secretions 78
      Bone Marrow & Brain Marrow 80
   Fire (Huo)—Mobilizing the Qi 84
      Mobilization of Qi 86
      Dao Yin and Tu Na 89
      Embryonic Breathing 90
      Natural Breath 94

Triple Warmer 95
The Eight Extraordinary Meridians 98
The Twelve Major Qi Cavities and Seven Chakras
    of the Body 105
Three Barriers on the Front and Back 110
Nine Restorations 113
True Breath 123
Returning Spirit to the Void 127
Conclusion 141

The Great Process for Refining the Elixir Treatise 145
    Upper Verses on the Great Process
        for Refining the Elixir 147
    Lower Verses on the Great Process
        for Refining the Elixir 177
Verses on Seated Meditation 195
Verses on the Sleeping Immortal 233
Ancestor Lu's One Hundred Character Tablet 263

History of Zhang Sanfeng 285
    The Creation of Taijiquan 287
    Legends of Zhang Sanfeng 289
    Teachings of Zhang Sanfeng 295
    The Ming Emperors and Zhang Sanfeng 298
    Written Records of Zhang Sanfeng 300
    Disciples of Zhang Sanfeng 302
    Dating the Text of *Refining the Elixir Treatise* 305
    Conclusion 305

Suggested Reading 307
About the Translator 309
About the Publisher and Sanctuary of Tao 316

Preface

My introduction to internal alchemy occurred in the early 1970s when I first read Lu Kuan Yu's *Taoist Yoga*.[1] Admittedly, I understood little of what the book was saying as the terminology was way beyond my understanding at that time. Later in 1979 while residing at the City of Ten Thousand Buddhas in Ukiah, California, I had the good fortune of listening to the abbot, Chan Master Hsuan Hua, address many questions about what participants in the Chan sessions were experiencing—such as sensing heat developing in the lower abdomen, noticing the movements of qi, and feeling vibrations within the body. All this reminded me of what I had read in *Taoist Yoga*, and my interest in internal alchemy was rekindled. Then in 1982 I was privileged to befriend and live with Taijiquan master T.T. Liang, and through him the teachings of internal alchemy sparked a lifelong preoccupation. Since then I have studied and practiced internal alchemy texts incessantly, resulting in the formation of this book.

I have yet to fully accomplish what the texts describe as "Forming the Elixir," and certainly haven't achieved any of the stages of immortality. My inner experiences connected to internal alchemy have been many, but they've also been

---

1 *Taoist Yoga: Alchemy & Immortality* by Lu K'uan Yu (Charles Luk) (Samuel Weiser, 1973).

Refining the Elixir

sporadic due to "life" getting in the way. Youthful endeavors, arrogance, laziness, and economic setbacks have been the main culprits for lulls in my practice, but I've found that with age and experience, my practice has become much more consistent and powerful.

Writing this book has also been a healing process, encouraging me further and, in many ways, bringing a sense of contentment I did not possess earlier in my life. I do not practice or study these teachings for the purpose of living forever, rather I follow them as a way to leave this world in better condition than when I arrived, and hopefully to complete the work of immortalizing my spirit. My life, especially my spiritual life, has been blessed. I was lucky enough to live at the City of Ten Thousand Buddhas for nine months while the great Chan master Hsuan Hua was still alive, becoming a disciple of his and meeting so many incredible people during my time there, and most fortunately to be there during Hsuan Hua's almost daily lectures on chapter 39 of the *Hua Yen Jing* (華嚴經, *Avatamsaka Sutra*), the "Travels of Sudhana (Jade Youth)." Then to have met and be invited to live with Master T.T. Liang and his family, to travel with him and become, as he claimed, "his adopted son." This also afforded me additional opportunities to meet with many other great teachers and persons, both in America and abroad.

In a curious way my connection to the practice of internal alchemy stems from an unusual endowment of mine. I am one of those rare humans who can remember

Preface

things from six months of age. I can remember the clothes I wore, the wallpaper behind my crib, throwing formula bottles, and a host of other things and events. This shocked my mother when I would describe memories from being in the crib. This ability has also allowed me to recall some of the sensations that occurred in my body during my adolescence and youth, and much of it is exactly what these ancient internal alchemists talked about in their teachings. Once I grasped what internal alchemy was, it became familiar to me and something I could do if I put forth the right effort. To this end I have sometimes failed and sometimes succeeded, but I console myself with the idea that all of it has been positively cumulative.

Although I put great effort into this book, it can only serve as an overview of the "Great Process." The true details of this practice are to be found and discovered in the internal alchemy texts written by the great masters of this art. My words can never hope to reach the height and profundity of their contributions, so for those who seek to pursue this practice, begin by studying the foundational works. For example: *The Scripture on Tao and Virtue* (道德經, *Tao De Jing*), *Zhuang Zi* (莊子), *Lie Zi* (列子), *Secret of the Supreme One's Golden Flower* (太乙金華宗旨, *Tai Yi Jin Hua Zong Zhi*), *Yellow Court Scripture* (黃庭經, *Huang Ting Jing*), and *Jade Tablet Decrees on Nature and Life* (性命圭旨, *Xing Ming Gui Zhi*), along with the weft texts of the *Yin Convergence Scripture* (陰符經, *Yin Fu Jing*), *Clarity and Tranquility of the Constant Scripture* (清靜常經, *Qing Jing Chang Jing*), *Jade*

Refining the Elixir

Pivot Treasury Scripture (玉樞寶經, *Yu Shu Bao Jing*), *Jade Emperor's Mind Seal Scripture* (玉皇心印經, *Yu Huang Xin Yin Jing*), and *The Exalted One's Treatise on Actions and Retributions* (感應篇, *Gan Ying Pian*).

These works provide the foundation for internal alchemy practice. As you become more adept, continue your studies with the *Scripture on Supreme Clarity* (太清經, *Tai Qing Jing*), Zhang Boduan's *Understanding Reality* (悟真篇, *Wu Zhen Pian*) and *Four Hundred Words on the Golden Elixir* (四百字金丹, *Si Bai Zi Jin Dan*), Wei Boyang's *Book of Zhou Seal of the Triple Unity* (周易參同契, *Zhou Yi Can Tong Qi*), and definitely *Master of Embracing Simplicity* (抱朴子, *Bao Pu Zi*) by Ge Hong (葛洪, 283–343 CE), the first recorded work on an individual's search for immortality, and his work *Biographies of Divine Immortals* (神仙傳, *Shen Xian Zhuan*).

Contained herein are four internal alchemy texts attributed to the Song dynasty (宋朝, 960–1279 CE) Taoist immortal Zhang Sanfeng, which, in my opinion, well represent the teachings of *Refining the Elixir*. First are the texts on *The Great Process for Refining the Elixir Treatise*, given in two sections, Upper and Lower. Then follow the *Verses on Seated Meditation*, *The Sleeping Immortal*, and lastly *Zhang Sanfeng's Commentary on Lu Zi's One Hundred Word Discourse*. My commentaries are included with each text. I have also written lengthy introductory sections to cover many aspects of the internal alchemy practice and tradition that haven't been gathered in one place before.

Preface

This book is not attempting to define a "one and only way" of performing internal alchemy, rather I wanted to present an overview of the concepts and processes so readers could comfortably select what practices they might wish to explore, or to help clarify the purposes of their existing practice. For the most part, this book is about trying to define internal alchemy in the most succinct, but thorough, manner I could provide.

The practice of internal alchemy is actually quite simple, but the theory and philosophy behind it can be complex. This book represents my perspective on internal alchemy. From more than forty years of study and practice, I have formulated my views of this intensive and extensive subject, and sometimes my interpretations are not always traditional or academic. Also, I hope the reader will understand and forgive some of the repetition that occurs throughout the book. This can't be helped as each of the four texts often address the same issues, and in many cases the explanations of certain terms are repeated for clarity of the subject at hand. This work is by no means a definitive exposition of internal alchemy, as the subject and existing Chinese sources are so numerous. But what is provided here, I believe, will greatly add to the perception and knowledge of all those practicing or having interest in internal alchemy.

Lastly, this has been a longtime work in progress (I began writing it in 2006), and I've tried to present these teachings in an understandable language and manner. In

Refining the Elixir

light of this approach, I also take responsibility for any errors or confusing aspects that may occur.

My reverent hope is that this book proves valuable to the reader, either providing some motivation to those who wish to undertake the study of internal alchemy or revealing some nugget of insight to those already engaged in the art.

Stuart Alve Olson
Spring 2016

Timeline of Zhang Sanfeng's Life

This overview of Zhang Sanfeng's life and the fuller biography at the back of the book are as important to study as the works he left behind. Zhang was one of the greatest internal alchemists in Chinese history whose attributed writings left an indelible mark upon the art and practice. He reportedly lived 170 years and in so many ways became the model of what we now think of as a Taoist "cloud wandering"[2] immortal.

Song (宋) dynasty (960 to 1279)
1247 Born either in the northeastern province
 of Liaoning or in the southeastern province
 on Dragon-Tiger Mountain.
 Name Used: Quan Yi (全一), birth name.
1256 At age 9, he started studying Buddhism
 under Chan master Hai Yun.
 Names Used: Jun Shi (君室), Jun Bao (君寶).

---

2   *Cloud Wanderer* (雲路, Yun Lu) refers to a Taoist who wanders about mountain regions looking for hermit teachers or is simply seeking to escape from all worldly affairs and live within nature.

Refining the Elixir

Yuan (元) dynasty (1279 to 1368)

1290 At age 43, he left his family and position as County Magistrate in Liaoning to cultivate the Tao.
Name Used: Yu Xu Zi (玉虛子), self-given cultivation name.

1294 At age 47, he met Xuan Du and was initiated as a Taoist priest.
Name Used: Zhang Tong (張通).

1303 At age 56, he faked his death at Golden Terrace Monastery in western Shensi.
Names Used: Zhang Tong, Xuan Xuan (玄玄).

1325 At age 78, he met Fire Dragon Immortal on Ge Hong Mountain.
Name Used: Xuan Hua (玄化).

1329 At age 82, he left Ge Hong Mountain and entered the Wu Dang Mountains. Created Taijiquan during these years.
Name Used: Xuan Hua.

1338 At age 91, he attained immortality.
Names Used: Xuan Hua, Zhang Sanfeng.

1339 At age 92, he left Wu Dang Mountain to cloud wander.
Name Used: Zhang Sanfeng.

Timeline of Zhang Sanfeng's Life

Ming (明) dynasty (1368 to 1644)

1379 The Jiang (姜) family reports Zhang (age 132) lived on their property in Sichuan province.
Name Used: Zhang Sanfeng.

1381 Reports of a Taoist priest called Dirty Immortal Zhang (age 134) start circulating throughout Sichuan and Guizhou provinces.

1385 At age 138, he escaped from Emperor Tai Zu, cloud wandered, and eventually went into hiding in Yunnan province until 1399.
Names Used: Qing Xu (清虛), Zhang Sanfeng.

1403 At age 156, Zhang met with Prince Jun.
Name Used: Zhang Sanfeng.

1410 At age 163, he reappeared either on Dragon-Tiger Mountain or Wu Dang Mountain.
Name Used: Zhang Sanfeng.

1417 At age 170, he ascended into the immortal realms.

Early Qing dynasty (清朝, Qing Chao, 1644–1912) painting of Zhang Sanfeng standing in meditation. Taken from *Collections on the Sect of Zhang Sanfeng Taoist Arts* (張三豐道術匯宗, *Zhang San Feng Tao Shu Hui Zong*). Original artist and source unknown.

Introduction

In present times most people are fairly certain about what meditation means, but when speaking about Taoist internal alchemy, especially in terms of it being a meditation, very few can define or explain it clearly.

In many ways, internal alchemy is a science, which isn't surprising because it developed from the work of the original scientists, Chinese alchemists, who had pursued the task of turning base metals into potable gold or seeking to create a physical compound called the Pill of Immortality (丹丸, Dan Wan). For a long time these pursuits were all external processes that made use of precise rituals, furnaces, cauldrons, and specialized ingredients. Later, internal alchemists framed their processes for creating their pill of immortality in the body through terms that were borrowed from the early alchemists.

The subject of alchemy in Taoism has two distinct approaches and traditions. One is the older and original form of actually using substances, mainly cinnabar, for concocting a medicine through metallurgical processes that would provide physical immortality, an actual pill of immortality for ingestion. Early alchemists believed that minerals were more powerful than herbs, and that herbs could only provide longevity, not immortality. The Song dynasty alchemist Ge Hong in his work *Master of*

Refining the Elixir

Embracing Simplicity provides an in-depth look at this tradition of metallurgical alchemy. Actually, early Taoism considered the metallurgical process, primarily that of producing potable gold as the basis for a pill of immortality, superior to the meditation methods of circulating qi in the body. Ge Hong states,

> The taking of medicines [potable gold] is the first and best requisite for enjoying immortality, but the associated practices of Mobilizing the Qi can greatly enhance a quick attainment of the goal. So if the medicine is not attainable, and only circulation of the breath can be practiced, a few hundred years of life could be achieved, provided the methods were carried out to their fullest measure.

The second approach, the basis of this book, is an alchemy based on using inherent biological substances of the body (called jing) along with the internal energies of the breath (qi) and spirit (shen) to forge a spiritual pill of immortality. Metallurgical alchemy had as its goal perpetual physical immortality, and the biological-spiritual alchemy (internal alchemy) equally promoted this perpetual physical immortality, but in the main was directed at the idea of immortalizing the spirit of a person so that even after death the spirit could function in clarity and direct itself to exist however it so chooses.

The processes for creating a metallurgical pill of immortality were quite intense and complex, taking months (or even years) to complete. The practices took

Introduction

great concentration and discipline, and have long been considered profound forms of meditation and cultivation in their own right.

In early Taoism, internal alchemy texts began to appear, such as the *Scripture on Supreme Clarity* and *Yellow Court Scripture*, along with subsequent texts of the *Yellow Emperor's Scripture on the Spiritual Elixir of the Nine Cauldrons* (黃帝九鼎神丹經, *Huang Di Jiu Ding Shen Dan Jing*), *Scripture of the Nine Elixirs* (九丹經, *Jin Dan Jing*), *Scripture on the Golden Elixir* (金丹經, *Jin Dan Jing*), and a numerous variety of other works directed at the process of meditative internal alchemy, compounds for producing a pill of immortality, and more religious-like rituals and guidelines for invoking the aid of spiritual immortals.

Remnants of the recipes and formulas of the old alchemists who attempted to turn base metals into gold or concoct a pill of immortality utilize metallurgical metaphors such as "true lead," "true mercury," "furnace," "fire times," and "cauldron." Differing works may rely on regenerative and reproductive metaphors for creating a "spiritual embryo" within the abdomen, a self-induced spiritual pregnancy. While other teachings present the idea of purifying and appeasing spirits in the interior body to assist in producing the Elixir Pill so the mortal can become immortal.

Yet another approach relies upon using the *Book of Changes* (易經, *Yi Jing*) as a guide for attaining immortality. There is also a method on restraining the three negative worm spirits in the body and illuminating the three positive

Refining the Elixir

bright spirits through the actions of good deeds. And still other methods use the practice of visualization of either a Golden Flower, Dragon Pearl, or Golden Pill of Immortality within the lower abdomen. So, throughout Taoism's long history hundreds of methods of internal alchemy have been written about and used by various sects and teachers, but the most popular texts and teachings generally fall into five main categories of methodology—each being represented by a major Taoist text.

1. Visualizations and invocations of inner spirits of the body to produce the Elixir of Immortality. This method of internal alchemy was introduced by Madame Wei Huacun (魏華存, 252–334 CE) in a work entitled *The Internal Illumination of the Yellow Court Scripture* (內景黃庭經, *Nei Jing Huang Ting Jing*). Although other Taoist teachers and schools had been exploring internal alchemy before her time, she is credited with having created the practice of employing the use of inner spirits to accomplish the goal of immortality.

In this method, the development of an interior world is used to create the means of purifying the body and mind for the state of immortality. The *Yellow Court* text is divided into two parts: the *External* and *Internal* illuminations. The *External Illumination* (attributed to Lao Zi) is divided into three sections that define the spirits of the Upper, Middle, and Lower Yellow Courts of the body (synonymous with the three Elixir Fields. The *Internal Illumination* text,

Introduction

written by Madame Wei Huacun, is divided into thirty-six chapters that define the processes and functions of the alchemy, namely using methods called Spiritual Force (耀靈, Yao Ling), Absorbing Mists (附霧, Fu Wu), and Thunder Rites (雷法, Lei Fa).

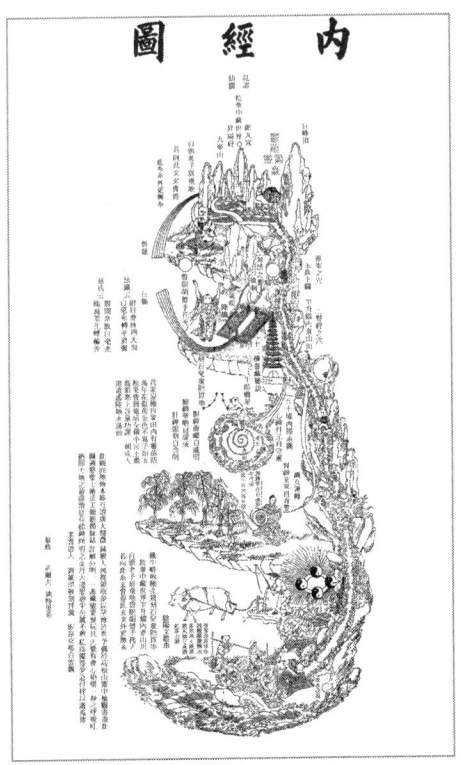

Illustration of the Nei Jing Tu (內經圖)
This "Internal Map of Channels" depicts the inner body and spirits as described in the *Yellow Court Scripture*. Source unknown, but most likely originating in fourth century CE.

Refining the Elixir

The actual date in which the *External Illumination* text was written is unknown, but it existed long before the time of Madame Wei Huacun as the text was mentioned in the *Master of Embracing Simplicity* by Ge Hong, but he makes no mention of Wei Huacun or of the Internal Illumination text of the *Yellow Court Scripture*.

2. Metallurgical terminology of the early alchemists. The *Jade Tablet Decrees on Nature and Life* (性命圭旨, Xing Ming Gui Zhi), the major text representing this area of internal alchemy, predominately draws from the external alchemy methods, using such metaphors as "lead" and "mercury" while also integrating regenerative terms like "spiritual child" and "forming an embryo within the lower Elixir Field." For the most part, the text is relating a method of circulating jing (essence, or fluids of the body) and qi (vital-breath energy) through the Eight Extraordinary Qi meridians (八奇經脈, Ba Qi Jing Mai) to achieve immortality. The *Jade Tablet Decrees on Nature and Life* makes clear the distinction between the meridian system of acupuncture (外丹, Wai Dan, or *External Elixir*) and the Eight Extraordinary Qi meridians associated with internal alchemy (內丹, Nei Dan, or *Internal Elixir*). Even though many meridians and acupuncture points share the same name and locations, the functions are entirely different. The Eight Extraordinary (or sometimes called "subtle psychic") meridians are best looked at as dry river beds that fill with melting snow or rain—or in internal

Introduction

alchemy terms, the meridians (dry river beds) fill with jing (snow and rain).

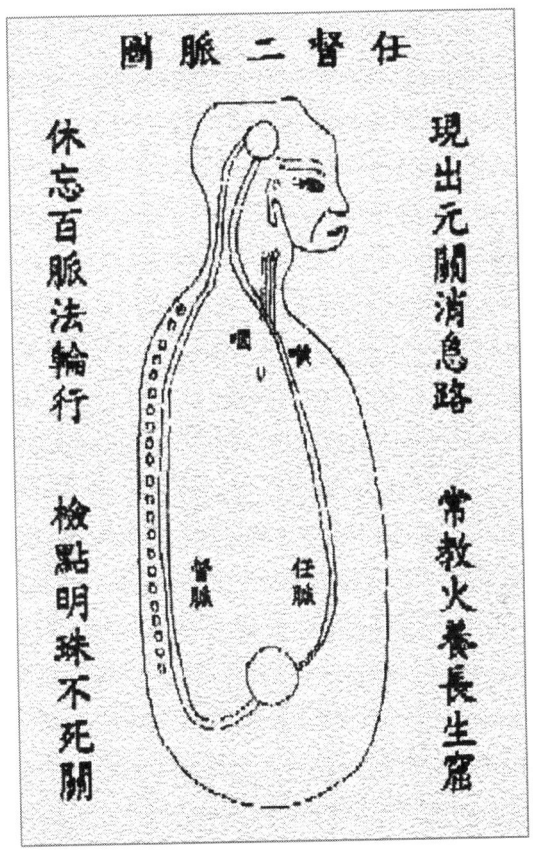

Map of the Two Meridians, Du and Ren
This drawing is showing the route of the Bright Pearl
(明珠, Ming Zhu) for obtaining immortality.
Early Ming dynasty (1368–1644 CE).

Refining the Elixir

3. Opening up the consciousnesses of the interior body and mind. The main idea of this category is best represented by the *Secret of the Golden Flower*, which teaches that when a person succeeds in opening what is called the "Heavenly Consciousness" (or Spiritual Mind), then the workings of the Three Treasures (jing, qi, and shen—essence, vitality, and spirit) can, through deep abstract contemplation, produce the Elixir of Immortality within the body. The method presented in this work is a combination of internal alchemy and Chan (Zen) Buddhist meditation, which is similar to the Taoist method of Sitting and Forgetting (坐忘, Zuo Wang). The purpose is to use the conscious and unconscious mind to reveal the Spiritual Consciousness. This Spiritual Consciousness is what can lead the cultivator to the experience of Returning Spirit to the Void.[3]

---

[3] See p. 127 for the section on this stage of internal alchemy.

Introduction

Sitting in Chan Pose
(坐禪圖, Zuo Chan Tu)[4]

---

4 Illustration from *Secret of the Supreme One's Golden Flower* (太乙金華宗旨, *Tai Yi Jin Hua Zong Zhi*). Attributed to Lu Dongbin of the Tang dynasty, but more likely written by Wang Chongyang (王重陽, 1113–1170 CE), founder of the Perfect Realization Sect (全真派, Quan Zhen Pai). This illustration represents the First Level of Meditation for the *Secret of the Golden Flower* Internal Alchemy Practice.

Refining the Elixir

Center top text
The peaceful comfort of Emperor Yao.
The supreme harmony of King Wen.
The ease and contentment of Confucius.
The resting and cessation of Zhuang Zhou.

Right side text
When sitting for a long period, just forget whatever you know. Suddenly you'll become aware of the [bright] moon on the Earth. A cool celestial wind will blow in, quickly arriving in the liver and lungs. Lean over to look into the deep water; nothing is hiding in the clear depths. Tiny fish swim within it, and silently they create an understanding with you.

Left side text
Without having any affairs when Tranquil Sitting, one day is like two. If you live for seventy years, it will then actually be 140. In sitting tranquilly few thoughts and desires can darken the mind, and so the qi can be nurtured and the spirit preserved. This is the all-important oral secret for cultivating perfection. Those who learn this can write it down.

Introduction

The Great Process for Refining the Elixir Treatise, and the other works associated with Zhang Sanfeng, fit into this category as they stress the importance of meditation and the focusing of the Mind-Intent (意, Yi)[5] upon specific qi centers of the body to open up the Eight Extraordinary Qi meridians. Of all the internal alchemy methods, the *Refining the Elixir Treatise* is the most structured and understandable. Zhang Sanfeng clearly shows that by progressing through certain stages, other functions will occur naturally. As he frequently states, "Do not worry about this, it will happen naturally," and by that he means the mind-intent will function spontaneously, and so there will be no need for an inner dialogue or anxiety about how to proceed.

As will be explored in this book, Zhang Sanfeng relates well the ideas of transforming from the mortal condition into a state of immortality through a progression of cultivation periods.

---

5   *Mind-Intent* is a term for the ability of reacting to a situation or attending to some purpose without any thought process, it being a trained, spontaneous, and natural response of the body and mind. In the case of internal alchemy, a practitioner, initially through focused mindful attention, pays attention to the lower Elixir Field, but from this repeated practice, the breath will spontaneously and without thought stay in the lower Elixir Field. On a much higher level, mind-intent is the function of the spirit once it has been illuminated, awakened to, or as some texts say "realized."

Refining the Elixir

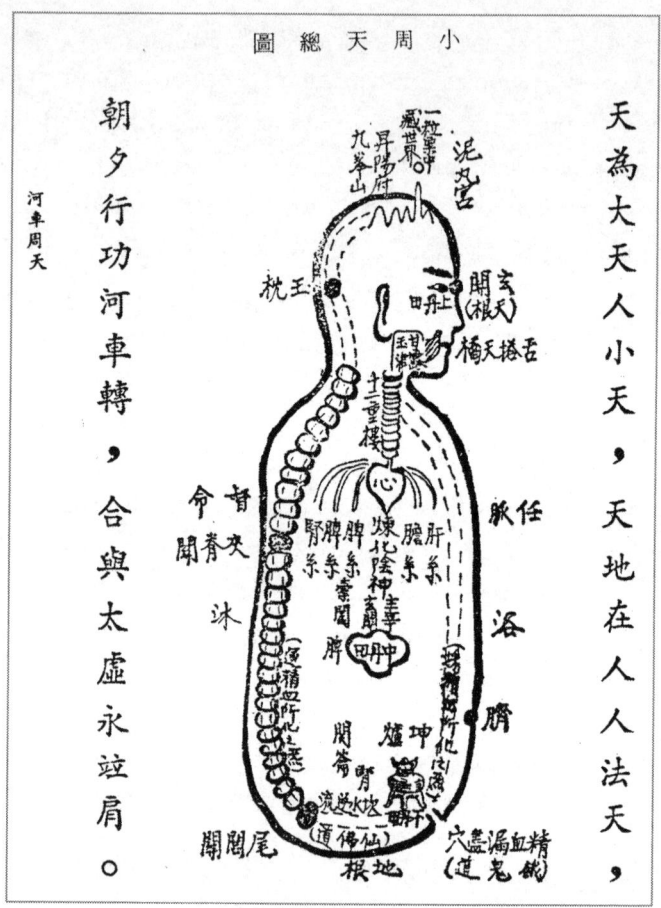

A Dragon Gate Sect (龍門派, Long Men Pai) drawing
of the Neidan meridian route and qi cavities
of the Lesser Heavenly Circuit.

Introduction

4. Regulating the internal spirits (good and bad) through right conduct and the performance of good deeds. This category is best represented by *The Actions and Retributions Treatise* and *The Supreme Exalted One's Classic on Eradicating the Three Corpse Spirits and Nine Worms for the Protection of Life* (太上除三尸九蟲保生經, *Tai Shang Chu San Shi Jiu Chong Bao Sheng Jing*).[6]

These works approach internal alchemy from the viewpoint of attaining a high level of spiritual virtue (power and influence)[7] so that immortality is bequeathed upon the practitioner by simulating the persona and activities of an immortal. Those of high spiritual virtue can overcome the ill effects of the Three Corpse Spirits and Nine Worms[8] of the interior body which support mortality and prevent immortality.

---

6   In Ge Hong's *Master of Embracing Simplicity,* he discusses the Three Corpse Spirits, Nine Worms, and particulars of the *Actions and Retributions Treatise,* yet he never mentions that work specifically. Rather, he cites three other works, but everything he states is almost verbatim from the *Actions and Retributions Treatise.* The texts he cites are *The Inner Precepts of the Book of Changes* (易內戒, *Yi Nei Jie*), *Master Red Pine Classic* (赤松子經, *Chi Song Zi Jing*), and *Talismans of Life from the River Map Records* (河圖記命符, *He Tu Chi Ming Fu*).

7   Virtue (德, De) in Taoism carries a much broader meaning in the Chinese than English. *De* is a spiritual power and influence developed through cultivation of one's spirit.

8   See *Actions & Retributions: A Taoist Treatise on Attaining Spiritual Virtue, Longevity, and Immortality,* Attributed to Lao Zi (Valley Spirit Arts, 2015).

Refining the Elixir

Illustration of the Three Corpse Spirits
(三尸圖, San Shi Tu)

上尸彭倨小名呵呵在頭上伐人泥丸丹田
The Upper Corpse [上尸彭琚, Shang Shi Peng Ju], with a common name of He He, dwells in the head and acts as a go-between for the Ni Wan and Dan Tian.

中尸彭質小名作子在人心領伐人絳宮中焦
The Middle Corpse [中尸彭質, Zhong Shi Peng Zhi], with the common name of Zuo Zi, dwells in a person's heart and acts as the go-between from the throat to the Crimson Palace and Zhong Jiao [Central Heater].

下尸彭矯李和在人胃是伐人下脚
The Lower Corpse [下尸彭矯, Xia Shi Peng Jiao], or Li He, dwells in a person's stomach and acts as the go-between for the legs.

Introduction

The Nine Worms (九蟲, Jiu Chong)[9]

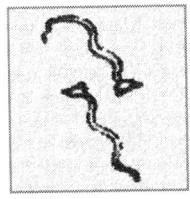

Crouching Worms
(伏蟲, Fu Chong)

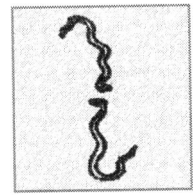

Winding Worms
(回蟲, Hui Chong)

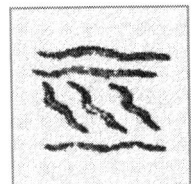

White Worms
(白蟲, Bai Chong)

Flesh Worms
(肉蟲, Rou Chong)

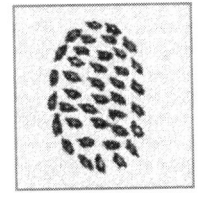

Lung Worms
(肺蟲, Fei Chong)

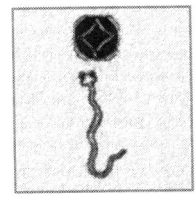

Stomach Worms
(胃蟲, Wei Chong)

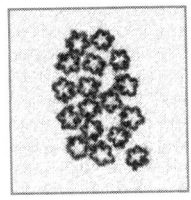

Cooking Pot Worms
(鬲蟲, Li Chong)

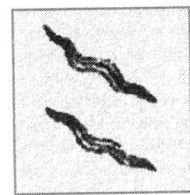

Crimson Worms
(赤蟲, Chi Chong)

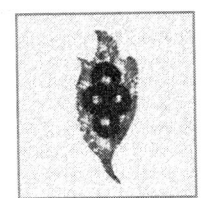

Dung Worms
(蟯蟲, Qiang Chong)

---

9   *The Supreme Exalted One's Classic on Eradicating the Three Corpse Spirits and Nine Worms for the Protection of Life* goes into great detail on the Nine Worm types, which aid the Three Corpse Spirits in creating illness and disease in a person's body. See *Actions & Retributions: A Taoist Treatise on Attaining Spiritual Virtue, Longevity, and Immortality* for more information.

Refining the Elixir

Within this teaching and method of subduing the Three Corpse Spirits and Nine Worms, the cultivator is doing the work of Seven Reversions (七返, Qi Fan) of the Seven Earthly Spirits, also called the Seven White Spirits (七魄, Qi Po), and Refining the Three Treasures (三寶, San Bao) of jing, qi, and shen, which on a deeper level is cultivating the Nine Restorations (九還, Jiu Huan) and Nine Revolutions (九轉, Jiu Zhuan). The details of these processes are covered later.

The Seven White Spirits (七魄, Qi Po)

1. 尸狗, Shi Gou (Dog Corpse)
2. 伏失, Fu Shi (Hidden Error)
3. 雀陰, Qiao Yin (Small Bird of Yin)
4. 吞賊, Tun Ze (Swallowing Thief)
5. 飛毒, Fei Du (Flying Poisons)
6. 除穢, Chu Hui (Dirty Excrement)
7. 臭肺, Chou Fei (Foul Smelling Lungs)

Introduction

The Hun and Po Spirits Diagram
(魂魄圖, Hun Po Tu)[10]

---

10 This illustration and text is thought to have originated within the Dragon Gate Sect (龍門派, Long Men Pai) in thirteenth century CE, but the theories of Three Hun and Seven Po began circulating as far back as third century CE.

Refining the Elixir

First block of text, right side

The Yang Spirit [陽 神, Yang Shen) is called "the Cloud Spirit" [魂, Hun]. The Yin Spirit [陰 神, Yin Shen] is called "the White Spirit" [魄, Po]. The Cloud Spirit is joined with the White Spirit, as they exist together in one another's room [organs of the body] and mansion [the body as a whole].

The Cloud Spirit is the spirit of the qi, it contains the abilities of clarity and turbidity, and is breathed by the mouth and nose. The exhale is the yang extending out [advancing] and the inhale is the yin bending back [converging].

The White Spirit is the spirit of Essence [Jing]. It contains the abilities of depletion and repletion, and gives the ears and eyes the ability to hear and see. Seeing is the clarity of yang, and hearing is the keenness of yin. From the perspective of life it is called "Essence" and "Qi." From the perspective of death it is called "Cloud Spirit" and "White Spirit." From the perspective of the entirety of Heaven and Earth it is simply called "Soul" and "Spirit."

"Spirit" [鬼, Gui] and "Cloud" [云, Yun] make the character for "Cloud Spirit" [魂, Hun]. "Spirit" [鬼, Gui] and "White" [白, Bai] make the character for "White Spirit" [魄, Po]. The cloud represents the wind, and wind is Wood [i.e., the liver]. The white represents the qi, and qi is Metal [i.e., lungs]. Wind disperses and so is light and pure. Being light and pure the White Spirit

Introduction

follows the ascent of the Cloud Spirit. Metal Wind is solid so it is heavy and turbid. Being heavy and turbid, the Cloud Spirit descends and the White Spirit follows. Therefore, sages use the Cloud Spirit to move the White Spirit. Common people use the White Spirit to grasp at the Cloud Spirit.

Middle block of text
In the daytime, the White Spirit resides in the eyes. In the nighttime the Cloud Spirit dwells in the liver. When it resides in the eyes a person can see; when it dwells in the liver a person can dream. For those who dream [and sleep] much, the White-Spirit is controlling the Cloud Spirit. For those who are often awake [alert and mindful], the Cloud Spirit is conquering the White Spirit.

    Therefore, because of the White Spirit there is Essence, and because of Essence there is the Cloud-Spirit. Because of the Cloud Spirit there is Spirit [神, Shen], because of Spirit there is mind-intention [意, Yi, the will], and because of mind-intention there is the White Spirit.

Third block of text, left side
The Five Activities [五行, Wu Xing] circulate unceasingly. As a result, my True Mind [真心, or Original Spirit] roams the Heavens for millions upon millions of years, it is the Illimitable [無極, Wu Ji].

Refining the Elixir

A seed and a sprout mutually create each other, but it cannot be known how many thousands of plants will be produced [from them]. Although Heaven and Earth are great, they cannot produce a sprout from a seed in nothingness. The female of a species and an egg mutually create each other, but it cannot be known how many myriads of birds will be born [from them]. Although yin and yang are subtle, they cannot make a female bird give birth to an egg without the male. Therefore, as Ten Thousand Things are being born, sages rely on their Before Heaven nature [to understand them], not their minds [the After Heaven temperament]. The Before Heaven nature does not sprout the mind.

When there's no mind, then there's no mind-intention; when there's no mind-intention, there's then no White Spirit. When there's no White Spirit, life is not received, and the Revolving Wheel [輪回, Lun Hui, of life and death] ceases forever.

5. Harmonizing the Yin and Yang (陰陽和, Yin Yang He)—also called Uniting Vital Energies (合氣, He Qi), White Tigress Green Dragon (白虎青龍, Bai Hu Qing Long), Refining the Rosy Clouds (煉霞, Lian Xia), or Clouds and Rain (雲雨, Yun Yu)—are teachings found in various works that approach the use of sexual energy to catapult the practitioners' jing to stimulate their qi. In chapter 5 of Ge Hong's *Master of Embracing Simplicity*, the following statement appears,

Introduction

One must also know the art of sexual intercourse to attain longevity. If through ignorance of the sexual arts the sexual secretions [jing] are frequently lost, then it will be very difficult to have the sufficient energy to Mobilize the Qi.

Taoism in antiquity made extensive use of sexual energy for the purposes of internal alchemy, health, and longevity, but due to the politics of Confucian, Buddhist, and Taoist clergy seeking imperial and aristocratic support, the sexual texts started being removed from the Taoist Canon (道藏, Tao Zang)[11] in the Tang dynasty and completed during the Ming dynasty.

Nonetheless, in almost all the other major categories of internal alchemy, there's usually a covert reference for sexual teachings. For example, "dual cultivation" originally meant the sexual congress of a male and female for the purpose of transmuting jing into qi. Later it came to mean (as seen in the *Jade Tablet Decrees on Nature and Life*) an individual making use of sexual energy (i.e., through self-stimulation) and meditation. This was deemed as a form of dual cultivation because the practice called for the retention of ejaculate to stimulate the function of Reverting Jing to Restore the Brain.

---

11 The *Taoist Canon* is a collection of texts and scriptures comprised of scrolls gathered from antiquity. The first collection of these materials was compiled sometime during the Song dynasty in 400 CE, containing about 1,200 scrolls, and the last version was completed during the Ming dynasty in 1444, which contained 5,300 scrolls.

Refining the Elixir

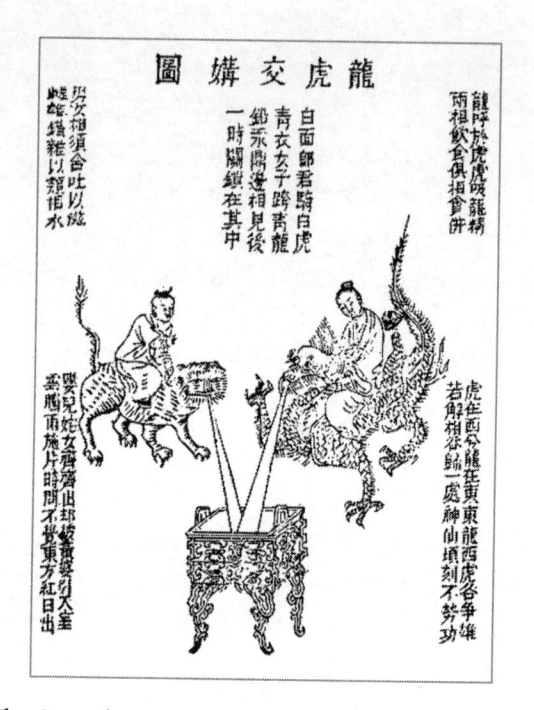

The Sexual Intercourse of the Dragon and Tiger
(龍虎交媾圖, Long Hu Jiao Gou Tu)[12]

The white faced boy rides upon the White Tiger.
The green robed girl bestrides the Green Dragon
When the lead and mercury unite in the cauldron,
instantly they are then congealed together.

---

[12] This image depicts Yang (the boy) within Yin (the tiger) and Yin (the female) within Yang (the dragon)—a unique way of illustrating the Yin-Yang Symbol (太極圖). The tiger and dragon are shown emitting their essences (jing and qi) into the cauldron, thus symbolizing reverting the jing and qi for sublimation of the spirit (神, shen). From the Ming dynasty print of the *Jade Tablet Decrees on Nature and Life*.

Introduction

Within all the works mentioned here, as well as many other internal alchemy texts, a great deal of overlapping of categories (or metaphors) occurs. References in the *Jade Tablet Decrees on Nature and Life*, for example, refers to the *Yellow Court* teachings, as does the *Secret of the Golden Flower*, and all the texts maintain a subtle reference to the Harmonizing the Yin and Yang teachings. In this work, Zhang Sanfeng clearly references other teachings and borrows terminology from them.

As all readers of internal alchemy texts discover, numerous metaphors are used to describe the internal functions and processes. The primary ones are found in the correlations of 1) a spiritual pregnancy, 2) metallurgical process, 3) mental creation of a spirit realm within the body, 4) the realization of the consciousness of the senses within, 5) the regulation of inner spirits, 6) a spiritual-sexual experience inducing inner illumination, and 7) a psychological absorption of cosmological imagery—such as in the *Book of Changes*.

Regarding the *Book of Changes*, you would be hard pressed to find an internal alchemy book that didn't include terminology from it. References to the Eight Trigram (八卦, Ba Gua) images of Qian (乾, Heaven ☰), Kun (坤, Earth ☷), Kan (坎, Water ☵), and Li (離, Fire ☲); the 64 Hexagrams (六十四卦, Liu Shi Si Gua, the six-lined images); and The Twelve Lunar Sovereign Images (十二卦月君, Shi Er Gua Yue Jun) are prevalent. So also are references to the Ho River Map and the Lo River Script (河

Refining the Elixir

圖洛書, He Tu Luo Shu), as well as correlations with the Five Activities (五行, Wu Xing), Ten Heavenly Stems (十天干, Shi Tian Gan), Twelve Earthly Branches (十二地支, Shi Er Di Zhi), and the Twenty-Eight Mansions (二十八宿, Er Shi Ba Xiu—the twenty-eight constellations and four celestial animals. These are all mandatory subjects of study as the *Book of Changes* is perceived as a map for internal alchemy cultivation.[13]

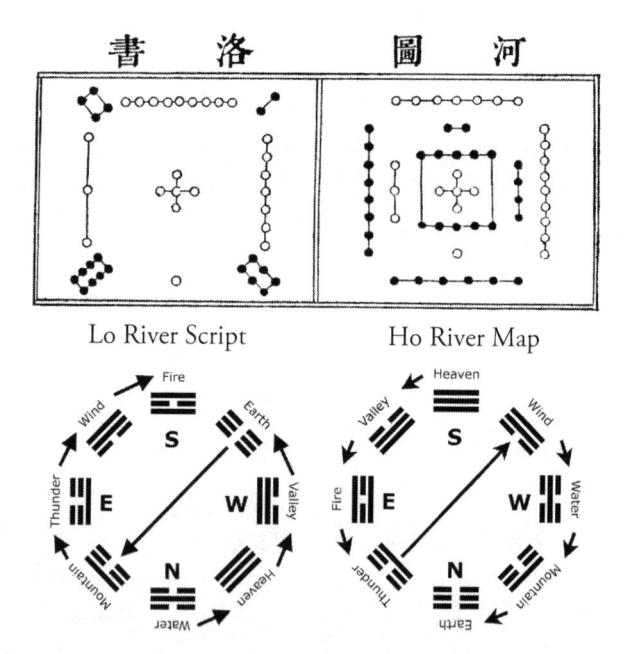

Lo River Script   Ho River Map

The After Heaven arrangement of trigrams developed from the Lo River Script and the Before Heaven from the Ho River Map.

---

[13] See *Book of Sun and Moon (I Ching)*, volumes I and II (Valley Spirit Arts, 2014) for explanations of all these associated subjects.

Introduction

Circular Arrangement of the Sixty-Four Hexagrams with the Four Quadrants of the Twenty-Eight Mansions

The inner circle shows the Center (中, Zhong) of the Universe, then the next circle shows the direction and Celestial Animal correspondences: North (北, Bei) is the Mysterious Warrior (玄武, Xuan Wu); East (東, Dong) is the Green Dragon (青龍, Qing Long); South (南, Nan) is the Red Bird (朱雀, Zhu Jiao); and the West (西, Xi) is the White Tiger (白虎, Bai Hu). The next circle are the names of the 28 constellations (called Mansions), and the outer circle are the correspondences of the 64 Hexagram images from the *Book of Changes*.

Refining the Elixir

The Twelve Lunar Sovereign Hexagrams

	#24	#19	#11	#34	#43	#1	#44	#33	#12	#20	#23	#2
	Fu	Lin	Tai	Da Zhuang	Guai	Qian	Gou	Dun	Pi	Guan	Bo	Kun
Earthly Branch	子 Zi	丑 Chou	寅 Yin	卯 Mao	辰 Chen	巳 Si	午 Wu	未 Wei	申 Shen	酉 You	戌 Xu	亥 Hai
Twelve Animals	Rat	Ox	Tiger	Rabbit	Dragon	Snake	Horse	Goat	Monkey	Rooster	Dog	Pig
Month	11	12	1	2	3	4	5	6	7	8	9	10
Hour	23-1	1-3	3-5	5-7	7-9	9-11	11-13	13-15	15-17	17-19	19-21	21-23

These twelve images not only relate to the months of the year, but they are used in internal alchemy to indicate the twelve two-hour periods of a day, showing the process of qi movement (mobilization of the qi) within the body throughout the day, called Firing Times in some texts.

The *Book of Changes* is quite cerebral for most people, however, and it takes a great deal of understanding of the workings of the book to bring any clarity into one's internal alchemy practice.

The great internal alchemist Wei Boyang (魏伯陽, 25–220 CE) delves deeply into the correlations with the *Book of Changes* in his work *The Seal of Triple Unity According to the Book of Zhou* (周易參同契, *Zhou Yi Can Tong Qi*). In most texts the inclusion of terminology from the *Book of Changes* has more to do with validating a work than with adding clarity. Since antiquity, no work in Chinese cultural and spiritual circles would have been afforded any merit or

Introduction

meaning unless it were correlated with the *Book of Changes* (and the Five Elements (五行, Wu Xing) for that matter).

For the most part, references to the *Book of Changes* are not that complicated (although the semantics can get quite complex), as the imagery is mostly used to create philosophical metaphors representing the aspects of Heaven, Earth, Water, and Fire, or in more internal alchemy terms the ideas of our Three Heavenly Spirits (魂, Hun, Qian ☰), the Seven Earthly Spirits (魄, Po, Kun ☷), our Essence (精, Jing, Kan ☵), and the Vital Energy (氣, Qi, Fire ☲).

Besides references to the *Book of Changes,* all teachings of internal alchemy discuss, in one form or another, Replenishing the Three Treasures (續三寶, Xu San Bao) to achieve Reverting Jing to Restore the Brain (還精補腦, Huan Jing Bu Nao), Mobilizing the Qi (運氣, Yun Qi), Illuminating the Yang Spirit (神陽明, Shen Yang Ming, and undergoing Nine Restorations and Nine Revolutions (九還, Jiu Huan and 九轉, Jiu Zhuan) of the Reverted Elixir (還丹, Huan Dan) through the body to attain immortality.

Although the early Chinese did not have the same terminology and understanding of medical, biological, chemical, hormonal, and anatomical structures that we do today, they obviously had a clear understanding of the functions within the body and a definite science behind it.

Even though I delve into the particulars of the processes later, it can be said that internal alchemy is a matter of first

Refining the Elixir

stimulating and heightening the effects of the Water element (jing) in the body. Second, it is the heightening and stimulation of the Fire element, the breathing functions (qi) within the body. Qi is the energy within us that animates our physical body, brings warmth to our body and fluids, causes the heart to beat, and the blood to circulate. Therefore, it is the qi (vital energy) that gives motion to the jing (essence) in our body. They equally rely on each other. Third, through learning intense and absorbed contemplation of the mind, the shen (spirit) brings forth a "spiritual power" (德, de, virtue) or as stated earlier, the Spiritual Consciousness.

In internal alchemy practices of Taoism, the essential stages for attaining immortality—in a very simplistic summary—come in two parts. The first part, or process, is to Replenish the Three Treasures. Once the Three Treasures are replenished, the processes of either Reverting Jing to Restore the Brain, Illuminating the Yang Spirit, or completing the Nine Restorations can take place. Replenishing the Three Treasures and then completing any of the other three processes enables the immortalization of the spirit (靈神, Ling Shen). This then is the short story behind internal alchemy.

To study Taoist internal alchemy texts and scriptures to learn the details of these processes, however, can be confusing. Readers find that the works are often written in mystical and cryptic language. In part, this is due to the fact that what is being explained is mystical, and therefore the language cannot be other than mystical, just as a medical

Introduction

book needs to be written in medical language. Some of these documents, then, were composed by mystics using mystical language, the technical language of the mystic, and so the writings could not be presented in understandable colloquial language.

Most texts were also written by teachers who were attempting to provide a document, a bulleted list of sorts, by which their disciples and students could cultivate, and therefore they assumed a level of knowledge and skill on the part of their readers and didn't need to detail the processes. It was also the case where writers were purposefully being cryptic so as to prevent unworthy students or other schools from stealing their teachings, and therefore wrote in a kind of secret code for worthy and trustworthy disciples.

Zhang Sanfeng, however, was in many ways an exception to the norm. In my opinion, he was one of the few early Taoist writers who attempted to write in a more understandable fashion, even though his language is still purely Taoist and appropriate to his time and influences.

Through focusing on his work and adding commentaries, my intention is to make clearer this subject of internal alchemy. Understandably, this is a departure from the traditions of obscuring these teachings, but I believe everyone is worthy to learn internal alchemy, everyone is inherently an immortal, and everyone knows in his or her innermost being what "Tao" is.

Although Taoist internal alchemy texts often rely on a mixture of terminology and metaphors, the central idea in

Refining the Elixir

all of them is about first placing one's entire mind-intent and spirit in the lower Elixir Field. Without acquiring a sense and sensation of this internal area, nothing further can be accomplished in internal alchemy.

The Great Process
大侯

A Ming dynasty painting of the Song dynasty alchemist Ge Hong making potable gold.

What Zhang Sanfeng calls the "Great Process" (大侯, Da Hou) is internal alchemy. In essence, it's about recreating the conditions and functions of an infant inside the mother's womb. We are at our best right before and shortly after leaving the womb because we are completely abiding by our Elixir Field (丹田, Dan Tian), the area where our umbilical cord was attached. As time goes on during our adolescence

Refining the Elixir

we lose this connection with the Dan Tian. We lose the sensations of the elixir flowing through our subtle meridians, the ability to let our whole body breathe as one unit and to produce pure saliva, and, most importantly, we lose our internal clarity of spirit. All these abilities dry up, so to speak, as we grow older and become more attached to and afflicted by the external world, leaving behind that internal world of the womb. In analogy, internal alchemy can be viewed as simply rediscovering that womb inside ourselves so to return to our original spirit.

One of the best examples of this idea is seen in the seated practice of Eight Sections of Brocade (八段錦, Ba Duan Jin),[14] wherein all the exercises simulate the activities an infant performs inside the mother's womb. Also consider that the umbilical cord, the lifeline for the nourishment of the child, is attached to the navels of both the mother and child. The umbilical cord extends into the womb and attaches to the navel of the fetus, and it is this point where the true Elixir Field is located. It's always been there even though we forget about it and no longer sense it.

People who experience astral projection, for example, can sense the umbilical cord being attached and readily apparent, at least in the etherial sense. I can attest to this, as I experienced leaving my body numerous times as a young man until my teacher Hsuan Hua helped me stop. I held no

---

[14] See *The Immortal: True Accounts of the 250-Year-Old Man, Li Qingyun* by Yang Sen (Valley Spirit Arts, 2014) for information on Li Qigong and his teachings of the Eight Brocades Exercises.

The Great Process

great desire for leaving the body, as it frightened me and I saw some things I would rather forget.

One of the more memorable and heart-pounding experiences occurred when I was eleven years old. I was sleeping but then completely fell off my bed, which startled me greatly. When I picked myself up to crawl back into the bed I was staring directly into my own face. I panicked and went crashing back into my body. For days after my back was sore along with a sharp pain directly inside my navel.

In all my experiences of leaving my body I could see this yellowish, sometimes violet, misty white cord descending from my navel. Also, all these experiences were preceded by a strong vibration throughout my body, yet I felt frozen. I would try and shake it off if I was conscious enough, but to no avail. Once the vibration started I would leave my body.

I have no great tales to tell, as I didn't travel too far away, just experiences within my home and on occasion I drifted above my house. Sometimes I would see, what I thought at the time, were devils. In retrospect they were more likely spirits, and some were really horrific looking.

I had these experiences frequently between the ages of six and twenty-nine. When I was fourteen my best friend's older brother, who overheard me talking about it, gave me his copy of *The Third Eye* by Tuesday Lobsang Rampa, which at least answered the question as to what I was experiencing—astral projection. From then on I began reading everything I could find on Tibetan spiritual teachings, but my ability to understand was limited, and I

Refining the Elixir

had no intent of cultivating as a Tibetan yogi. Rather, I read in hopes of finding a way to stop it altogether.

Finally, when I was twenty-nine years old and went to the City of Ten Thousand Buddhas where the incredible Chan master Hsuan Hua was teaching, he simply rubbed the top of my head during a meditation session, smiled kindly and said, "It will happen no more. Better you figure out this world than another one right now." And it did stop. The best result from those experiences was the knowledge I gained of how important my navel was, or as Taoists call it, the Elixir Field (丹天, Dan Tian) or the Gate of Life (命門, Ming Men). For that I am truly grateful for my out-of-body experiences, because to this day I can still sense this etherial connection at my navel, as that vision was consistent in all my astral experiences.

Important Terms in Internal Alchemy

In most Taoist internal alchemy texts the location of the Elixir Field is either kept secret, misleading, or confused. Such works erroneously explain it as being 1.3 inches into the body and/or three inches down from the navel, but these locations accord with acupuncture of External Alchemy (外丹, Wai Dan). The actual location of the Elixir Field, in internal alchemy, is three inches below (or behind) the navel when measured by a person in a supine position, not standing. It is the exact location of where the umbilical cord connected to the navel. Texts that aren't hiding the location will say it is either 1.3 inches in from the navel, as Zhang Sanfeng states in the *Refining the Elixir Treatise*, or that it is three inches in from the navel (below the navel if lying down).

This cavity, or qi center, called the Elixir Field in the lower abdomen, is often referred to in internal alchemy texts as the point of the Original Spirit (元神, Yuan Shen), Original Cavern (元洞, Yuan Dong), or Original Ancestor (元祖, Yuan Zu), and many other names as well. This cavity or point of attention must be brought to fruition if any other developments of forming the elixir are to be accomplished. This point was the gateway of our embryonic and fetal development, and so as well it is the gateway point for creating what Taoism calls a "spirit embryo," (神胎, shen tai) the actualization and experience of the Taoist goal of spiritual immortality (靈仙, ling xian).

Dan (丹, Elixir)

The meaning of the term "Elixir" (丹, Dan) must be looked at carefully as it is the root term for all of Taoist alchemy. In Chinese antiquity, its original meaning was "the hue of a sprouting plant," referring to the yellowish and whitish color of a bud bursting forth from a seed. Eventually, the term came to be used for denoting the ingredient processed in a crucible or stove of the alchemist, cinnabar, the color red, and a pill conferring immortality, of which all these terms were used by the ancient alchemists in their search for

Refining the Elixir

turning base metals into gold or forming the pill of immortality. In the ideogram for dan (丹), the one dot in the upper section is indicating the seed or pill, and the surrounding ideogram is the pot or cauldron aspect.

There are two types of Dan (Elixir) in the body. The first is called the "After Heaven" (後天, Hou Tian) and this is the Dan we acquire after the umbilical cord is cut. This Dan is classified as Wai Dan (外丹, External Elixir). The qi of this type of Dan can be manipulated in acupuncture. It also refers to the jing we make use of in trying to maintain our health and bodies. These types of jing and qi can dissipate and be damaged, so they do not bring about immortality. Rather, they support mortality.

The second type of elixir refers to "Before Heaven" (前天, Qian Tian), the Dan we had before the umbilical cord was cut. Internal alchemy teachings call it Reverted Elixir (還丹, Huan Dan), which results from cultivating and obtaining the True (真, Zhen) or Primordial (元, Yuan) Jing and Qi. This Dan manifests our True or Original Spirit, thus allowing us to achieve immortality.

Now in terms of what process the elixir (or cinnabar, as some texts call it) is being cultivated, there are three stages or formations of it. The first is called *Replenished Elixir*, and it means that our Three Treasures are strengthened and generating good health; the second is called *Refined Elixir*, and it means the components of jing and qi are united and begin moving in the body, bringing longevity. The third is called *Reverted Elixir*, and this is the actual medicine, as it were, of producing immortality.

Tian (田, Field)

The ideogram for "field" (田, tian) shows the crosshair sections (quarter sections) of the field in which the seeds (dan) are grown. In Taoism the character is showing the field inside the body where the two subtle qi meridians of the Renmai (任脈, Function Meridian) and Daimai (帶脈, Belt Meridian) intersect in the lower abdomen behind the navel. Hence, the term Elixir Field (Dan Tian) is actually two ideograms designed to be a map-like indicator of where the Original Cavity is actually located.

In early Taoist internal alchemy literature the area of the navel and directly behind it on the back of the body (kidneys) was called the "Gate of Life" (命門, Ming Men), wherein the Elixir Field was situated between them. During the stage of an embryo becoming a fetus, the first set of organs to develop are the kidneys. The left kidney (called Dragon Fire, 龍火, Long Huo) nourishes and maintains balance for the functions of the Five Viscera. The right kidney (called Tiger Water, 虎水, Hu Shui), properly called the Gate of Life (命門, Ming Men), maintains the regenerative forces of the body. In males, the right kidney generates the energy for semen production and sexual vitality. In females, the right kidney also generates sexual vitality, and it's where the fetal membrane for forming the fetus and the umbilical vesicle

Refining the Elixir

occur. In early Taoist texts the kidneys are described as the seat of sexual/regenerative energy.[15] The jing (精) is stored and developed there, which explains why the area was called the Gate of Life.

On top of each kidney reside the adrenal glands. To early Chinese medical doctors, the adrenals would have appeared simply as part of the kidneys, not as separate glands. Taoists have long said that if the kidneys (the storehouse of jing) were made strong, heated, and qi was directed to them, a great power would be experienced and the Elixir could then be directed up the spine and into the brain. In Taoist internal alchemy texts this is called "Reverting Essence (Jing) to Restore the Brain." This may just be my opinion, but it seems logical that a crucial part of the process for Mobilizing the Qi, or Reverted Elixir, up the spine has a lot to do with the stimulation of the adrenal glands enabling it to occur.

---

[15] The meridian pulse of the kidneys issues from the middle of the soles of the feet, the Bubbling Well (湧泉, Yong Quan) cavity. In Chinese medicine this cavity is used for the suppression of excessive sexual energy, such as for treating rapists in prison, nymphomania, and other sexual disorders. In Taoism, many Dao Yin exercises make use of rubbing the Bubbling Well cavity for the balancing of sexual energy in the kidneys.

The Great Process

Ming Men (命門, Life Gate)

This is the original term for the navel. It is called "Life Gate" because it is the very location of where the umbilical cord attaches to the mother and to the fetus's navel, and is thus the source of the infant's nourishment and life.

Sheng Men (生門, Mortality Gate)

The location of the Sheng Men is one inch behind the navel. It's also referred to as the "Life" or "Mortality" Gate because if this qi center, or cavern, is punctured, death immediately ensues.

Jing Men (精門, Essence Gate)

This qi cavern lies between the two kidneys along the lower spine and is directly behind the navel, about seven inches back. It's called "Essence Gate" because it is the seat of regenerative energy for the kidneys, the first set of organs developed by a fetus in the mother's womb.

Chinese medicine assigns the left kidney (and adrenal gland) as promoting the health and nourishing of all five internal organs through the processing of the blood, and the right kidney is what provides the regenerative/sexual energy.

Refining the Elixir

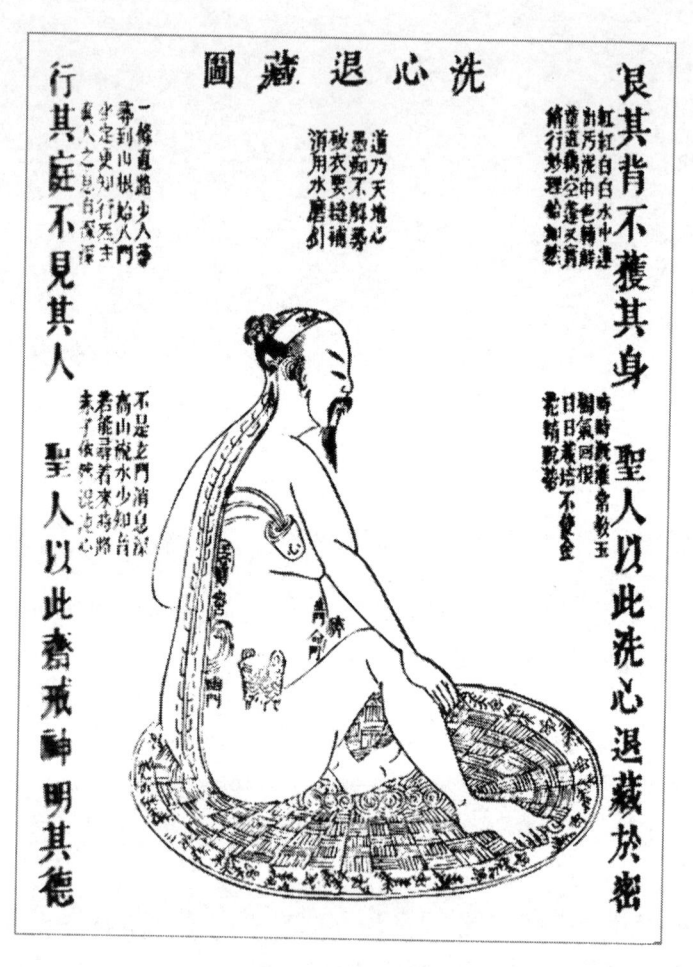

Washing the Heart (Mind) Through Reverting and Storing
(洗心退藏圖, Xi Xin Tui Cang Tu)
From the Ming dynasty printing of the *Jade Tablet Decrees on Nature and Life*. The abdomen area shows the characters indicating the location of the navel (臍, qi), Gate of Mortality (生門, Sheng Men), and Gate of Life (命門).

The Great Process

This process of Reverting Jing to Restore the Brain is also referred to as Reversing (or Reverting) the Illumination as seen in the following illustration, which provides a much closer look at the specific areas along the Dumai meridian in the context of Neidan terminology.

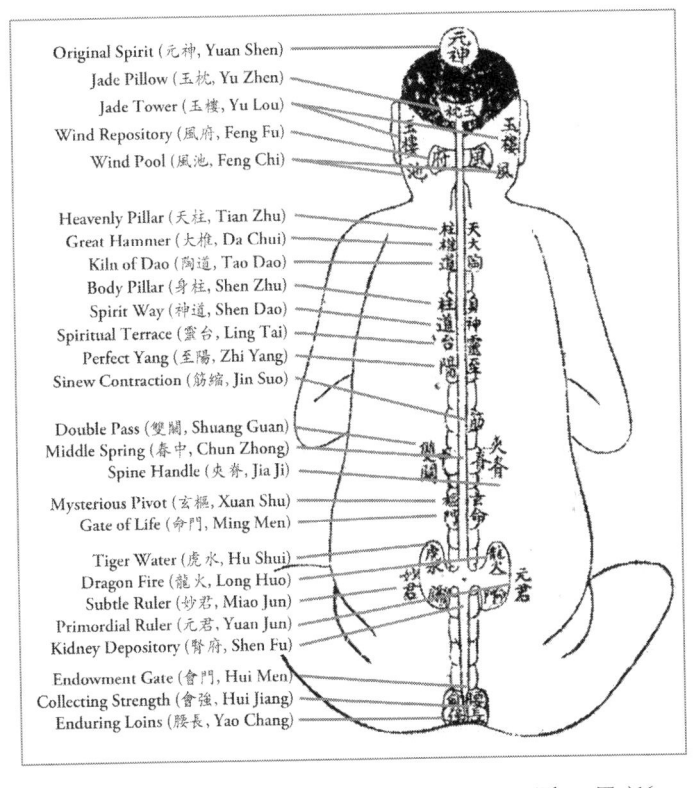

Original Spirit (元神, Yuan Shen)
Jade Pillow (玉枕, Yu Zhen)
Jade Tower (玉樓, Yu Lou)
Wind Repository (風府, Feng Fu)
Wind Pool (風池, Feng Chi)

Heavenly Pillar (天柱, Tian Zhu)
Great Hammer (大椎, Da Chui)
Kiln of Dao (陶道, Tao Dao)
Body Pillar (身柱, Shen Zhu)
Spirit Way (神道, Shen Dao)
Spiritual Terrace (靈台, Ling Tai)
Perfect Yang (至陽, Zhi Yang)
Sinew Contraction (筋縮, Jin Suo)

Double Pass (雙關, Shuang Guan)
Middle Spring (春中, Chun Zhong)
Spine Handle (夾脊, Jia Ji)
Mysterious Pivot (玄樞, Xuan Shu)
Gate of Life (命門, Ming Men)

Tiger Water (虎水, Hu Shui)
Dragon Fire (龍火, Long Huo)
Subtle Ruler (妙君, Miao Jun)
Primordial Ruler (元君, Yuan Jun)
Kidney Depository (腎府, Shen Fu)

Endowment Gate (會門, Hui Men)
Collecting Strength (會強, Hui Jiang)
Enduring Loins (腰長, Yao Chang)

Reverting the Illumination (返照圖, Fan Zhao Tu)[16]

---

16 From the *Great Spiritual Grotto Scripture* (大洞真經, *Da Dong Zhen Jing*).

Refining the Elixir

San Bao (三寶, Three Treasures)

The development and refinement of jing (精, essence, spirit of vitality of the body) and qi (氣, vital energy and animating energy of the breath) when brought to fullness are directed by the shen (神, spirit, intellectual operations of the mind). Jing, qi, and shen are collectively known as the Three Treasures, and they are the components that, in their reverted condition, form the Elixir. When they are brought to fullness and the cultivator taps into their original state (the Before Heaven, innate, or primordial aspects of jing, qi, and shen), the Elixir will then be felt moving within the body. But this is not a substance, rather a sensation, or as Zhang Sanfeng states, "like steam rising in the body." If it were a substance, there would be no need to cultivate it within your own body. We could simply retrieve it by a syringe from a person who had formed the elixir and inject it into our own body. Unfortunately, this isn't possible.

Through the internal alchemy of Replenishing the Three Treasures, two phases of work can be observed: the Fire (火, Huo) and Water (水, Shui) processes. *Fire* implies the production of heat (炁, qi) within the body (called Mobilizing the Qi), and *Water* the development of secretions (液, yi) creating the sensations of fluid movement in the body (called Reverting Jing).

The Great Process

Dumai (督脈, Control) and Renmai (任脈, Function) Meridians

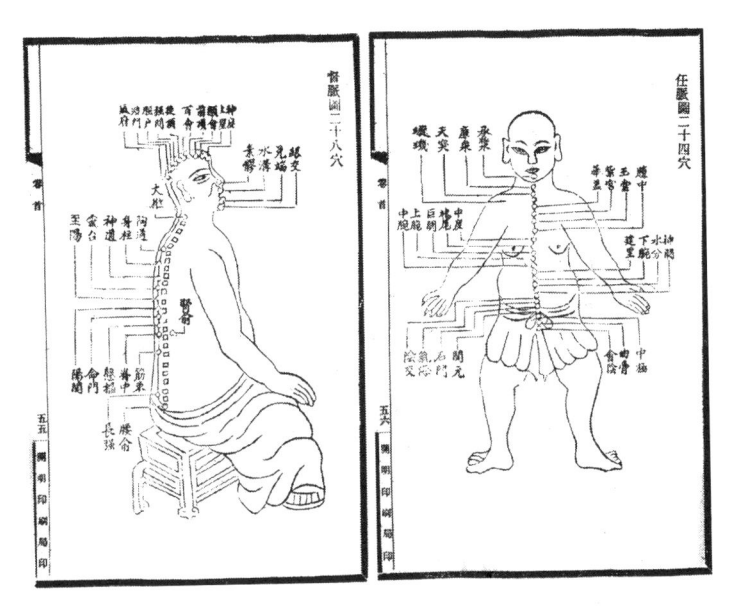

Illustrations of the Dumai (left side) and Renmai (right side) meridians with their associated qi cavities. From *The Yellow Emperor's Internal Medicine Classic* (黃帝內經, *Huang Di Nei Jing*), attributed to the mythical Yellow Emperor (黃帝, Huang Di, 2698–2598 BCE). The work, however, was more likely written in the Han dynasty (漢朝, 206 BCE–220 CE). The *Nei Jing* is still required reading for medical students in China.

Refining the Elixir

These two meridians play an important role in both the External Elixir and Internal Elixir systems. The Dumai runs midline along the spine from the Tail Gateway cavity up to the Hundred Gatherings cavity in the head. In internal alchemy, these two meridians are the channels through which the elixir will flow.

In the External Elixir system these meridians are connected by a series of qi centers (acupuncture points). The Dumai has twenty-eight points along its path and the Renmai has twenty-four. In the Internal Elixir system these External Channels become part of the pathway through which the elixir flows, and when this occurs they are called Extraordinary Vessels (奇經脈, Qi Jing Mai). In analogy, the External Channels can be viewed as a small stream, a trickle as it were, running through a dry riverbed. Once the flood gates open and the riverbed becomes filled with water and the river flows, the small stream is just absorbed into it. The meridians carry the same names, but are completely different in function.

The Dumai, as an Extraordinary Vessel, has six major subtle (or psychic) qi centers along its path, and the Renmai has six as well. Cultivating these two Extraordinary Vessels for the Reverted Elixir to flow through is the goal for achieving immortality. With the External Elixir, they produce good health.

The practices of internal alchemy are primarily about the opening, purifying, and activation of these two Extraordinary Vessels.

The Fire and Water Processes
火水侯

To explain the meanings of Fire and Water (Jing and Qi) it must first be clear how these two terms are applied in the practice of internal alchemy. The terms for *Fire* and *Water* are somewhat confused in many of the writings I have reviewed. Some of this confusion seems purposeful and in other cases is simply a lack of knowledge.

In internal alchemy there are two distinct areas of practice. The Water aspect of practice is developed through the processes and methods of Reverting Jing to the Brain, and the Fire aspect is developed through the processes and methods of Mobilizing the Qi. Even though these are distinct from one another, their effects, functions, and applications take place somewhat simultaneously. Meaning, when the jing is made strong, the qi is likewise strengthened, and vice versa. When both the jing and qi are transmuted into the elixir, the shen then attaches itself to form the Spiritual Embryo (胎靈, Tai Ling), Pill of Immortality (仙丸, Xian Wan), Dragon Pearl (龍珠, Long Zhu), or a Droplet of (Congealed) Yang Shen (凝陽神, Ning Yang Shen). Various teachings refer to this aspect of the shen's attachment differently. Despite the terminology used, it is the seed of becoming immortal.

Refining the Elixir

Harmonizing the Male and Female Essences
(男女精協和, Nan Nu Jing Xie He)

If the image of Kan [坎, Water, ☵] is over filled, then Li [離, Fire, ☲] completes Qian [乾, Heaven, ☰]. The positions of Heaven and Earth [坤, Kun, ☷] are then established. The origin is restored and it returns to the source.[17]

---

[17] From the *Jade Tablet Decrees on Nature and Life*. These verses are saying that when the feminine (Kan) becomes filled (replenished) with the Water element (the saliva, sexual secretions, blood, and marrow), this will complete the male, the Fire (Li) element (the Qi and breath), and so becomes pure Yang (Heaven/Qian, the Yang spirit). When this occurs, the male (Heaven, Yang) and female (Earth, Yin) are then positioned in their proper places and are in harmony. When harmonious, their origin (Before Heaven/prenatal/innate) condition is restored and so one can enter the Tao (Returning to the Source).

The Fire and Water Processes

Fire is referring to heat and sensations internally derived from this heat. Heat is created from the breath (qi) in the lower abdomen. This idea of developing heat and qi through the breath was first written about in the Shang dynasty. Someone had engraved on a sword handle a set of verses titled *The Cure* (治, Zhi), which tells the story of a man who was experiencing pain in his wrist. The man describes clenching his fist tightly, gazing intently at the point of pain while holding his breath for a short period, and then quickly opening his fist and exhaling while visualizing the pain leaving the area. After a few attempts of doing this, the pain not only left, but he also noticed something strange, the area on the wrist felt warm and tingly. He continued his practice of focusing and so on until he could with his mind move the heat up his arm and into all the reaches of his body. *The Cure*'s verses mark the beginning of all Internal and External Arts in China, and it best describes the Fire Process.

In the practice of internal alchemy there are Four Stages of Refining the Elixir, and the Fire and Water Processes occur within them.

The first stage, normally called *Setting Up the Foundation,* concerns itself with Replenishing the Three Treasures of jing, qi, and shen. In some internal alchemy texts, this stage is characterized by the practice of Opening the Three Barriers (Elixir Fields) on the front of the body. These three Elixir Fields of the head, torso, and abdomen must first be restored, energized, and opened.

Refining the Elixir

The second stage is about Refining Jing to Transform the Qi. This idea of refining the Essences of the body relates to what some internal alchemy books call Opening the Three Barriers (Qi Cavities) on the back in the kidneys, middle of the back, and the occiput areas.

The third stage, Refining the Qi to Transform the Shen, entails forming and reverting the elixir.

The fourth stage, Returning Spirit to the Void, contains the processes of nourishing the formed spiritual fetus and/or pill of immortality.

The Four Stages of Internal Alchemy Practice (四分內丹法, Si Fen Nei Dan Fa)

The internal alchemy text *Records on the Transmission of Tao from Zhong and Lu* (鍾呂傳道記, *Zhong Lu Chuan Tao Ji*)[18] presents a progressive list for the practice and completion of internal alchemy. This influential work has been adopted by almost all schools of the Neidan tradition. It relates the ideas of cultivating through Four Stages of practice:

---

[18] Zhongli Quan (鐘離權) and Lu Dongbin (呂洞賓) lived during the Tang dynasty. They are the two main figures in the popular group known as the Eight Immortals (八仙, Ba Xian).

The Fire and Water Processes

Setting Up the Foundation Illustration[19]
(築基圖, Zhu Ji Tu)

Right-side text

Even though the yin is orphaned and the yang friendless, they complete the Tao.

孤陰寡陽雖成道

The yin and yang have not yet harmonized. Before being cultivated they are separated like an orphan and widower, but when replenished they are what will complete the Tao for becoming an immortal.

---

19 This illustration comes from the Gold Mountain Sect (金山派, Jin Shan Pai) in the text *Establishing Life Treatise* (立命篇, *Li Ming Pian*). Written sometime during the early Qing dynasty.

Refining the Elixir

Left-side text
The Dual Cultivation of Nature and Life occurs like a turning wheel.

性命雙修出若輪

Life (命, Ming) is the cultivating practices of jing and qi leading to immortality; Nature (性, Xing) is the awakening of the Original Spirit that results from cultivating Life. So it is like a turning wheel: Nature relies on Life, and Life on Nature.

Circle on the chest
Ocean of Blood (血海, Xue Hai)

The heart replenishes the blood.

On the breasts
Ocean of Vitality (氣海, Qi Hai)

The lungs replenish the vitality.

Circle on the abdomen
Ocean of Essence (精海, Jing Hai)

The kidneys replenish the Jing.

Outside the circle (horizontal)
Ocean of Heat (炁海, Qi Hai)

The abdomen produces the heat (炁) to mobilize the Qi (氣).

Outside the circle (vertical)
Before Heaven (先天, Xian Tian)

The Before Heaven resides in the lower abdomen, the Elixir Field.

The Fire and Water Processes

1) Setting Up the Foundation (築基, Zhu Ji)
This primarily means practicing the methods of Replenishing the Three Treasures, Three Barriers on the Front, and any of the Nourishing-Life Arts (養生術, Yang Sheng Shu), such as meditation, Dao Yin exercises, Taijiquan, qigong, and so forth. The outcome of this stage is mainly seen as acquiring Free Circulation of Qi (氣遍週, Qi Bian Zhou), sensations of the Three Elixir Fields on the front of the body, and to be able to sit quietly without experiencing confusion or dullness.

2) Refining Jing to Transform the Qi (煉精化氣, Lian Jing Hua Qi)
This stage includes the practices of Reverting Jing to Restore the Brain, Mobilizing the Qi, and Nine Restorations.

3) Refining Qi to Transform the Spirit (煉氣化神, Lian Qi Hua Shen)
In this stage, the processes of reverting the elixir and circulating it to create the immortal fetus or pill of immortality begin to occur.

4) Returning Spirit to the Void (神還虛, Shen Huan Xu)
This stage means reaching the goal of internal alchemy, becoming a realized immortal wherein the cultivator can manifest transformation spirits and has Returned to the Tao.

Refining the Elixir

In connection with the Four Stages of Refining the Elixir are the three designated states, or aspects, of the Three Treasures as they concern the cultivation of the elixir. These *Coarse* (俗, Su), *Subtle* (微, Wei), and *Celestial* (天, Tian) stages overlap somewhat within a person's cultivation of the elixir, but they are distinctly different in definition, and in how they function and are viewed within the Four Stages described above. For example, Stage 1 is primarily about gaining some skill over the coarse aspects of the Three Treasures. Stage 2 implies the cultivator is gaining skills with the subtle aspects of the Three Treasures. In Stage 3, the cultivator is still working with the subtle stage of the Three Treasures, but now on the level of having reverted the After Heaven Elixir into the Before Heaven Elixir. In Stage 4, the celestial aspects are fully engaged.

At this point, it's important to note that this book deals primarily with the *coarse* and *subtle* stages of internal alchemy, as the *celestial* designation is quite abstruse. It is far better, and necessary, for a cultivator to achieve the goals of the coarse and subtle states first.

When thinking about the Four Stages of Refining the Elixir, the cultivator first works with the coarse aspects of the Three Treasures. Defined as the actual secretions and fluids of the body, regulating the breath, and focusing of the mind. In the subtle stage, the cultivator works with the refined secretions to stimulate the qi in the body (Mobilization of the Qi), and strengthen the mind-intent process. In the celestial stage, the jing, qi, and shen have

The Fire and Water Processes

been reverted to their Before Heaven, or innate, condition. At this point, the cultivator's Three Treasures are those of an immortal, no longer the coarse and subtle versions of the mortal condition.

The above description is actually what is meant by the circulation of the elixir nine times through the Dumai and Renmai Extraordinary Meridians, because first there is the replenishing of the coarse aspects of jing, qi, and shen, then the three subtle aspects function (or revolve), and finally the three celestial versions take place. From the developments (or revolutions) of these three stages, the elixir is congealed and comes to enter the Elixir Field.

This process may also be called Depositing a Drop of Yang Spirit, Creating the Pill of Immortality, or Forming the Spiritual Immortal Fetus, along with numerous other metaphors. It is not just the simple matter of circulating the qi through the Dumai and Renmai meridians of the body. The elixir must be formed and refined. Three energies times three processes equals the idea of Nine Revolutions. In analogy, internal alchemy teachings will equate this with the metallurgical process of harvesting iron ore (coarse), smelting it down to iron (subtle), and finally refining it into pure steel (celestial), which goes back to the methods of sword making—another metallurgical process from which internal alchemy texts are drawn.

Keeping the above explanations in mind, the coarse stage, or *Replenishing Process*, applies to the processes of regenerating saliva, sexual secretions, marrow, and blood

Refining the Elixir

and the simultaneous development of qi to begin the process of Transmuting the Jing into Qi.

The subtle aspect, or *Refining Process,* occurs after the elixir has descended into the Elixir Field through the process of Replenishing the Three Treasures down the front of the body through all Three Passes. The "Three Passes," or "Barriers," are the upper, middle, and lower Elixir Fields (third eye, solar plexus, and lower abdomen regions respectively).

Once this descent and replenishing of the Three Treasures has taken place, the subtle aspect of reversing the flow of jing and qi through the subtle meridian up the spine can be undertaken. This phase, called "Three on the Back," is what Taoism refers to as "Reversing" the movement of the jing and qi upwards and thus opposite of the mortal yin energy that is always descending. So the way of immortality is about reversing the movement of energy. The goal here of sending essence (jing) and vital energy (qi) up the spine and into the brain refers to the process of Reverting Jing to Restore the Brain.

When the experience of Reverting Jing to Restore the Brain is complete, then the Celestial stage, or *Reverting Process,* occurs, wherein the jing and qi are reverted into the Elixir of Immortality, and this is where the Spirit begins forming the spiritual embryo in the lower Elixir Field. At the outset of this Reverting Process there are two internal experiences that indicate the process is underway. First, a rumbling vibration is felt in the lower abdomen (Elixir Field),

The Fire and Water Processes

and second, a loud thunderous clapping sound will be heard in the head (Muddy Pellet). In the *Book of Immortal's Longevity of Ten Thousand Years* (萬壽仙書, *Wan Shou Xian Shu*) is the verse, "A rumbling at the birth of awakening, the sound of thunder claps in the Muddy Pellet." This is the beginning of becoming an immortal.

In the defining of these three stages it can also be likened, in a simplistic paraphrase, as to how Ge Hong in his work *Master of Embracing Simplicity* sums up the fundamentals of understanding the metallurgical process. Within his definition the processor first refines lead and mercury (鉛汞, Qian Gong) into cinnabar (丹, dan), then through a smelting process reverts the cinnabar into potable gold (金液, Jin Ye) for ingesting, calling it the Reverted Elixir. So, in internal alchemy the process follows a similar approach: taking jing and qi to simulate the lead and mercury, the jing and qi are processed into a refined elixir, and from there processed into an internal elixir, called the Reverted Elixir.

When undergoing the Coarse, or Replenishing, Process, cultivators may experience a variety of possible sensations, such as feeling increased heat in the palms and feet, increased warmth in the abdomen, tingling sensations within various qi centers (sometimes described like ants crawling along meridians), profuse sweating (especially along the spine and temples), and producing tears in the eyes. Men may experience erections during meditation, and with women, the breasts swelling. Saliva production can

Refining the Elixir

increase, and the nose may run. The top of the head (the fontanel we had as infants) may pulse and feel warm, and the same goes for the third-eye region.

Most importantly, the cultivator will experience the sensation of heat rising up the spine. There will also follow the experience of internally seeing different colors swirling about, rising and descending throughout the interior of the body. These are psychological effects of the spirit awakening, and the cultivator shouldn't attach great significance to them. Just let these experiences happen. Let them come and go, nothing more. Just as when experiencing the sensation of steam-like vapors rising and moving about the interior of the body, let it occur. In analogy, it will simply condense and turn to a more substantial, watery-like sensation, but this can't be manipulated or forced as it will occur of its own volition.

Eventually, with continued and consistent practice, there will be the sensation of a very substantial watery, steam-like, or vaporous flow rising up the spine of the body. This is the process and sensation of Reverting Jing to Restore the Brain. From this point, the ideas behind the Nine Restorations take place. These two are the essential processes of Refining Jing to Transform the Qi and Refining Qi to Transform the Shen.

From the above discussion it should be clear that the elixir is first comprised of the components of refined saliva, sexual secretions, marrow, blood, and so on. These all fall under the definition of "essence" (jing) and when refined and replenished, they have restorative and regenerative effects on the body. Keep in mind that the explanations of these processes refer only to the coarse aspects of refining the elixir.

No matter how this is all approached or defined in Taoist texts this coming together of True Jing (Essence) and True Qi (Vitality) means a new immortal spirit is being formed. Or, in other words, it is about re-establishing or re-discovering the Original Spirit we had before the umbilical cord was cut.

Water (水, Shui)–Reverting Jing

Water is the metaphor for essence (精, jing). The ideogram for jing is comprised of three radicals. On the left side is the character *mi* (米) for "rice" or "seed." The upper right character is *zhu* (主), "the sprouting of life." The bottom right is a variant for *dan* (丹), the "elixir." The lower right variant can also be viewed as *yue* (月), the "moon." The meaning then, in context of the female, relates to the moon cycle (menstrual flow), and so equally applies to "female essence" rather than the common definition of just male essence, or "sperm."

Jing is primarily defined by the coarse fluids of the body—saliva, blood, marrow, tears, sexual secretions, and so on—but the term also applies to food (including herbs) and nourishment of the body. Root plants are especially helpful, and various fruits, vegetables, and grains are crucial towards

Refining the Elixir

the development of jing, while starches and sugars damage the jing. In noting this connection to food and nourishment, and the importance of how integral saliva is in the breaking down of foods within the small intestine for digestion and absorption, it's easy to see why Taoist internal alchemists saw jing as equal to the development of qi and spirit.

The Water element, or jing, aspect includes saliva, sexual secretions, blood, bone marrow, brain marrow, brain fluids, tears, sweat, hormones, spinal fluids, adrenals, fluids of the endocrine system, and a host of other fluid-based chemicals and hormones within the body.

The human body is comprised of four-fifths fluids, the same as the Earth. These fluids are all classified as jing in Taoism. In Replenishing the Three Treasures, the jing comes first. It is paramount to internal alchemy. When the jing is brought to fullness, the qi is attracted and will be accumulated. However strong the jing is correlates with how strong the qi will become. By extension, the qi will then make the jing even stronger. When the qi is accumulated, these fluids (jing) all become stimulated and thus function on an optimum level. It is a mistake by cultivators to assume internal alchemy is just a matter of conserving sexual secretions and accumulating qi as the process for attaining the Elixir of Immortality. Our biological secretions, chemicals, and hormones play a very important role. We cannot separate the idea that when we seek to raise qi along the spine, we are equally affecting and making use of adrenals, spinal fluid, and blood. It is in this

The Fire and Water Processes

context that internal alchemy becomes a science in its own right—an internal alchemical science, as these fluids along with the accumulation of qi are the components/ingredients for forming the elixir. Just like the processors of antiquity who used base metals and minerals in attempts to form potable gold, they were applying science. From this standpoint, internal alchemy is a science, the science of self-promoted health, longevity, and immortality.

Blood (血, Xue)

Xue, 血, blood, shows in the lower ideogram of *Min* (皿), "a vessel in which to feed from and be nourished." The upper stroke represents the idea of fullness and overflowing. Xue is then an aphorism for depicting a fluid giving abundant nourishment to the body (the blood).

Blood, and the proper circulation of it, is one of the most important factors of a person's health and well-being. When the blood circulates well, new blood cells are created, the body maintains warmth, and all three systems of blood flow (arteries, veins, and capillaries) nourish the muscles, sinews, and organs of the body. In internal alchemy the increased blood circulation and heat derived from correct breathing aids in increasing and regenerating bone and brain marrow. Qi, as my teacher liked to define it, is like a "latent oxygen within the blood." This is a very good analogy because without qi the blood can neither be warmed nor could it move. Blood and qi mutually depend and rely on each other. The cultivator of internal alchemy

Refining the Elixir

first seeks to achieve what is called "Free Circulation of Qi," and this means getting the blood and qi to circulate throughout the entire body, not just in the meridians. This is how the jing is strengthened by the qi. In Taoist terms, it's the process of "transmuting jing into qi."

Females dissipate their jing through the menstrual blood, and males through semen, so in internal alchemy women are instructed to lessen their menstrual flow to the point of just spotting. Reverting to the state of when they were young and the first signs of their menstrual period (經期, jing qi) began to appear, or as Taoist texts refer to it as "Entering the Moon" (入月, Ru Yue), a term used to describe a young female during her first experience of menstrual flow. Men on the other hand need to lessen and limit the frequency of ejaculation to restore their jing.

Saliva (液, Yi)

Taoists consider saliva as one of the main components of jing, and this is for two reasons: 1) when we chew food, saliva is stimulated to help break down the food, which aids in digestion; 2) saliva also helps breaks down fats in food and so aids in keeping the body at a healthy weight.

Infants primarily survive on and receive most of their basic nutrients from saliva. Observe how much saliva an infant constantly produces and you'll understand how important this substance is to the body. Saliva is not a bodily excrement, it's a nutrient.

The Fire and Water Processes

In Taoism there's an important practice called "Refining the Jade Secretions" (練玉液, Lian Yu Yi), which is based on the notion that all the fluids of the body are a Jade Secretion. The reason for the description of jade is because in Chinese culture it is considered as valuable as gold. Jade is healing, and just wearing it is said to promote good health. Even deeper is the belief that jade is said to be refined dragon semen (jing) left by dragons who inhabit a mountain. Referring to body fluids as being jade then carries the idea that the secretions are cultivated and refined into jade, and so the body will become immortal and indestructible just like dragons and the jade they produce.

This concept is also found in what Taoists call "white jade" (白玉, bai yu), the jade-like remnants found in the ashes of accomplished adepts after cremation. White jade are formations of crystal-like bone fragments, which Taoists consider as evidence of the adept's successful cultivation, whereas a non-cultivator's bones turn completely to ash and dust from cremation.

Within the practice of Refining the Jade Secretions, an important point of instruction is to keep the tongue connected to the upper palate. This will stimulate the salivary gland to keep the throat moist during long meditation periods. It also creates a connection of the

Refining the Elixir

Renmai Meridian with the Magpie Bridge Cavity[20] (鵲橋穴, Que Qiao Xue), so the qi can flow directly through the mouth. It likewise opens up the areas underneath the tongue, directly on each side of the frenulum that attaches the tongue to the lower palate. On the right side is the Golden Saliva Cavity (金津穴, Jin Jin Xue) and on the left side is the Jade Fluid Cavity (玉液穴, Yu Ye Xue). These cavities when stimulated properly produce a sweet tasting nectar called the "Upper Peak Medicine," "Sweet Dew," "Jade Juice," or "Divine Water." Other traditions call it "Amrita." Keeping the tongue raised onto the upper palate is crucial for acquiring this medicine. In fact, it is only when the saliva thickens, turns pure white, and takes on this sweet taste can it be considered as refined and reverted.

A main reason for practicing Refining the Jade Secretions is to make the saliva thicker and more whitish in color, rather than letting it remain clear and thin in consistency. Making the saliva more substantial produces a greater effect when ingesting it. This aspect of Refining the Jade Secretions is part of many qigong practices, including

---

[20] *Magpie Bridge* comes from the story of the "Cowherd and Weaver Maiden." The Weaver Maiden is the daughter of the Jade Emperor and Western Royal Mother. When she falls in love with a mortal, the cowherd, her parents are upset and forbid her to see him. Eventually they give in because she is so insistent and they allow her to see him once per year, on the seventh day of the seventh moon (Double Seven Festival Day). They construct a bridge across the Milky Way between the stars Altair and Vega where Cowherd and Weaver Maiden are allowed an annual meeting.

The Fire and Water Processes

Li Qingyun's Eight Brocades and Chen Tuan's Four Season Qigong & 24 Dao Yin Exercises.[21]

Anytime an exercise calls for rousing the tongue about the mouth to build up the amount of saliva, then to rinse the saliva back and forth along the tongue, and finally to swallow (or gulp) it down into the Elixir Field—this is one of the processes for Refining the Jade Secretions.

A rarely mentioned principle of the practice is to focus on the Mysterious Well (玄井穴, Xuan Jing Xue), a point directly in the center of the clavicle, when swallowing the saliva. After gathering the saliva in the mouth, put your attention on the Mysterious Well Cavity, contract the nose, suspend the head, and sense that the saliva is being gulped straight down from this point through the esophagus, called the Twelve-Story Pagoda (十二重樓, Shi Er Zhong Lou), and in some texts the Mysterious Receptor (玄迎, Xuan Ying). Then the saliva is sensed passing through the solar plexus, the Bright Palace Cavity (絳宮, Jiang Gong) and from there directed into the Lower Elixir Field. Focusing and swallowing in this way enables the saliva to travel down the esophagus correctly and thus affect the Renmai properly.

---

21 See *The Immortal: True Accounts of the 250-Year-Old Man, Li Qingyun* by Yang Sen (Valley Spirit Arts, 2014) and visit the Sanctuary of Tao's website (sanctuaryoftao.org) to learn about Chen Tuan and gain access to the Four Season Qigong & 24 Dao Yin Exercises as part of the Celestial Membership Program.

Refining the Elixir

Keep in mind that in this process of Refining the Jade Secretions, the saliva is warmed through the rousing and rinsing of it, which means there is then qi within the saliva. As Taoists say, "Fire and Water Harmonized," or "Union of Essence and Vital Energy." Heating the saliva is crucial to refining it.

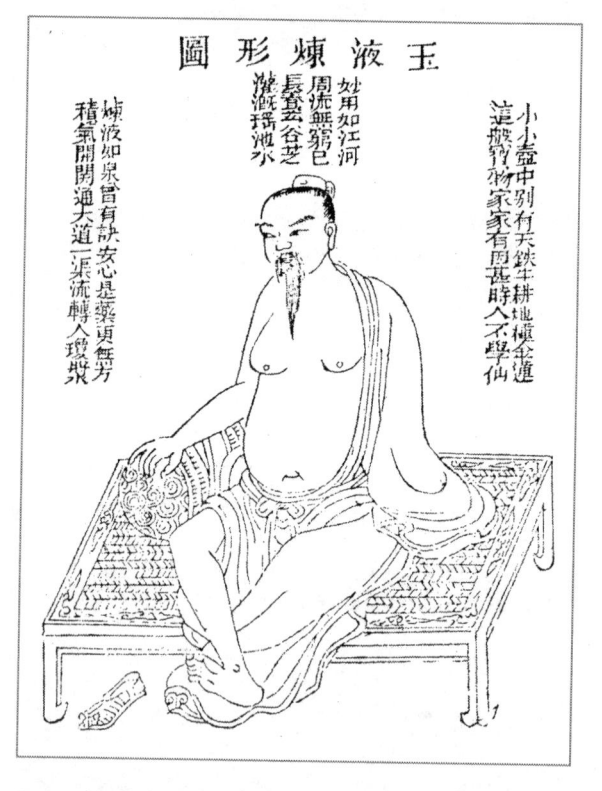

Image of the Body Refining the Jade Essences
(玉液煉形圖, Yu Yi Lian Xing Tu)

The Fire and Water Processes

Right side panel text
Within, there exists a distinct Heaven in a minuscule gourd.
> 小小壺中別有天
> Xiao Xiao Hu Zhong Bie You Tian

The Iron Ox plows the earth to plant the golden lotus.
> 鉄牛耕地種金蓮
> Niu Geng Di Zhong Jin Lian

This is like the treasures of a home.
> 這般寶物家
> Zhe Pan Bao Wu Jia

When the home is established, who then does not study immortality?
> 家有固甚時人不學仙
> Jia You Gu Shen Shi Ren Bu Xue Xian

Center panel text
Like rivers and streams the uses are so profound.
> 妙用如江河
> Miao Yong Ru Jiang He

Circulating and flowing without limit or cessation.
> 周流無窮已
> Zhou Liu Wu Qiong Yi

Constantly nourishing the herb of longevity in the Mysterious Valley,
> 長養玄谷芝
> Zhang Yang Xuan Gu Zhi

Refining the Elixir

and irrigating the water of the Jade Pool.
灌溉瑤池水
Guan Gai Yao Chi Shui

Left side panel
Refining the secretions is like fountain springs gathering together.
煉液如泉曾
Lian Yi Ru Quan Zeng

There is a secret for a calm mind, and it is to have endless joy.
有訣安心是樂更無方
You Jue An Xin Shi Le Geng Wu Fang

Accumulate the qi, open the passes, and penetrate the Great Tao.
積氣開関通大道
Ji Qi Kai Guan Tong Da Tao

A person's nectar flows and turns about the one wheel.
一渠流轉人瓊漿
Yi Ju Liu Zhuan Ren Qiong Jiang

Tears (淚, Lei)

The *Jade Tablet Decrees on Nature and Life* includes instructions for producing tears in the eyes. The eyes are surrounded by tear ducts that are normally stimulated by different emotions, like crying from sorrow or having tears

The Fire and Water Processes

of happiness. Some tears are also triggered by smells, such as from cutting an onion, and others by focused attention. Taoism professes that tears produced from intense focused attention—such as by staring into a crystal, gazing at a wall, or looking at a candle flame, and by specific procedures for the rotation of the eyes—are considered the restorative tears for healing, cleansing, and invigorating the five internal organs (heart, lungs, liver, spleen, and kidneys). Tearing, the removal of saline in the tear ducts of the eyes, is considered in internal alchemy as a cleansing of the Five Organs and the Four Components (四分, Si Fen)—the body (體, Ti), breath (息, Xi), Hun (魂, Heavenly Spirits), and Po (魄, Earthly Spirits), normally referred to as the Cloud Spirits (Hun) and White Spirits (Po) respectively. Tears, then, are an important aspect of cultivating jing in the body. If the five internal organs are not healthy, immortality cannot be achieved.

Sweat (汗, Han)

Normally we perspire from either strenuous exercise or work, and sometimes during a sickness where there are hot and cold sweats. Internal alchemists seek the type of sweat produced from breathing and stillness because it is stimulated by the qi. This type of sweating also proves to be crucial in not only elevating blood circulation (which generates new cells) but also is crucial in the production of regenerating marrow in the bones and brain.

Refining the Elixir

In internal alchemy the production of sweat through abdominal breathing (performed in seated meditation, qigong, and Taijiquan) is called Free Circulation of Qi—explained in the section on Bone Marrow. After taking up any internal alchemy or meditative practice, at some point the experience of profuse sweating will occur. Although this gradually subsides, most students are amazed by how much sweat can be produced from just breathing while either sitting quietly or moving slowly in unison with the breath. Profuse sweating is a result of Mobilizing the Qi in the body and is an indicator that the student is acquiring the stage of free circulation of qi.

Sexual Secretions (淫水, Yin Shui)

Endocrine glands produce internal secretions such as hormones (內分泌腺, Nei Fen Mi Xian). Exocrine glands produce external secretions such as saliva (外粉泌腺, Wai Fen Mi Xian).

In internal alchemy the translation of endocrine glands would apply to the production of energy needed for sexual stimulation, and exocrine glands to the actual substance of sexual secretions. With males, the goal is to refine the semen and with females, the menstrual blood. Males can refine their semen by practicing "retentions" (精保, jing bao)—meaning, a purposeful stoppage of ejaculation. In the *Plain Girl Classic* (素女經, *Su Nu Jing*) it lists the benefits of retaining ten ejaculations, but this method needs to be engaged in carefully and with utmost discipline.

The Fire and Water Processes

For women the dissipation of jing occurs through menstruation (月事, Yue Shi), not her sexual secretions, and is especially damaging if the menstrual flow is erratic, heavy, or painful. Males lose jing from unregulated ejaculation, and females from unregulated menstrual flow. Being the opposite of males (陽, yang), females (陰, yin) need the regular experience of orgasms to balance their essence and vital energy, which is to harmonize the yin with the yang. Conversely, males need to harmonize their yang with the yin.

Taoists have long theorized that the sexual secretions of a female produced during orgasm is the most natural means for stimulating the jing and qi of her body. It's also the case that females externally express their qi through the breasts (during heightened sexual stimulation the breasts and areoles swell). In males, the external expression of qi is through the occurrence of an erection. In both cases it is blood and qi producing a reaction—erections in males and swelling of the breasts in females.

Master T.T. Liang best summed this up in the following eloquent statement, "For males, stimulation is far more beneficial than dissipation. For females, stimulation is far more beneficial than suppression." The implications of this statement should be clear to everyone.[22]

---

22 See *Daoist Sexual Arts: A Guide for Attaining Health, Youthfulness, Vitality, and Awakening the Spirit* (Valley Spirit Arts, 2015) for more information on female reduction of menstrual flow and male retention of semen.

Refining the Elixir

Bone Marrow (骨髓, Gu Sui) & Brain Marrow (腦髓, Nao Sui)

Bone marrow is a soft fatty substance within the cavities of the bone where blood cells are produced. During the aging process this substance begins to dry up and the production of blood cells begins to decline. In our youth, bone marrow is plentiful and so the bones are pliable. As we age and the marrow gradually dries, the bones weaken and turn brittle.

Taoist internal alchemists have long recognized the health and longevity effects of heating the bones to cleanse and strengthen the marrow, but this cannot be done with dry heat or external heating processes. It must be done internally with the blood and breath/qi for the marrow to truly replenish.[23] In Taijiquan texts this is related in the statement that the arms become like "iron bars wrapped in cotton." In Buddhism, the Shaolin Monastery tradition especially, there is the practice of Marrow Cleansing (洗髓, Xi Sui) attributed to the first patriarch of Chan Buddhism, Bodhidharma. Both of these references are directed at the process of increasing bone marrow.

The essence and initial process of marrow rejuvenation begins with the free circulation of qi, which starts with focusing the breath in the lower abdomen—just as infants do. Watch an infant breathe and you'll notice that even the fingertips seem to expand and contract slightly with each

---

[23] Note that carbonized soft drinks have an eroding effect on the marrow and bones and the immune system. When the marrow is weakened, a person's general health is also diminished.

The Fire and Water Processes

inhalation and exhalation, and the breath is always in the lower abdomen (the infant is still psychologically relying on the umbilical chord).

When we breathe from our lower abdomen, the fluids of the body are heated much more readily and fully. Our breath is naturally warm, and so from heating the blood, especially with our breath, blood circulation increases. Heated fluids move. Cold fluids stagnate, so by increasing the heat of the blood it's better able to flow throughout the arteries, vessels, and capillaries. It's also the case that when blood circulation is increased, new cells are generated within the organs and muscular system of the entire body.

Again, as Master Liang so aptly described, "The qi is like a latent oxygen within the blood for health and stamina." His statement not only acknowledges that qi is within the blood, but also that the qi has the potential to be actualized. Instead of it remaining a latent energy, the qi becomes kinetic when heated. This warmed blood and active qi can then spread into all the sinews and joints of the body. Over time, the sinews and joints become saturated with new fresh blood and qi, and then gradually (with continued practice) the heat of the qi will begin to penetrate into the bone and marrow, thus making it softer, moister, and more pliable. This then is the basis for cleansing the marrow, and for the attainment of Free Circulation of Qi.

Brain marrow, in Taoism, was always considered the brain matter itself and the fluids surrounding it. The brain

Refining the Elixir

is the center of the nervous system and of the primary sensory organs of vision, hearing, equilibrium, taste, and smells. In internal alchemy the practice of Reverting Jing to Restore the Brain begins with the stimulation of the Tail Gateway (a gland inside the anus, called the kundalini gland in yoga). As the jing and qi ascend the spine, they affect the kidneys and stimulate the adrenal glands on top of the kidneys. The spinal fluids are then stimulated to open up the Spine Handle (middle of the back directly across from the heart) and the Kiln of Tao at the top of the spine, which connects with the neck vertebrae and brain stem. The fluids in the back of the brain at the occiput (Jade Pillow) then affect the brain itself, thus stimulating the release of the rare gonadotropin hormone from the hypothalamus, which produces the effects of illumination and euphoria. Also, between the Jade Pillow and the Muddy Pellet is the region of the fontanel area we had on top of the head as infants. Called the Ocean of Brain and Bone Marrow (髓骨海, Sui Gu Hai), it hardens over time and traps the Heavenly Spirit (Hun) inside the body. The infusion and heat of the jing and qi to this area replenishes the brain and bone marrow. When this region of the head begins to feel warm with tingling sensations or feelings of being energized, it's a sign of the jing being reverted and the Yang Spirit being illuminated.

In brief, the meaning of "reverting jing" has to do with the stimulation, rejuvenation, and heightening of the responses of all the fluids mentioned under the heading of

The Fire and Water Processes

Jade Secretions. Jing is the fluid aspect and qi is the heating aspect. When jing reaches its optimum state, the kundalini gland and adrenals are activated and so can push up this energy along the spine, affecting the spinal fluids, and once in the brain, the brain marrow and fluids surrounding the brain, as well as stimulating the release of hormones in this ecstatic state. This process is similar to how heated blood affects the bone marrow. In internal alchemy texts, the terminology to describe this would be: "The refined jing transmutes into accumulated qi and thus rises up the Dumai meridian into the brain causing an illumination of the spirit." Internal alchemy, then, is as much about producing and stimulating chemical reactions (the Jade Secretions) in the body as it is about heating and mobilizing the qi.

In Eight Brocades practice a verse in the text reads, "When the Dragon Moves, the Tiger Naturally Flees." This verse is an analogy for what was discussed above. Meaning, when the elixir rises up the spine, this is the *Dragon Moving* (龍行, Long Xing), a metaphor for the yang positive energy (the refined jing and qi, the elixir) rising up the spine into the top of the head (brain). The *Tiger Naturally Flees* (虎自奔, Hu Zi Ben) is a metaphor for the yin negative energy having been eliminated, which means it can no longer influence death and so immortality can be obtained. In this verse the ideas of "reverting" and "reversal" are seen. From the time people are born and the umbilical cord is cut, we are on the path of yin descent, leading from birth to death.

Refining the Elixir

Each moment and day, we descend closer to death. Internal alchemy is about reversing that process, so when we accomplish Reverting Jing to Restore the Brain, we are drawing closer to attaining immortality. We can equally fall back into the yin descent, however, if we don't continue and maintain the practice and progress into the stage of Transforming Qi into Spirit. Everything prior to that stage (and what has been discussed so far) is, for the most part, about Transmuting Jing into Qi.

Fire (火, Huo)–Mobilizing the Qi

The Fire (qi) aspects of internal alchemy relate to the functions of the breath in connection with internal heat generated from the breath. There are two distinct ideograms used in Taoist internal alchemy texts for indicating qi: 炁 and 氣, and each carries a distinct meaning. The reason for this is that the first ideogram of qi (炁) is a variant term specifically about the heat generated from breathing. This ideogram is based on two radicals, *wu* (无) and *huo* (火). Wu is negative, meaning "non," or "without." Huo means "fire" or "heat." So this ideogram (炁) translates as "formless heat" or "empty fire." While the second term for qi (氣) is an ideogram depicting "breath, air, gas, vapors, or steam," such as when rice is being cooked in a pot and the vapors of steam rise from it.

The Fire and Water Processes

This first ideogram of qi (炁) was originally used in Taoism as a charm, a secret character used on talismans (符, fu), and so was borrowed by internal alchemy writers as a kind of secret indicator for the effects of the breath in connection with the Fire Process of cultivation. Whereas, the second ideogram (氣) was used to indicate the qi of the Mobilizing the Qi practices. The difference then in how Taoist texts use these two terms is usually that the first ideogram (炁) is relating the effects of just heat produced in the body and the second version (氣) for the qi that circulates in the body. There's also the case of many internal alchemy writers not making any distinction and just using qi (氣) to describe all processes and functions.

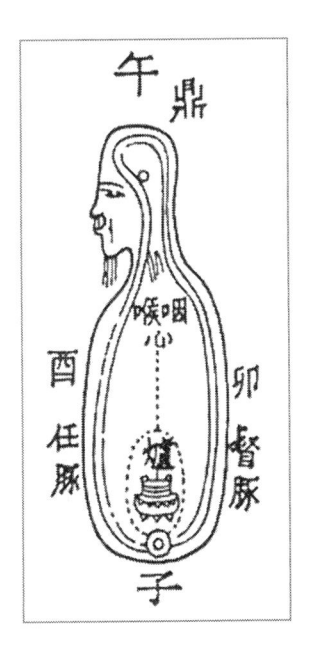

Refining the Elixir

This image from the *Jade Tablet Decrees on Nature and Life* is showing the internal alchemy functions and positions of the Furnace (爐, Lu) in the lower abdomen; the Cauldron (鼎, Ding) in the head; the throat (咽喉, yan hou), and beneath the heart (心, xin); on the back of the body Dumai (督脈) and on the front Renmai (任脈). Surrounding the body are the Four Components of Wu (午), You (酉), Mao (卯), and Zi (子), the four firing (heating) times in the day for cultivation practice. In the hour of Wu (11:00 a.m. to 1:00 p.m.) the cauldron is heated, in the hour of Zi (11:00 p.m. to 1:00 a.m.) the Furnace is heated, in the hour of Mao (5:00 a.m. to 7:00 a.m.) the Dumai is heated, and in the hour of You (5:00 p.m. to 7:00 p.m.) the Renmai is heated.

Mobilization of Qi (運氣, Yun Qi)

The ideogram compound of Yun Qi occurs in all the earliest internal alchemy books. Actually, without the use of this term, no true internal alchemy practice can function. It speaks to the very essence of the practice, so great importance is placed upon mobilizing the qi. Because Yun Qi plays a role in all the specific processes of internal alchemy, whether talking of Water or Fire methods, the following explanation describes it best:

In Taoism each person is considered to be a "Small Heaven" (小天, Xiao Tian) and so when inhaling pure air (清氣, Qing Qi) and swallowing it with some effort, it descends into the Elixir Field, and then into the coccyx (會陰, Hui Yin, Gathering Yin, the perineum). This is a qi

The Fire and Water Processes

cavity that in young persons is permeable, but in older people becomes obstructed and filled with fatty tissue, which is why Taoist texts call for continually swallowing the pure air until the blockage is removed. Once pure air can move through the Gathering Yin qi cavity, it is directed to move up the back of the body through the Double Barrier (雙關, Shuang Guan, or sometimes called the Spine Handle) in the middle of the back, and then up to the occiput (玉枕, Yu Zhen, the Jade Pillow). From there it will pass over the crown of the head to the Heavenly Door (天門, Tian Men), also called the Mysterious Barrier (玄關, Xuan Guan, the third eye, or the middle of the brow). From here it finally finds its way out through the nostrils and is now deemed as foul air (惡氣, E Qi). New pure air is then inhaled again and the process repeats.

Called "performing revolutions of the Small Heaven" (or "microcosmic circuit of qi," or "Lesser Heavenly Circuit"), it is actually the initial process of setting the qi into motion within the body, hence Mobilizing the Qi. To be clear, this is not the circulation of the Elixir in Nine Revolutions. At first, Mobilizing the Qi is mostly a purely imaginary process and one of its main purposes is to clear the pathways, meridians, and cavities in the body (most importantly the Dumai and Renmai meridians) for when the elixir is formed, which occurs in Stage 3 of internal alchemy practice, "Transmuting Qi into Shen."

Mobilizing the Qi is still part of the second stage, "Transmuting Jing into Qi." It is External Elixir (外丹, Wai

Refining the Elixir

Dan) because the Internal Elixir (內丹, Nei Dan) has not yet formed. The qi being cultivated here is more in keeping with the first version 炁, not 氣, because Mobilizing the Qi is largely about creating the sensations of heat within the body, meridians, and cavities.

The most essential part of Mobilizing the Qi practice is in the aspect of gathering qi into the mouth, the swallowing of it, and how to visualize its descent on the front of the body. Regarding swallowing the breath/qi, there's the idea of swallowing saliva (jing) and of swallowing breath (qi)—two separate practices, but similar in application.

To swallow the breath, make an inhalation through the nose to fill the lower abdomen with air. Simultaneously, visualize the qi as a pure, white, and cloud-like substance gathering in the mouth. Then making sure the head is suspended slightly upwards and there's a slight contracting of the nose, gulp the qi down with some force. The actual swallowing, however, is sensed as coming from the area of the Mysterious Well (玄井, Xuan Jing), located in the top middle area of the clavicle bone, and then focused on as it descends through the solar plexus (Bright Palace, 炯宮, Jiong Gong) and into the lower Elixir Field. Great attention must be given to feeling the qi descending through these areas, because just as the saliva becomes more substantial so will the qi in the mouth. Once the elixir is formed this cloud-like visualization will be seen as a "dragon pearl," "yellow sprout," or a "golden flower" moving through the Dumai and Renmai meridians. The practicer need not put

The Fire and Water Processes

too much energy into sensing its descent into the Gathering Yin cavity, or the other subsequent areas, because once it has fully entered into the Elixir Field there is a natural movement of the qi to these areas.

Dao Yin (導引) and Tu Na (吐呐)

The term Dao Yin literally translates as "leading and enticing"—meaning, to lead and entice the qi to certain areas of the body. Eight Brocades, Wind and Dew, Four Season Dao Yin Exercises, Five Animal Frolics, Taijiquan, and various other forms of breath-induced movement exercises are all Dao Yin. It's one of the primary functions of internal alchemy, as most of the initial functions are in fact a purposeful leading and guiding of the qi.

Although Tu Na (吐納), also called Bellows Breathing (橐籥息, Tuo Yue Xi), translates as "exhaling and spitting out." In application it is like "blowing-out and drawing-in"—meaning, one exhales the unclean air (Tu) and when inhaling, takes in clean air (Na). The main function is to gather the vital energy (qi).

In practice, Tu Na means to inhale through the nose (Na) into the lower Elixir Field and then with pursed lips exhale by blowing out (Tu).

In internal alchemy, Tu Na is found in the regimes of *Listening to the 24 Breaths, Exhausting One Breath,* and in the *Six Healing Sounds*.

With the practice of Listening to the 24 Breaths, position the palms of the hands over each ear, in a cupping-

Refining the Elixir

like fashion to create a sea-shell type of sound effect. This cupping serves to block out external noises and allow the breath to be heard purely internally.

In practicing Exhausting One Breath (as found in Eight Brocades practice), the exhalation is lengthened for as long as comfortably possible to rid the lungs of foul air (惡氣, E Qi).

For instructions on the Six Healing Sounds, see my translation of *The Immortal: True Accounts of the 250-Year-Old Man, Li Qingyun* by Yang Sen (Valley Spirit Arts, 2014).

Embryonic Breathing (胎息, Tai Xi)

Within the various types of Taoist meditation breathing, the two main regimes are Natural Breathing (自息, Zi Xi) and Embryonic Breathing[24] (or Reverse Breathing). In the processes of gaining the skills of Free Circulation of Qi, the manner of Natural Breathing is most useful. When moving on in the practice to actually begin circulating the Elixir (the refined jing and qi) through the Extraordinary Meridians, then Embryonic Breathing is more useful. As

---

[24] Within Embryonic Breathing is the practice of *Closing the Breath* (閉氣, Bi Qi), sometimes called *Tortoise Breathing* (龜息, Gui Xi). This and other breathing methods are not critical to the purposes of this book, but information on them is available at the Sanctuary of Tao's website (sanctuaryoftao.org) in the Celestial Member area under the heading "The Nine Breathing Methods for Mobilizing the Qi."

The Fire and Water Processes

Li Qingyun said, "Immortality begins with embryonic breathing."

It is called Embryonic Breathing because it is exactly how we breathed within out mother's womb. When the fetus draws in oxygen and nutrients from the blood of the placenta through the umbilical cord, the abdomen must be drawn in, inhaling and contracting the abdomen, to aid the process and ensure the reception of oxygen and blood. If the abdomen were expanded during inhalation it would cause a pushing back of the oxygen and blood into the placenta. So, in internal alchemy it is this type of embryonic breath that creates and nourishes the spiritual embryo with jing and qi, a similar process of drawing in blood (jing) and oxygen (qi). Natural breathing is how we started breathing after the umbilical cord was severed.

Note that many internal alchemy texts state, "Use the After Heaven to acquire the Before Heaven." In part, this statement is referring to our breath. The idea is that we first learn to gain Free Circulation of Qi through Natural Breathing (or called After Heaven Breath) and then it becomes possible (because the qi has been accumulated) to begin the work of Embryonic Breathing (Before Heaven Breath) to circulate the jing and qi through the Extraordinary meridians of Dumai and Renmai, the Microcosmic Orbit.

Refining the Elixir

Image from the *Jade Tablet Decrees on Nature and Life* depicting the Spiritual Fetus.

There are some particulars to performing Embryonic Breathing correctly. The basic idea is to contract the abdomen when inhaling and expand it when exhaling, the exact opposite of Natural Breathing. Embryonic Breathing naturally pushes the energy (jing and qi) up the back of the body along the spine into the brain. Natural Breathing is designed to keep the energy (jing and qi) in the lower abdomen to open the lower Elixir Field (Dan Tian). With Embryonic Breathing, imagine your abdomen is like a balloon and, in analogy, something squeezes the balloon causing the upper portion of the balloon to rise and expand.

The Fire and Water Processes

When doing so roll the eyes upwards as if to gaze at the upper brain area, the tongue is held against the upper palate, and when inhaling lift the anus upwards slightly. These are the physiological aspects of internally raising the energy in the body. Psychologically, the mind imagines and visualizes the energy rising from the lower abdomen up into the brain. In these respects Embryonic Breathing is simple, but to get rid of the sensations of forcing and overextending the inhalation is much more difficult.

It's worth stating again that Embryonic Breathing should only be used when actually beginning the practice of Reverting Jing to Restore the Brain, not during the practices of Replenishing the Three Treasures, or during meditation in general. My teacher was adamant about this because he had witnessed many practicers who believed Embryonic Breathing would accumulate qi faster and constantly practiced it, only to end up trapping negative energy in their head and causing various ills in the body. Keep in mind that each type of breathing has its function and time for use. As the great meditation master Yinshizi commented in his book on meditation,[25] "We begin with

---

25 See *Clarity & Tranquility: A Guide for Daoist Meditation* for a translation of the writings on the Tranquil Sitting meditation method of Master Yinshizi. It presents the material in an augmented, edited, and reformatted manner. This new arrangement is a bit more succinct than the original, especially to the beginner, and is in essence an expanded version of the method of meditation prescribed by Yinshizi in his original work, *Yinshizi's Tranquil Sitting Method* (因是子靜坐法, *Yin Shi Zi Jing Zuo Fa*), published in 1914 in China.

Refining the Elixir

Natural Breathing, progress to Embryonic Breathing, and then when the work is done, revert to Natural Breathing." Embryonic Breathing is very powerful, and because of that power we must be careful in using it.

Natural Breath (自息, Zi Xi)

There are two types of Natural Breathing: Yin Natural Breath (陰自息, Yin Zi Xi) and Yang Natural Breath (陽自息, Yang Zi Xi). The difference between them is that Yin Natural Breathing maintains a longer exhalation than inhalation, and Yang Natural Breathing maintains a longer inhalation than exhalation.

When inhaling, the abdomen expands, and it contracts during the exhalation. Each breath is inspired and expired through the nose with the tip of the tongue placed on the upper portion of the inside of the mouth. Natural Breathing is accomplished simply by putting all of your attention into the lower abdomen (Dan Tian) so that there is no forcing of the breath to be deep and slow, rather it will be the mind-intent which regulates the breathing.

The first rule of Natural Breathing is just that, to be "natural." Do not force the breath to be either long or deep. Let this happen naturally through practice. Use the mind-intent to keep the breath in the lower abdomen. Use the abdomen like a balloon or bellows to expand and contract it equally. Do not just push out the front of the stomach on the inhalation and pull it inward on the exhalation. Rather, on the inhalation you should sense an expansion of the

The Fire and Water Processes

breath on the lower spine, sides of the body, and front of the abdomen. On the exhalation, you should feel the contraction in a similar manner.

As you progress with Natural Breathing there will be a sense of the entire body breathing, feeling the inhalation expanding the very skin and muscles of the entire body, from the toes to the fingers, and contracting when exhaling. This is a very beneficial stage to reach as it will bring greater sensitivity and qi to the body.

Triple Warmer (三焦, San Jiao)

In one of the oldest Chinese medical texts, *The Yellow Emperor's Internal Medicine Classic,* the San Jiao is viewed as the passageway of heat and fluids throughout the body. In the section titled "Elementary Questions," it states, "The San Jiao holds the office of the sluices, and manifests as the internal waterways."

The San Jiao is divided into three sections within the body: Upper (neck and head), Middle (torso), and Lower (abdominal area and below).

Unlike all the other organs of the body, the Triple Warmer is purely ethereal, not material. If a surgeon were to dissect the body, the San Jiao could not be found.

Refining the Elixir

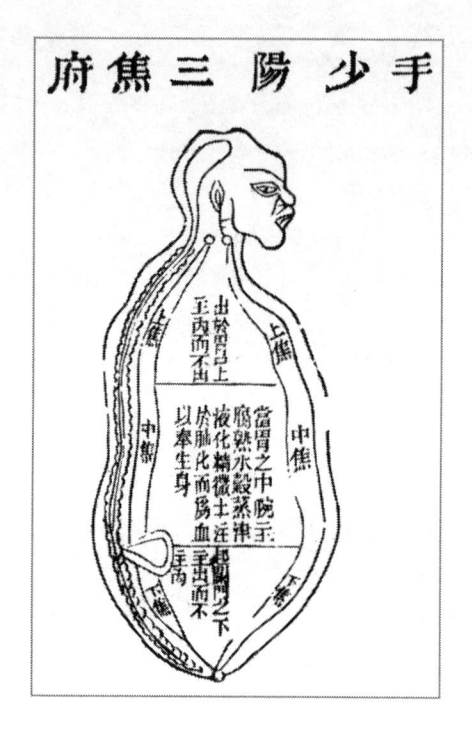

Image showing the three divisions of the Triple Warmer, Upper (上焦, Shang Jiao), Middle (中焦, Zhong Jiao), and Lower (下焦, Xia Jiao). From *The Yellow Emperor's Internal Medicine Classic*.

The Triple Warmer is considered to be a metabolism mechanism, similar to an old-fashioned waterwheel that is turned by incoming water to produce energy, such as with a mill apparatus for grinding grain.

In the analogy of a waterwheel, the San Jiao functions for the metabolizing and digestion of food. It's not limited

The Fire and Water Processes

to work with just the gall bladder, spleen, or kidneys, but is like a general metabolizer for a variety of metabolic needs of the body, and it's closely associated with the functions of transportation and transformation in the metabolizing of incoming food.

In internal alchemy descriptions of the San Jiao, it's responsible for the circulation of heat and as the mobilizer of fluids and secretions throughout the body. In brief, it is the modus operandi of qi and jing in the body, and therefore is a very important organ of the body, especially concerning the development of internal alchemy.

Eight Brocades texts mention the River Cart (河車, He Che) Method. Based on the idea of the waterwheel, the characters 龍骨車 (Long Gu Che) interestingly translate as "Dragon Bones Cart," which carries the idea of a dragon twisting and turning its bones as it maneuvers through the sky. The context of the waterwheel in internal alchemy is just that, like the functioning of a real waterwheel. The momentum of water propelling in downward and upward actions is not unlike what has been discussed here. For example, in internally alchemy we are either swallowing qi or saliva from above and then letting it descend, which then propels the energy of jing and qi to travel upward. Equally, since the San Jiao acts as the mobilizer of heat (qi) and fluids (jing) in the body, it operates the River Cart in internal alchemy, not just an inner visualization and mind-intent for its occurrence, but is one of the functions of the San Jiao.

Refining the Elixir

The Eight Extraordinary Meridians (八奇經脈, Ba Qi Jing Mai)

The subtle meridians are similar to dry riverbeds. Once full of flowing water, they've since dried up, leaving only an imprint in the ground of their path. This is the same with the subtle meridians of the human body. Like dry riverbeds they can again be filled with flowing water if snows melt from the mountaintops and the water flows down into them. As discussed, the initial stage of internal alchemy is based on the rising of heat and the descent of water, just like the melting snows of mountains filling dry riverbeds.

The question most people have when attempting to cultivate internal alchemy is how to acquire this elixir so it can flow through these subtle meridians?

First of all, there's nothing fixed or rote about it. After a person successfully refines the jing and brings the replenished Three Treasures down the front of the body, the Furnace (abdomen) and Cauldron (solar plexus) are ready to smelt (refine) the components into the elixir. This will be quite apparent to the cultivator because when sitting in meditation there will be several signs of this being accomplished. Some might feel a strong vibration in the lower abdomen, some might experience an internal sound, like the rumbling of thunder, and some might experience the feeling of something very solid and substantial, like a small ball, pulsing within their lower abdomen. There is no guarantee of these sensations, but most people experience some or all of them.

The Fire and Water Processes

Even if never experiencing any of them, this doesn't mean the elixir isn't being formed. Everyone has different endowments and different levels of internal sensitivity, but the one experience everyone undergoes is the feeling of something steam-like rising in the body. This sensation is warm and moving like a gentle and flimsy breeze—and is the first real sign that the elixir has been formed and is starting its ascent in the body. Still, this is not actually the fully formed elixir that feels like moving water. The steam effect needs to be cultivated until it condenses, so to speak, into a more watery feeling sensation.

The reality of all this is not a matter of trying to produce the elixir, rather it is allowing the elixir to form from your previous work of Refining the Jade Secretions, Replenishing the Three Treasures, guiding the descent of qi through the Three Barriers on the Front, and leading the ascent of the qi through the Three Barriers on the Back. That is the work. The rest is about patience and continued repetitive practice, much like a hen brooding over her egg. The embryo in the egg was created, but to hatch it requires her continued patience and brooding.

Refining the Elixir

The Eight Extraordinary Neidan Meridians
(內丹奇經八脉, Nei Dan Qi Jing Ba Mai)

In these drawings the first two meridians (Heaven and Earth) show the routes for the Lesser Heavenly Circuit, the focus of this book.

The Greater Heavenly Circuit (大天周, Da Tian Zhou) makes use of the seventh and eighth meridians (Mountain and Thunder). Generally speaking this circuit is stimulated through Heel Breathing (跟息, Gen Xi) practice.

The remaining four meridians—Fire and Water, Valley and Wind—are categorized as Mobilized Reverted Elixir (運返丹, Yun Fan Dan), as they are activated during the stage of when the elixir is reverted. They will naturally open when the Lesser Heavenly Circuit is complete.

The Fire and Water Processes

Heaven (Qian) ☰
Control Vessel
(督脉, Du Mai)

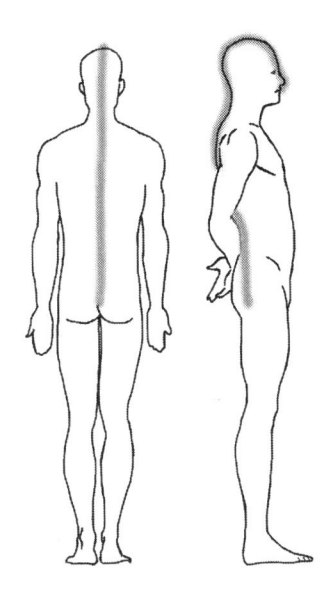

Earth (Kun) ☷
Function Vessel
(任脉, Ren Mai)

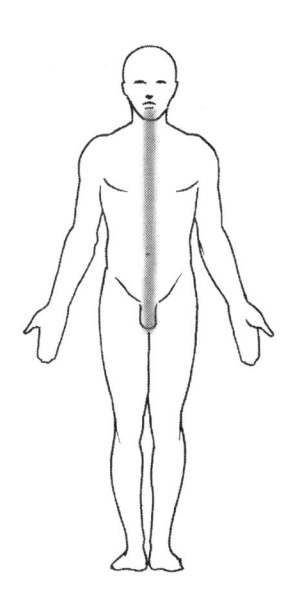

Refining the Elixir

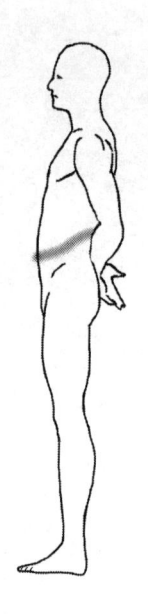

Fire (Li) ☲
Belt Vessel
(带脉, Dai Mai)

Water (Kan) ☵
Penetrating Vessel
(冲脉, Chong Mai)

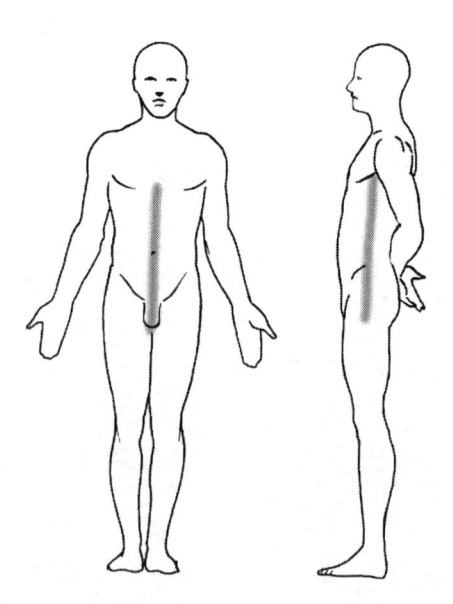

The Fire and Water Processes

Valley (Dui) ☱
Yang Preserving Vessel
(陽維脈, Yang Wei Mai)

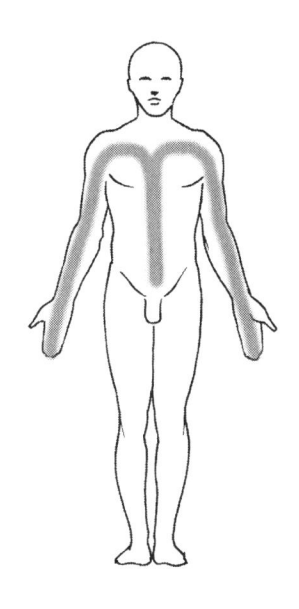

Wind (Xun) ☴
Yin Preserving Vessel
(陰維脈, Yin Wei Mai)

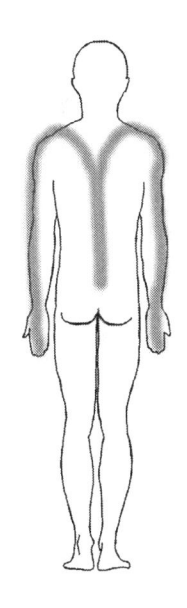

Refining the Elixir

Mountain (Gen) ☶
Yang Heel Vessel
(陽蹺脉,
Yang Qiao Mai)

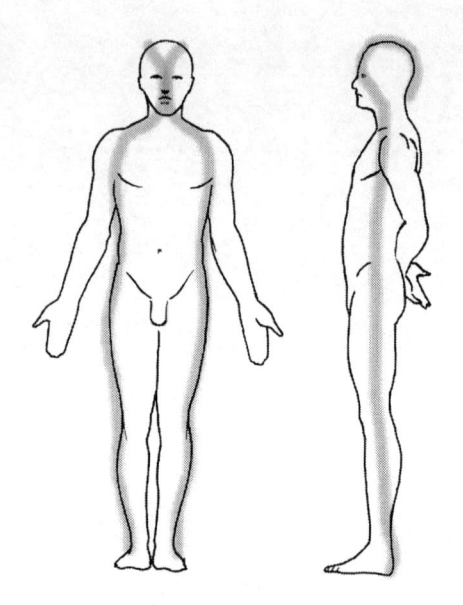

Thunder (Zhen) ☳
Yin Heel Vessel
(陰蹺脉,
Yin Qiao Mai)

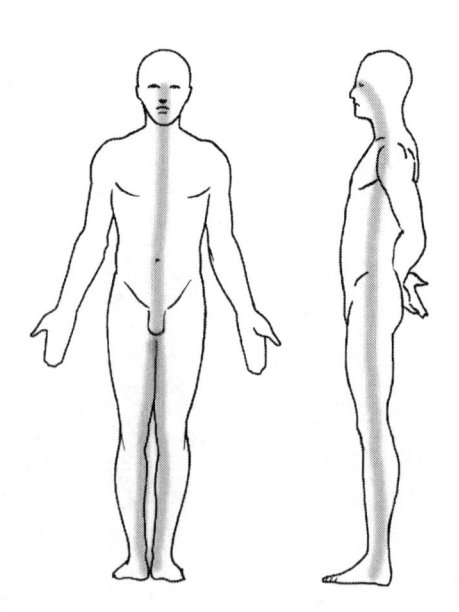

The Fire and Water Processes

The Twelve Major Qi Cavities (十二大氣穴, Shi Er Da Qi Xue) and Seven Chakras (七輪, Qi Lun) of the Body

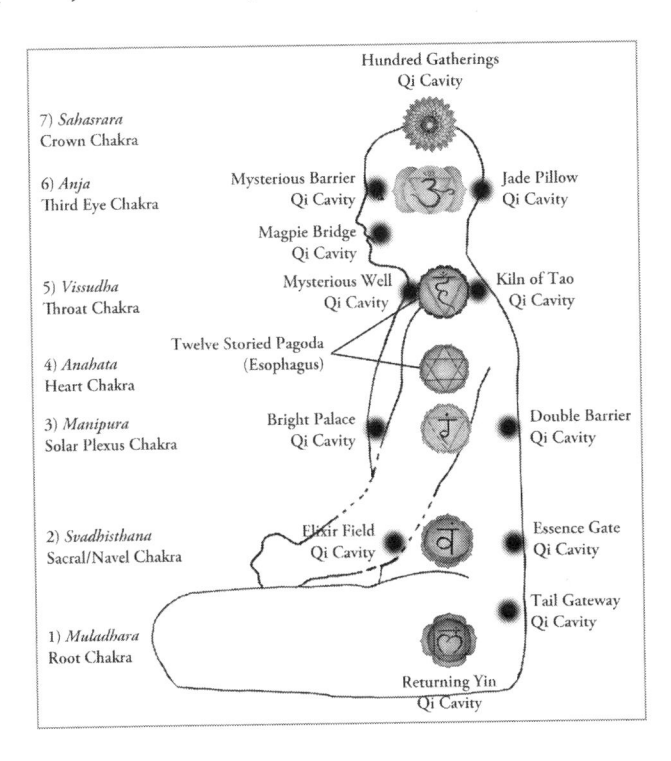

Seven Chakras (left side):
- 7) *Sahasrara* — Crown Chakra
- 6) *Anja* — Third Eye Chakra
- 5) *Vissudha* — Throat Chakra
- 4) *Anahata* — Heart Chakra
- 3) *Manipura* — Solar Plexus Chakra
- 2) *Svadhisthana* — Sacral/Navel Chakra
- 1) *Muladhara* — Root Chakra

Twelve Major Qi Cavities:
- Hundred Gatherings Qi Cavity
- Mysterious Barrier Qi Cavity
- Jade Pillow Qi Cavity
- Magpie Bridge Qi Cavity
- Mysterious Well Qi Cavity
- Kiln of Tao Qi Cavity
- Twelve Storied Pagoda (Esophagus)
- Bright Palace Qi Cavity
- Double Barrier Qi Cavity
- Elixir Field Qi Cavity
- Essence Gate Qi Cavity
- Tail Gateway Qi Cavity
- Returning Yin Qi Cavity

These twelve qi cavities are the major areas along the Dumai and Renmai meridians of internal alchemy. Cultivators need to pay attention to each cavity. They are, in analogy, like crimps in a garden hose, so directing the breath and producing heat in them helps clear the Dumai and Renmai meridians. This practice of *Opening the Twelve Major Qi Cavities* is performed during the Setting Up the Foundation

Refining the Elixir

Stage of Replenishing the Three Treasures. Practice it in conjunction with the following exercises of *Three Barriers on the Front and Back* and the *Nine Restorations*.

Begin in a seated meditation posture and start with the lower Elixir Field. Direct the attention to the cavity for nine breaths, and then move on to the next area and repeat the focused breathing. Continue in order until all twelve cavities have been stimulated, cycling through the full set three times.

1. *Dan Tian* (丹田, Elixir Field). Also referred to as the lower Elixir Field, the lower Yellow Court, and Central Palace. The area of the Elixir Field in internal alchemy is approximately three inches back from the navel. In kundalini yoga this is part of the second chakra, *Svadhisthana*, the Sacral/Navel Chakra.

2. *Hui Yin* (回陰, Returning Yin). This is the coccyx area of the perineum between the legs, the soft fleshy space between the anal opening and the base of the genitals. It is the first chakra in kundalini yoga, *Muladhara*, the Root Chakra.

3. *Wei Lu* (尾閭, Tail Gateway). In internal alchemy this cavity is located about 2 1/2 inches inside the anal tract on the upper side. The Tai Gateway is the source and first qi cavity of the Dumai meridian. In kundalini yoga it is called the "kundalini gland," which is contained in the second chakra, *Svadhisthana*, the Sacral/Navel Chakra.

The Fire and Water Processes

4. *Jing Men* (精門, Essence Gate). This area is between the upper part of the two kidneys, directly across from the Elixir Field. It's in the adrenal glands, residing on top of each kidney, where the elixir divides into two streams within the Dumai. These two streams are called White Tiger (白虎, Bai Hu, the right side) and Green Dragon (青龍, Qing Long, left side). These two areas, Essence Gate and Elixir Field, comprise the second chakra, *Svadhisthana*, the Sacral/Navel Chakra.
5. *Shuang Guan* (雙關, Double Barrier). Also called the Spine Handle (夾脊, Jia Ji). This area is in the middle of the back and is directly across from the solar plexus on the front of the body, the Jiang Gong cavity. It is at this juncture where the White Tiger and Green Dragon channels cross over each other to change sides along the spine. In kundalini yoga this area is the third chakra, *Manipura*, the Solar Plexus Chakra.

Twelve Storied Pagoda (十二重樓, Shi Er Zhong Lou) is not considered a singular qi cavity, rather an area running from just above the solar plexus (Bright Palace) and beneath the throat (Mysterious Well), the esophagus, and is sometimes referred to as the Mysterious Receptor (玄迎, Xuan Ying). In kundalini yoga this is the fourth chakra, *Anahata*, the Heart Chakra.

Refining the Elixir

6. *Tao Tao* (陶道, Kiln of Tao). The very top of the spine and base of the neck where a large bone protrudes. The White Tiger and Green Dragon channels join together as the elixir enters into the neck bone. The Kiln of Tao and Mysterious Well are across from each other and represent in kundalini yoga the fifth chakra, *Vissudha,* the Throat Chakra.
7. *Yu Zhen* (玉枕, Jade Pillow). This cavity resides in the occiput, and is considered in internal alchemy as the most difficult of all cavities to open. The Jade Pillow and Mysterious Barrier are directly across from each other and represent in kundalini yoga the sixth chakra, *Anja,* the Third Eye Chakra.
8. *Bai Hui* (百會, Hundred Gatherings). This is also called the Muddy Pellet (尼丸, Ni Wan). The area for this runs from the center of the brain up to the top of the head. It equates with the "soft spot" area we had as infants. Bone gradually forms over this area sealing in the spirit. Taoists say that if this spot is warm when a person dies, it means the Hun Spirit has ascended to a higher spiritual plane (immortal paradise), but if cold it means the Po Spirit descended through the feet into the ghost or animal plane. It is the Hundred Gatherings area that produces the illumination experience in internal alchemy. In kundalini yoga it represents the seventh chakra, *Sahasrara,* the Crown Chakra.

The Fire and Water Processes

9. *Xuan Guan* (玄關, Mysterious Barrier). This is the area between the two eyes and brow, approximately one inch back. The Jade Pillow and Mysterious Barrier are directly across from each other and represent in kundalini yoga the sixth Chakra, *Anja*, the Third Eye Chakra.
10. *Que Qiao* (鵲橋, Magpie Bridge). This cavity is centered on the upper palate of the mouth. It connects with the Renmai meridian, Mysterious Well, and the Twelve Storied Pagoda, the esophagus, The Magpie Bridge is one of three cavities (the other two being the Kiln of Tao and Mysterious Well) represented in kundalini yoga as the fifth chakra, *Vissudha*, the Throat Chakra.
11. *Xuan Jing* (玄井, Mysterious Well). This cavity is centered in the bottom of the throat along the clavicle. The Kiln of Tao and Mysterious Well are across from each other (along with the Magpie Bridge) and represent in kundalini yoga the fifth chakra, *Vissudha*, the Throat Chakra.
12. *Jiang Gong* (絳公, Bright Palace). This cavity is located about one inch inwards of the solar plexus area, directly beneath the ribs in the center of the body. In kundalini yoga this area is the third chakra, *Manipura*, the Solar Plexus Chakra.

Refining the Elixir

Three Barriers on the Front, Three Barriers on the Back (前三關後三關, Qian San Guan Hou San Guan)

The practice of this process is really quite simple, but very effective. As with Opening the Twelve Major Qi Cavities, it is simply a matter of directing the breath to each of the areas.

Instructions for Three Barriers on the Front:

In a seated and upright position, lower the head slightly downward and raise the back when exhaling, and then return to an upright position when inhaling. With Embryonic Breathing, focus all your attention on the Hundred Gatherings (Bai Hui). Inhale and exhale 12, 24, or 48 times.[26]

Next, focus on the Bright Palace (Jiang Gong) and inhale and exhale 12, 24, or 48 times.

Lastly, focus on the lower Elixir Field (Dan Tian), inhaling and exhaling 12, 24, or 48 times.

Instructions for Three Barriers on the Back:

In a seated, upright position, raise the shoulders slightly while contracting the neck downward when inhaling, and return to an upright position when exhaling. With Embryonic

---

[26] For the descent along the Renmai, yin numbers are used for counting the breaths of each pass. Lowering the head and raising the back is a physiological way of aiding in the descent of the qi.

The Fire and Water Processes

Breathing, focus all your attention on the Tail Gateway (Wei Lu), inhaling and exhaling 9, 18, or 36 times.[27]

Next, focus on the Double Pass (Shuang Guan). Inhale and exhale 9, 18, or 36 times.

Lastly, focus on the Jade Pillow (Yu Zhen) while inhaling and exhaling 9, 18, or 36 times times.

Three on the Front, Three on the Back

Translated from *The Immortal: True Accounts of the 250-Year-Old Man, Li Qingyun*[28]

The Three Passes on the Front [前三關, Qian San Guan]:

The Upper Pass [上關, Shang Guan], the Muddy Pellet [泥丸, Ni Wan]. It is the aperture of the source of the heart and the Sea of Original Nature [源性海, Yuan Xing Hai].

The Middle Pass [中關, Zhong Guan], the Yellow Court [黃庭, Huang Ting]. It is the aperture of the correct position and the central yellow.

---

27 For the ascent along the Dumai, yang numbers are used for counting the breaths of each pass. Raising the shoulders and contracting the neck downwards is a physiological way of aiding in the ascent of the qi.

28 This procedure and translation may appear differently in other internal alchemy works. Sometimes the three front barriers are the *Mysterious Barrier, Bright Palace,* and *Elixir Field,* and the three barriers on the back are the *Essence Gate, Double Pass,* and the *Hundred Gatherings.*

Refining the Elixir

The Lower Pass [下關, Xia Guan], the Crystal Water Palace [水晶宮, Shui Jing Gong]. It means the aperture of the Elixir Field [丹田, Dan Tian] and Ocean of Qi [氣海, Qi Hai].

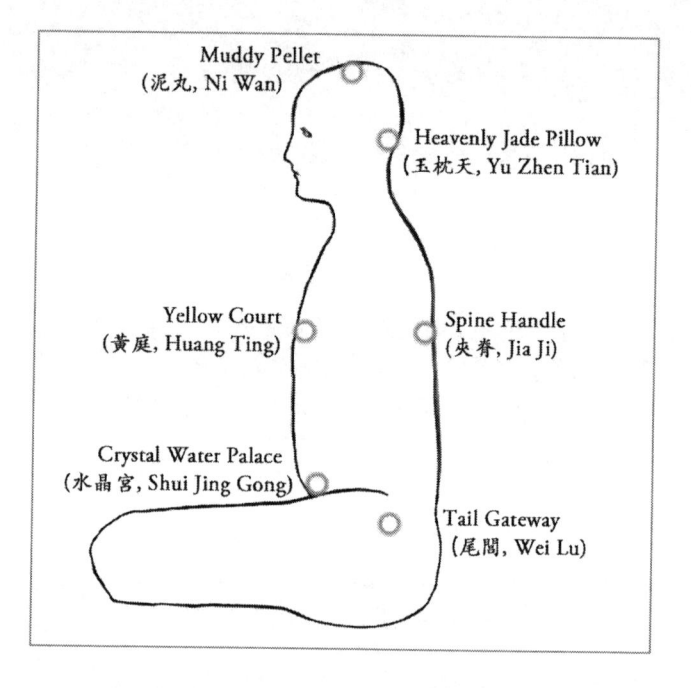

Muddy Pellet (泥丸, Ni Wan)

Heavenly Jade Pillow (玉枕天, Yu Zhen Tian)

Yellow Court (黃庭, Huang Ting)

Spine Handle (夾脊, Jia Ji)

Crystal Water Palace (水晶宮, Shui Jing Gong)

Tail Gateway (尾閭, Wei Lu)

The Three Passes on the Back [後三關, Hou San Guan]:

The Lower Pass [下關, Xia Guan] is the Tail Gateway [尾閭, Wei Lu]. It is the aperture of the Du Meridian, Supreme Mystery [太玄, Tai Xuan].

The Middle Pass [中關, Zhong Guan] is the Spine Handle [夾脊, Jia Ji]. It is the aperture of the Life Gate [命門, Ming Men] and Double Pass [雙關, Shuang Guan].

The Fire and Water Processes

The Upper Pass [上關, Shang Guan] is the Heavenly Jade Pillow [玉枕天, Yu Zhen Tian]. It is the aperture of the Valley of the Muddy Pellet [谷泥丸, Gu Ni Wan].

Nine Restorations (九還, Jiu Huan)

The Nine Restorations derived from the metallurgical methods of Nine Crucibles (九坩, Jiu Gan), a very extensive subject in alchemy. In "Gold and Cinnabar," chapter 4 of *Master of Embracing Simplicity,* Ge Hong recounts the methods and formulas that make use of nine crucibles for the production of potable gold through processing mercury into cinnabar, and then the cinnabar into potable gold (金液, Jin Ye), which would then be ingested for attaining immortality. He gives numerous examples of formulas for doing this, with various other ingredients and processes, but the use of Nine Crucibles, Nine Turnings (九轉, Jiu Zhuan), Nine Processes (九侯, Jiu Hou), Nine Reversions (九返, Jiu Fan), Nine Flowers (九華, Jiu Hua), Nine Bright Elixirs (九光丹, Jiu Guang Dan), and numerous other such terms are normally found within the formula name or process. These metallurgical terms were borrowed later by internal alchemists for their methods. This subject, as stated, is quite extensive and not the purview of this book, but it's worth noting correlations and similarities between the metallurgical processes and the biological-based methods of internal alchemy.

The use of the number nine is presented in various ways within different alchemy texts. Sometimes it is just about

Refining the Elixir

circulating the qi nine complete times through the Dumai and Renmai meridians, calling it the Lesser Heavenly Circuit (小天周, Xiao Tian Zhou, or Microcosmic Orbit). Other texts term it in the practice of restoring the Nine Essences (九精, Jiu Jing) to revert them into a positive yang energy, rather than negative yin, or as it is stated in a cryptic language in internal alchemy works, "Use the After Heaven [temporal] to bring forth the Before Heaven [innate]." *Refining* is the temporal, and *reverting* is the innate.

One of the more unique methods of Nine Restorations is found in the practice of visualizing Nine Cauldrons (九鼎, Jiu Ding) that relate to nine specific areas of the body (along the meridians). The following practice of Refining the Nine Cauldrons comes from the *Jade Tablet Decrees on Nature and Life*. The illustration with the translation depicts the Nine Cauldrons. Each cauldron is associated with a circle that contains the character xin (心) for "heart-mind"—except the ninth cauldron which is all white. The images progress from right to left—from black to white, obscured to the opaque.

The Nine Cauldrons, or Crucibles, are "sacrificial vessels" cast by Yu the Great, legendary founder of the Xia dynasty (夏朝, Xia Chao, circa 2070 BCE to circa 1600 BCE), who had the precious metals of each nine provinces in his kingdom made into cauldrons. This later became the basis for Nine Palaces Numerology of Feng Shui.

The metaphor of the elixir in the original text below is equating the sun as though it were a liquid. This is

The Fire and Water Processes

interesting in that the two main components of the elixir are fire and water, light and liquid.

The reader should note there are several meanings in this text concerning the term Dan (丹, the elixir). There is the "elixir" derived from cultivating, a sensation of a fluid flowing through the body. There is the "elixir" used to express a vibrant red color, the color of cinnabar and molten metals. There is also the "elixir" of the sun's red brightness, the same color seen internally by a practitioner when cultivating the elixir.

Refining the Nine Cauldrons
(煉九鼎, Lian Jiu Ding)

First Cauldron Transmission
Scouring the mind ground of the heart-mind [心, xin], refining the Golden Elixir [金丹, Jin Dan], and cessation of thought is the first barrier. Cutting off thought spontaneously severs the consciousness of passions. One must know of the tranquil waters [水靜, Shui Jing], without waves great or small.

Refining the Elixir

Second Cauldron Transmission
When the Ancestral Cavity [祖竅, Zu Qiao][1] opens, one enters dark obscurity. Kan [坎, Water] and Li [離, Fire], Lead [鉛, Qian = Water] and Mercury [汞, Gong = Fire], are like clouds moving of their own accord, the Nature[2] of True Fire[3] knows the time for refining. From this refinement comes Qian [乾, Heaven][4] from the Western directions, the moon is then half full.

Notes
1. *Ancestral Cavity* is the lower Elixir Field, three inches behind the navel.
2. *Nature* is Xing (性). True disposition as used in the meaning of Xing Ming, *Nature and Life*.
3. *True Fire* (真息, Zhen Xi) is the primordial breath, the breath coming from the lower Elixir Field.
4. The terms *Kan, Li,* and *Qian* are from the *Book of Changes.* Qian (Heaven) is actually assigned to the northwest direction and Dui (Valley) to the west in the After Heaven arrangement of the Eight Trigrams.

Third Cauldron Transmission
From the external it penetrates directly to the core. People of the world have seldom heard of it, as they only seek the leaves and branches, not the root. From this place it approaches calmly and steadily. From one flash of Divine Light [靈光, Ling Guang] will gradually illuminate you.

The Fire and Water Processes

Fourth Cauldron Transmission
The Yang Raven [陽烏, Yang Wu] following the Sea Bed [海底, Hai Di][1] demonstrates its strength of the spirit's incredible power. This is the correct time for the fourth transformation of the Golden Elixir. Steal the Primordial [先天, Xian Tian, Before Heaven] True Seed [真種子, Zhen Zhong Zi] and carry it upon the Waterwheel up along Cao's mountain stream.[2]

Notes
1. The *Yang Raven* (or crow) is the elixir and the *Sea Bed* is the initial lower region of the Renmai, moving into the perineum up to the Wei Lu.
2. The *Waterwheel* is another name for the River Cart (河車, He Che), and *Cao's mountain stream* (曹溪, Cao Qi) is the Dumai channel up the spine into the brain.

Fifth Cauldron Transmission
At this time the Golden Crystal [金晶, Jin Jing] ascends in flight. With a numinous brilliant light the door at the crest of the head[1] opens. Three flowers gather[2] at the summit[3] and the dragon and tiger[4] begin cooking. The pearl[5] descends into the Yellow Court [黃庭, Huang Ting][6] and forms the Sagely Embryo [聖胎, Sheng Tai].

Notes
1. *Crest of the head* is indicating the Mysterious Pass (玄關, Xuan Guan), the third eye.
2. *Three flowers* is referring to the *San Yuan* (三元), the Three Origins.

Refining the Elixir

   This represents the three Hun spirits residing at the top of a person's head.
3. The *summit* is the Ni Wan (泥丸), Muddy Pellet cavity atop the head.
4. *Dragon* and *tiger* here refers to the two points behind the eyes, left and right.
5. The *pearl* is the droplet of Yang Shen (陽神), the Spirit of Vitality.
6. The lower Elixir Field.

Sixth Cauldron Transmission
The Golden Raven [金烏, Jin Wu] flies into the Vast Cold Palace [廣寒宮, Guang Han Gong].[1] The White Tiger [白虎, Bai Hu] displays its massive power while awaiting on the Red Dragon [赤龍, Chi Long].[2] The Red Dragon exerts its strength and returns to the Golden Cauldron [金鼎, Jin Ding]. In the Dragon's palm is held a spirit pearl [神珠, Shen Zhu] and its eyes glow red.

Notes
1. *Cold Palace* is the Moon Palace of the Goddess Chang O.
2. Other texts on this line say, "While awaiting on the Green Dragon," not *Red Dragon*.

Seventh Cauldron Transmission
In the tenth month the immortal embryo [胎靈, Tai Ling] comes forth. The Infant requires three years of Way's Milk[1] [法乳, Fa Ru]. Concealed in hibernation, residing in the breath, it is warmed and nurtured. Just as the dragon on the bottom of the pool sleeps embracing the pearl.

The Fire and Water Processes

Note
1. The character Fa (法) is used in Buddhism as Dharma. In Taoism it is used as another term for Tao (道).

Eighth Cauldron Transmission
When Yang reaches its apex and yin diminishes, the elixir is then complete. The spiritual light glows bright and the Golden Court [金庭, Jin Ting] is brilliantly set aglow. Separating from its host the Infant emerges from the Bitter Sea [苦海, Ku Hai]. Freely ascending to the summit of the Kunlun Mountains [崑崙].[1]

Note
1. The *Kunlun Mountains* represent the highest peaks of the Himalayas, and in internal alchemy the top of the head.

Ninth Cauldron Transmission
There is no elixir, there is no fire, nor is there any gold. Discard the hammer and pincers[1] as there is nothing to hold onto. My original true face returns. The place of the unborn body is just a shining wheel.

Note
1. This is a metallurgical metaphor depicting the blacksmith's hammer and pincers used in forging metals. The pincer metaphor shows the blacksmith attempting to grasp and hold in place an object being shaped, but finds nothing to grasp onto.

Refining the Elixir

Commentary

The sun is Heaven's elixir. If you were to put black in it and shake it up, the sun could not shine. The heart-mind is the brightness [丹, Dan, the elixir] of people. When daily affairs cloud it, the heart-mind cannot shine. Therefore, what is called "refining the elixir" is actually the removal of debris to restore the heart-mind's original substance and the spontaneity of its Heavenly Mandated [天命, Tian Ming] Qi [氣, vital life energy].

The Heavenly Mandated Nature [the disposition] is our True Gold, which everyone must have. The physical Nature [of our disposition] is the impurities within the gold, which even those of superior wisdom are not without. Just as the fires we use of ethical daily affairs and human relationships refine it, so too is the physical Nature [disposition] purged daily. When the physical Nature [disposition] is purged daily, the Heavenly Mandated lifespan will spontaneously show itself.

There is no time when the mind is not with the Tao, no time when the Tao is not used to refine the mind. This is the requisite method of study of the ancient Great Sages and Worthies. These are then clear instructions for refining the mind, so to refine the Nature one hundred times over [until complete].

The Fire and Water Processes

These Nine Cauldrons were interpreted in internal alchemy not only in psychological terms for refining the mind, but also as a physiological exercise within the practice of Reverting Jing to Restore the Brain. The first cauldron was visualized in the Elixir Field, the second cauldron in the Returning Yin, the third cauldron in the Tail Gateway, the fourth cauldron in the Essence Gate, the fifth cauldron in the Double Pass, the sixth cauldron in the Kiln of Tao, the seventh cauldron in the Jade Pillow, the eighth cauldron in the Hundred Gatherings, and the ninth cauldron in the Mysterious Barrier.

In focusing on each cauldron, the cultivator should envision potable gold within them and a violet colored mist coming off of them. The practicer would perform several rounds of this visualization, going from one cauldron to the next, employing Embryonic Breathing of either 9, 18, or 36 breaths for each cauldron, and usually repeating the process nine times during one session.

Then there are the methods of Reverted Elixir in Nine Cycles (九轉還丹, Jiu Zhuan Huan Dan), and numerous other methods all using the idea of "nine," such as tripods, heavens, lords, flowers, efflorescences, radiances, palaces, grottos, pearls, chambers, and so on. Despite the varying associations, the basis of all these practices comes down to the matter of processing the elixir into a yang (陽) positive energy, and yang is represented by the number nine (from the *Book of Changes*), instead of the common human condition of having a yin negative (number six) energy.

Refining the Elixir

Turning this elixir from yin to yang is the idea behind the term "reverting." From the moment the umbilical cord is cut we are in a yin (陰) descent towards death, and so reverting this to a yang ascent away from death is the central idea behind internal alchemy leading to immortality. Therefore, creating Congealed Yang Spirit (凝陽神, Ning Yang Shen), or One Droplet (點子, Yi Dian) of Yang Spirit, can only take place within the context of nine processes, such as nine months to complete the gestation of a fetus in a pregnancy. It takes nine generations to complete an ancestral blood line. It takes nine complete circulations of the elixir within the Extraordinary Dumai and Renmai meridians to refine it to the point of congealing and producing the one droplet that can enter into and fuze within the lower Elixir Field to create an immortal fetus (胎仙, Tai Xian).

The meaning of Nine Restorations is not just about the idea of circulating the qi through the External Dumai and Renmai meridians nine times, even though this is the actual process of Replenishing the Three Treasures on a Coarse Level. However, when speaking about the elixir circulating through the Extraordinary Dumai and Renmai meridians it can be thought of as manifesting a self-induced spiritual-immortal pregnancy within your own womb (Elixir Field). Interestingly, male cultivators who, when attaining the elixir, acquire what is called a qi belly, and there is also a tendency for the left eye to close frequently, a response of the body seeking to preserve the yang positive energy.

The Fire and Water Processes

Females who attain the elixir acquire fuller breasts and a slimming of the waist.

The Nine Restorations actually has more to do with the undertaking of Replenishing the Three Treasures three times (totaling nine processes), Refining the Jing to Transform the Qi three times (another nine processes), and Refining the Qi to Transform the Shen three times (nine more processes).

Likewise, the Nine Jing are also being refined, which includes 1) saliva, 2) blood, 3) sweat, 4) tears, 5) bone marrow, 6) brain marrow, 7) sexual secretions, 8) adrenals, and 9) spinal fluids. When these Nine Jing are refined, and nourished and mobilized by the qi, the Reverted Elixir is formed. Once formed, the shen (spirit) will naturally cause it (a spontaneous kinetic reaction) to circulate through the newly formed and opened Extraordinary Meridians of the Dumai and Renmai nine times in order to congeal it, or as my teacher aptly described it, "Once the sperm is inside the woman, the sperm cells mobilize towards the egg of their own accord. There is no method, it is just a natural and spontaneous reaction."

True Breath (眞氣, Zhen Qi)

The meaning of True Breath is actually one of the best kept secrets in internal alchemy. Usually, it's explained with the idea that it's our Before Heaven (primordial breath), which is true except this doesn't explain how to bring it forth. *Breath* is normally just considered as breathing and many

Refining the Elixir

cultivators just become stomach pushers, as I was initially. During my first meeting and lesson with Master Liang, he questioned me on what kind of breathing I had learned at the monastery. I had to tell him I was never taught about breathing or meditation, as there were no classes on such things. One had to learn by assimilation.

He chuckled and said, "Just for monks I presume." Then he asked me to stand and breathe. When I did so he moved next to me, placing one hand on my lower abdomen and another on my lower back. Then he said to just breathe a few times. After a short while, he walked away laughing and said, "Half alive, half dead."

When I pressed him on what he meant, he told me, "I only felt the front of your stomach push out when you inhaled and go in when you exhale, but I felt nothing on your lower spine. It should be like a balloon, all parts expand and contract when air is blown in or when it is released. You cannot expect the qi to go somewhere if you cannot bring the breath there. They are one in the same."

Much later when I felt I had really accomplished this kind of breathing, I went to him (admittedly to show off). When I demonstrated for him, he again just chuckled and told me, "It is wonderful you can breathe this way, but it is not the True Breath. You are still using your lower back and stomach muscles to breathe."

Then he told me something so valuable I was reluctant for years to even speak of it. He said (in paraphrase):

The Fire and Water Processes

Imagine your Elixir Field in your lower abdomen is a small balloon and your abdomen is like a larger balloon. Your inhalation should be completely focused upon and generated by the small inner balloon, so it expands. Your exhalation should equally be as though deflating and releasing some air from the balloon. Internally feel as though it is your Elixir Field causing the expansion and contraction of your abdomen, not your external muscles. Like blowing up a small balloon within a larger balloon. This is True Breath because it is coming from within your Elixir Field. This is where your breath came from when you were in your mother's stomach, so it is called Before Heaven. If you can practice this, you will get something.

This piece of instruction made all the difference in the world in my meditation practice. Although I had read numerous texts that all used the term "True Breath," or the "One Breath" (一氣, Yi Qi), but I had never connected that with the idea of breathing from within my Elixir Field, rather I realized I had been breathing around it, not from within it. This is so very Taoist to breathe as we did in our mother's womb.

Returning Spirit to the Void
神還虛

The final goal of internal alchemy is this idea of Returning Spirit to the Void. The Taoist text *Clarity and Tranquility of the Constant Scripture*[29] defines it as "being so tranquil there is not even the perception of tranquility," also stating, "it is even void of the concept of voidness." There really isn't much that can be said to describe this state, and most internal alchemy texts do not attempt it, as it is beyond words.

Lao Zi himself in the *Scripture on Tao and Virtue* calls it "the nameless," and only says he used the term "Tao" as an expedient. Lao Zi explains immediately that this Tao can neither be spoken of nor can it be determined by some fixed or rote practice: "The Tao that can be Tao[ed] is not the Constant Tao."

Internal alchemy texts say so little on the subject because it's not a matter that can be thought through or calculated in any fashion. It is as Lao Zi explains, "active non-action." As my teacher said, "Sit until you have no awareness of sitting, then you are getting close to it."

This stage of internal alchemy is mostly identical to the practice of Chan (Zen), but this doesn't mean that you can

---

29 See *Clarity & Tranquility: A Guide for Daoist Meditation* by Stuart Alve Olson (Valley Spirit Arts, 2015).

Refining the Elixir

出 胎 圖

Spiritual Embryo Departing
(出 胎 圖, Chu Tai Tu)
Image depicts the transformation and release of the Spiritual
Infant. From the *Jade Tablet Decrees on Nature and Life*.

Returning Spirit to the Void

just go sit in a Chan session and Return Spirit to the Void. It doesn't mean you can just skip over the three initial stages of internal alchemy and go straight to this final stage. Actually, someone could potentially do this, but Chan is far more difficult for the majority of us. Personally I wish everyone would go to a Zen place and sit. This is good, really good, but to actually achieve Returning Spirit into the Void, or as a Chan Buddhist would call it, "Entering Sunyata" is quite another matter.

Since making this comparison of Returning Spirit to the Void and the goal of Chan as being identical, it brings up the question of why does internal alchemy have three stages of preparation and Chan is just about sitting? There are four possible answers to this question:

1) Chan Buddhists are not attached to the ideas of health, longevity, and immortality. Taoists do have an attachment to these matters because they want to be healthy and live long enough to immortalize their spirit. This means they will have more opportunities to achieve the goal of Returning Spirit to the Void.

2) Chan is a direct method of cultivation. If reaching the top of a mountain is the metaphorical idea of achieving enlightenment, then Chan Buddhists will simply climb straight up the mountainside, grasping onto anything to pull themselves upward. Taoists would find the path of least resistance and walk up to the top. Same goal, different methodology.

Refining the Elixir

3) Internal alchemy is very much like a preparation for achieving the goal of Returning Spirit to the Void. Within both Taoism and Buddhism there is a long-standing debate over whether or not cultivators should follow the idea of "first in the body then in the mind" or "first in the mind then in the body." Internal alchemy is about cultivating body and then mind, while Chan goes straight to the mind.

4) Buddhists have a root belief that life is suffering and so they cultivate the Eightfold Path to end that suffering. Taoists see life as something to be appreciated for what it is, accepting the sufferings and blessings of life with equanimity. In the *Scripture on Tao and Virtue*, Lao Zi says,

> When following the Tao, one identifies with the Tao. When following Virtue, one identifies with Virtue. When people identify with the Tao, the Tao will gladly accept them. When people identify with Virtue, Virtue gladly accepts them. If you identify with loss, loss gladly accepts you.

In this context, the difference in approaches comes down to one's perception and acceptance. Taoists go with the flow of life and Buddhists try to turn the conditions and suffering of life.

When reading the biography of the famous Taoist internal alchemist Zhang Boduan (張伯端, 987?–1082), author of *Realization of Reality* (悟真篇, *Wu Zhen Pian*) and *Four Hundred Words on the Golden Elixir* (金丹四百字, *Jin Dan Si Bai Zi*), it's not surprising to learn that in his elder years

Returning Spirit to the Void

he retired to a Chan Buddhist monastery. The great immortal Lu Dongbin also spent a great deal of time with Chan Buddhists, as did Zhang Sanfeng himself. This wasn't because they thought Chan Buddhism was superior, rather they saw that Returning Spirit to the Void was identical in practice with the Chan goal of entering Sunyata (the voidness of the void). The Taoist meditation practice of Sitting and Forgetting (坐忘, Zuo Wang) is akin to Chan meditation. The ideogram for Chan, 禪, literally means "abstract contemplative absorption."

There's also a great similarity between the Taoist ideal of living in the "naturally just so" (自然, zi ran)[30] and the Buddhist ideal of living in "perfect freedom action," wherein there is no more attachment to worldly matters and life is lived in the moment, completely free of fear. In the *Heart Sutra*[31] it states, "Enlightened beings, relying on the Profound Perfection of Wisdom are without hindrance. Because they are without hindrance, they are without fear

---

30 Lao Zi in the *Scripture on Tao and Virtue* states, "The Tao models itself on the naturally just so." The naturally-just-so is the very spontaneous, creationist aspect of everything. To live in the naturally-just-so is pointing at the idea of going with the flow of life and to live in accordance with the workings of nature, Heaven and Earth, and by our spirit—all of which are part of the Tao and the entrance to it.

31 *The Heart of the Profound Perfection of Wisdom Sutra* (般若波羅蜜多心經, *Bo Re Bo Luo Mi Duo Xin Jing*). *Prajñāpāramitāhṛdaya* in Sanskrit.

Refining the Elixir

and have gone beyond all distorted dream thinking; ultimately, to final blissful extinction [nirvana]."

In Taoism, living in the "naturally just so" is also being without fear, without hindrance, and without the illusory mind—or simply said, it's about "Entering the Tao."

The Infant Manifests Its Form Illustration
(嬰兒現形圖, Ying Er Xian Xing Tu)[32]

---

[32] From *Secret of the Golden Flower*. This illustration represents the Second Level of Meditation for the *Secret of the Golden Flower* Internal Alchemy Practice.

Returning Spirit to the Void

Right side bold vertical characters
Now that the elixir [丹, dan] has been cooked,
a loving mother is needed to nourish the Infant.

Left side bold vertical characters
One day you will fly about in the clouds. Only then
will you see the True Person [真人, Zhen Ren] in
salutation to the Highest Sovereign [上帝, Shang Di].

Top center text
Now, the True [真, Zhen] for insects with nictitating
membranes is that they gestate larvae for dragonflies.
They transmit their passions [情, qing] by mating
amongst the flower petals, where they exchange their
essence [精, jing]. From this they mix their vitality
[氣, qi] and unite their spirits [神, shen]. So even
the smallest of things can obtain the True.

Top right text
The spiritual name of the qi cavity [氣穴, qi xue]
is Infinite Storehouse [無量藏, Wu Liang Zang]. The
storehouse encompasses the aperture [竅, qiao] and
the aperture encompasses the Void [空, Kong] so I
ask: "The [person] in the midst of the Void is the elder
noble of what clan?" It says: "It is you, the master."

Refining the Elixir

Top left text
The hidden dragon [卧龍, wo long] completes its transformation into a flying dragon [飛龍, fei long]. When the transformation is manifested, the spirit connects and cannot be exhausted. One morning it will leap out from a pearly light [珠光, zhu guang], and the body will spring directly into the Virtuous Azure Palace [紫德宮, Zi De Gong].

Bottom right side
Whether walking, standing, sitting, or lying down, "Hold onto the male and keep to the female, continuously it [Tao] appears to exist."[1] If you concentrate on this point then it is at this point.

Note
1. From Lao Zi's *Scripture on Tao and Virtue*.

Bottom left side
The Spiritual Waters [神水, Shen Shui] absorb into the plant to irrigate it, the external and internal are then uncontaminated. Constantly nurture the spiritual body.

Returning Spirit to the Void

The gist of internal alchemy, at least in the essential practice of it, relies on attaining two skills: *Returning the Light* (回光, Hui Guang) and *Reversing the Hearing* (返聽, Ting Zhuan), so as to contemplate and sense everything internally, whereby the spirit is then completely retained internally. In chapter 5 of *Master of Embracing Simplicity*, Ge Hong says of the attributes of a spiritual cultivator, "Listening in reverse, they hear most clearly; gazing inwards, their seeing is free of blemishes."

Returning the Light is sometimes referred to in Taoism as obtaining the Heavenly Mind or Consciousness (天心, Tian Xin) and in Buddhism, the Dharma Eye. In the *Secret of the Golden Flower,* it states, "Emptiness is not empty, it is full of light." This light is created by the Original Spirit. Normally when we close our eyes we only see darkness with a spattering of light flashes. This is the deluded mind. When the Original Spirit begins to awaken, the opposite occurs. Everything seems brighter with a spattering of dark blemishes. Lao Zi referred to this as "pure whiteness appears blemished." The more we meditate and cleanse our minds of extraneous thoughts, the brighter and clearer our mind becomes. Without this light we simply cannot obtain the Heavenly Eye (天眼, Tian Yan) or gain realization of the eye consciousness.

Reversing the Hearing, or sometimes referred to as, Turning the Hearing Inwards, means being able to listen to ourselves internally to obtain the Heavenly Ear (天聆, Tian Ling) or gain realization of the ear consciousness. Have you

Refining the Elixir

ever heard your heart beat, heard the sound of the inhalation and exhalation within the lower abdomen, heard blood flow through your arteries, or heard the sound of thunder (when either ingesting saliva or breath) in your Elixir Field, or what Lao Zi called, "Hearing the spirits of the valley?" Sometimes in deep meditative states the cultivator will hear people talking in the distance, like an unrecognizable conversation. A few times while sitting, I heard the distant, and quite beautiful, sounds of monks chanting for brief periods. So, if we get quiet enough internally, we can hear these spirits of the valley.

When Returning the Light and Reversing the Hearing are accomplished, the spirit is retained internally and there will be no more leaking out or outflows of the spirit. To put this in a more practical view, look back to our childhood when our minds were bright and full of imagination. We could mentally envision everything, and we could daydream intensely. Even our hearing was cutoff a great deal of the time, such as when playing and our mother would shout several times about lunch being ready, but our spirits were so absorbed in the play we couldn't hear her. Then as we grow older the negative effects of anxiety take over, and so our sight and hearing consciousnesses are deadened, so much that by the time we are in our late teens only the sight and ear organs and the functions of them operate, not the consciousness or spirit of them.

Regarding the idea of anxiety being the root cause that prevents us from Returning the Light and Turning the

Returning Spirit to the Void

Hearing Inwards, anxiety creates false or wrong thinking, which in turn creates perplexities in our mind. Once we have perplexities, thoughts of greed, anger, and ignorance come rushing forth, so I normally advise my students that when they first sit down to meditate to give themselves a few moments to get rid of the inherent anxiety about sitting. Every meditator will go through some sort of anxiety about sitting, such as thoughts about how they only have so much time to sit so an alarm should be set, or thinking about things they need to do after they sit, or thoughts about past events, or attempting to problem solve while sitting. The worst is what I call waiting for the bell. During retreats I can sometimes feel certain participants in their minds screaming about when is the damn bell going to be rung? Thoughts like did the bell ringer fall asleep or drift off in deep tranquility? Why hasn't the bell been rung yet? It can get very tense and even to the point of anger in some. This is anxiety rearing its ugly head. Meditators should simply tell themselves they don't care about anything other than the method at hand—to constantly just be mindful of their sitting, or in Taoist terms to "sit and forget." Forget everything except the Original Spirit within the Elixir Field. These words on anxiety are very important because without letting go of anxiety there is no possibility of cultivating internal alchemy or Chan.

The very basis of Returning Spirit to the Void is found directly in the experiences of Turning the Hearing Inwards

Refining the Elixir

and Returning the Light, so I will attempt to explain how these are accomplished in contemplative cultivation.

First, in the *Yin Convergence Scripture* it states, "Blind people hear well, and deaf people see well." This is because the organs of either the eyes or ears are not operating, but the consciousnesses of the eyes or ears remains. Since the consciousness energy is no longer expended externally, it becomes heightened internally. In Taoism, the spirit follows the mind-intent, so when we look out at things or direct our hearing outward, the spirit follows. Likewise, it's said that the spirit expresses itself through the eyes, the qi through the mouth, and the jing through the ears. So, returning the light internally strengthens the spirit. Guarding the speech preserves the qi, and turning the hearing inward nourishes the jing. Taoism is not advocating becoming blind, mute, or deaf, but it is advocating the skill of not being distracted by external sights and sounds. Being fully absorbed in the consciousnesses of sight and sound means you won't be distracted by or attached to either of them. Sights and sounds of the external world are the main obstacles for full realization of our internal world, the province of internal alchemy.

Suppose you are sitting by the ocean, and your ears hear the sound of the waves rolling up onto the shore, and when the waves retreat, there is silence. The function of the ear hears the sound, and the consciousness of the ear experiences the silence. By fully focusing and absorbing our attention on the silence, the sound gradually dissipates.

Returning Spirit to the Void

Sounds are only heard because we habitually attach ourselves to the organ and its function, and disregard the consciousness. The consciousness is actually the strongest of the three components of seeing or hearing. For example, when we dream we hear and see things in an unconscious state, they are purely created in the mind—more precisely, in the consciousness of the sense organ. Ears or eyes can only function if there is a functioning organ for them, but the consciousnesses of both operate even if there is no organ or function.

For internal alchemy, the experience of Reversing the Hearing and Returning the Light is not solely about guarding the spirit or nourishing the jing, but ultimately about realizing and experiencing sight and sound (and the other senses) purely as consciousnesses. Much is said in Taoism about this state of absorption, such as Zhuang Zi's description of a sage sitting in meditation appearing to be like dried wood or cold ashes, and that even if Mt. Tai fell before him it would cause no reaction.

Of course, we all want good sight and good hearing as these functions protect us. The sense organs of sight, sound, smell, taste, touch, and mind all allow us to function as a mortal being. On one hand, they protect us, they're a source for great pleasures in life and are receptors for knowledge, and they do allow us to appreciate life in its fullest sense. On the other hand, they are the source of delusion and the main hindrances to attaining immortality.

Refining the Elixir

So, the dilemma for most cultivators, Taoist or Buddhist, is whether to fully engage with the functions of the sense organs or to cut them off. The simple answer is neither, yet simplicity can be very complex, and more often than not simplicity protects itself from being discovered. We need only look to Lao Zi's advice for confirmation: "Hold onto being [existence] and keep to non-being [non-existence]."

In other words, hold onto the function and keep to the consciousness. More aptly put, appreciate the functions of the sense organs when engaged in external affairs, yet revert to the consciousnesses of the sense organs when engaged in internal affairs. Even more simplistic, eat when you're hungry, and sleep when you're tired.

Now, when you sit in meditation, return the light and revert the hearing inwards to gain awareness of the consciousness of the sense organs. When engaged in your daily activities, be fully aware of the distractions and hindrances the sense organs can cause. Doing so brings you directly to the Middle Way.

In the Middle Way, we do not harm the spirit—and when the spirit is not harmed, it can return to the Void.

Conclusion

The whole process of internal alchemy, especially in the structure Zhang Sanfeng presents, is really not that complicated. If we look at it purely from the standpoint of first Replenishing the Three Treasures, then learning to Revert Jing to Restore the Brain, and then practicing the Nine Restorations, we are well on our way towards immortalizing our spirit. Although the theory is fairly straightforward, the actual long-term and disciplined practice proves to be the downfall of most practitioners.

No one can really say exactly what internal alchemy is, at least not in the context of it being a regimented and guaranteed step-by-step process, and I feel as though I have only scratched the surface in my explanation of this art, science, and philosophy of internal alchemy. Much of internal alchemy equally relies on a person's endowments, temperament, sincerity, and discipline. Just as taking piano lessons is no guarantee a person will become a concert pianist, or a person studying art will become a Picasso. The ability to focus in a one-pointed manner, for example, can elude many practitioners until they undergo an extended period learning to completely focus. Some people are born with certain endowments that make internal alchemy easier and others are not, but this doesn't mean you can't succeed. Anyone can gain great benefit from the practice provided he

Refining the Elixir

or she learns to focus and follow the specifics. As Zhang Sanfeng says, "People who have few extraneous thoughts can obtain the elixir quickly, but those who are inundated with extraneous thoughts are slow to obtain the elixir. The method is simple and quite easy."

Suffice to say, when we were in our mother's womb we were naturally performing internal alchemy and had no extraneous thoughts, but after being born we are constantly being distracted and forget what was natural to us. Cultivating, then, is really a matter of remembering and recalling our primal beginnings so we can approach and gain a glimmer of the meaning of what is meant by *Realization of Reality* (悟真, Wu Zhen) in internal alchemy.

Realization of Reality can be somewhat explained by how we recognize what is conscious and unconscious. When dreaming during the unconscious state we perceive thoughts, experiences, and images as real. When awake and experiencing the conscious state, we also believe our thoughts, experiences, and forms are real. Which state, conscious or unconscious, is truly real? Actually neither, as both are just extremes of the mind, not the true reality of our spirit. When we experience the spirit, we see matters of the unconscious and conscious states as mere illusions of the mind. Experiencing the spirit is what Taoism refers to as a "mystical state." The mystical state is "reality," for it doesn't adhere to or depend on the conscious or unconscious mind because the ego has vanished. When the ego vanishes we are selfless—and selflessness is the state of being of an immortal.

Conclusion

The cultivation of internal alchemy is a path to that mystical state—the *True* or *Reality*. Zhuang Zi attempts to explain this in his famous "Butterfly Dream,"

> I, Zhuang Zhou, was dreaming I was a butterfly dreaming that I was Zhuang Zhou, but when I awoke I did not know if I was Zhuang Zhou having dreamt I was a butterfly dreaming of being Zhuang Zhou, or if now I am really a butterfly just dreaming I am Zhuang Zhou.

In the end, Zhuang Zhou sees that neither the butterfly or himself nor the states of dreaming or being awake are reality. Reality can only be perceived in the mystical state beyond the conscious and unconscious. In internal alchemy this is Returning Spirit to the Void, the final stage of cultivating immortality, and is the Realization of Reality.

In "The Immortal" chapter in *Master of Embracing Simplicity*, the great alchemist Ge Hong perfectly sums up internal alchemy:

> The method of immortals consists of having a true desire for attaining clarity and tranquility, being unattached to possessiveness and contention, cultivating the ability to see and hear internally, and to be free of being entranced by the emotions.

These four simple statements truly are the essence of what it means to cultivate immortality, and if the reader gets nothing else from this work, I sincerely hope this verse is retained by all those seeking the Tao.

The Great Process for Refining the Elixir Treatise
煉丹大候篇
Lian Dan Da Hou Pian

Upper Verses on the Great Process for Refining the Elixir

煉丹大候說上

Now putting forth the skills and initiatives [for the Great Process] there can be no rote activities, because these activities are just temporal [After Heaven]. Presently in Taoism many have fallen into this deterioration. Therefore, few in the world can transmit the True [teachings of the Great Process].

夫功夫下手. 不可軌於有為. 有為都是後天.
今之道門. 多流此弊. 故世罕傳眞.

Translator's Commentary
Even though there must be a constant and disciplined approach to refining the elixir it cannot be a rote practice. A rote practice would be something like scheduling yourself to sit for an hour three times a day, every day. Refining the elixir cannot be done this way, you must sit when the need arises and for as long as it takes to complete the work, otherwise it becomes like a job where you punch in and out like clockwork. The work of refining the elixir is a process of going with the flow.

The term *gui* (軌) translated here as "rote" is not quite correct, as gui also means a "track," "course," "trail," and "path," so this line could also be translated as "there can be no set path of action."

The Great Process takes a great deal of intuition to complete, and so it is not a question of just doing step A to step Z and immortality is guaranteed. As the *Jade Pivot Treasury Scripture* (玉樞寶經, *Yu Shu Bao Jing*) states, "Everyone has different endowments, and so their qi and fate are naturally different." Cultivators must find their own path and not just follow a rote and fixed course.

When Zhang says that *Taoism has declined into rote activities* he was directly speaking to those sects of Taoism that imitated the Buddhist cultivators of his day who had fixed times and schedules for sitting. Other Taoist sects considered Chan (禪, Zen) meditation sessions, especially those that would run for consecutive days and weeks, as being merely exercises in spiritual gymnastics.

Zhang thought this was counterproductive to the practice of refining the elixir. Keep in mind, however, that the meditative work undertaken by a Buddhist adept seeking enlightenment is different from a Taoist seeking to refine the elixir of immortality. Taoists like Zhang Sanfeng believed that a cultivator should sit as if they were a hen brooding on an egg until it hatches—doing the work when it needs to be done.

Upper Verses on the Great Process

As will be pointed out later, this text shows how the process of refining the elixir is done in stages. First, there is a two-week period of settling the mind, then a three-month period of forming and developing the Field of Elixir (丹田, Dan Tian), and lastly a ten-month period for refining the elixir. This doesn't mean that following this regime will result in immortality. It is just the process, and it may have to be repeated numerous times over the course of a cultivator's lifetime (hence the need for cultivating health and longevity), with periods (sometimes years) in between for study, contemplation, cloud wandering, or just living in the naturally just so.

Likewise, Zhang states that rote activities are *temporal*. In the Chinese text the term for temporal refers to After Heaven (後天, Hou Tian). This is a correct translation in part, but it goes much further in meaning than temporal. After Heaven refers to what is acquired through practice and experience, whereas Before Heaven (先天, Xian Tian) implies what is inherited through natural endowments and primordial influences.

The Tao is not something that can be experienced by rote methods, formulas, or activities, so Zhang Sanfeng here is commenting on some of the Taoist schools of his time as falling into rote activities and patterns of cultivation (imitating the regimes and ascetic practices of Chan Buddhists),

Refining the Elixir

and so they really can't speak or transmit the truth about Tao itself.

In older, traditional Taoism, before it became a monastic system, the mountain and forest hermitages, the small regional and local temples, or the individual hermit living alone in an isolated hut all had one thing in common. They refused to be governed by schedules and fixed manners for cultivation. Visitors who stayed at these immortal abodes would relate how surprised they were that there were rarely meditation halls, rather each monk simply meditated in his own private room, and was left undisturbed for as long as he wished. Cultivators made their own choice of how they wished to cultivate, with complete non-interference by others. Zhang Sanfeng would have been accustomed to these traditions of cloistered hermits and cloud wandering Taoists, so the idea of Taoist monasticism and all its rote activities would have perplexed him.

Even though this idyllic way of living in non-interference would be the perfect environment in which to refine the elixir, it is beyond the possibility for most of us living in today's society. Normally, we need the support of groups and fixed schedules for meditation. Most of us were born into a fast-paced and goal-orientated environment and, likewise, a society that often sees no value in crossing your legs

Upper Verses on the Great Process

and doing nothing for any period of time. Add to these factors that culturally and spiritually we are very much different from people of ancient China, we simply are starting from the negative side of zero concerning matters of internal cultivation. None of this existed in our upbringing, so the starting point is to find support and be involved with other people who share the same interest. Left to our own devices our practice will fall apart very quickly. Even though Zhang Sanfeng was critical of fixed schedules for sitting, they are beneficial for beginners who need group support when starting out in their practice. Zhang was dealing with devoted Taoists, not necessarily people just trying out meditation to see if they like it. In this regard, scheduled times for group meditation is valuable.

Also, do not become attached to non-doing, because non-doing causes a descent into a false emptiness. Presently in Buddhism many have fallen into this deterioration and therefore there are now few [true] Buddhists in the world.

亦不可着於無為．無為便落頑空．今之佛門．
多中此弊．故天下少佛子．

Translator's Commentary
The notion of "active non-action" (為無為, wei wu wei), or acting though non-aggression, non-contention, non-interference, and non-conformity,

Refining the Elixir

comes from Lao Zi in the *Scripture on Tao and Virtue*, but it was never meant to be a negative dynamic, rather a positive one. Zhang Sanfeng is talking about cultivators who erroneously think that non-doing means doing nothing but siting in emptiness to become enlightened. This is just getting attached to a false, or perverse, state of emptiness, not the "true emptiness" or "Void" of the Tao. Zhang was admonishing Chan Buddhist cultivators of his day because he believed they were confusing the experience of emptiness with enlightenment. Actually, the meaning of "Sunyata" in Buddhism is identical with the idea of True Voidness (眞虛, Zhen Xu) in Taoism.

The problem is that emptiness is erroneously considered as empty, but True Voidness is the emptiness even within emptiness. A good analogy for what this means is to consider the function of a cup, which is actually only useful in terms of its emptiness. The form of the cup is what gives the emptiness its value, but this is false emptiness because it is still dependent upon form, and regarding meditation form, the cup in this case is represented by a self, by others, and by a life.

As long as a person maintains these distinctions, emptiness will always be false. True Voidness cannot be viewed as having any form that gives it function, so in True Void there is nothing that can

Upper Verses on the Great Process

be held onto or grasped, no doing and no non-doing, no form and even no formlessness. You cannot comprehend it, you cannot examine it, you cannot grasp it, and, most importantly, you cannot contain it. This speaks to the old adage, "Cultivation is like climbing up a hundred foot greased flagpole. Entering the True Void is like leaping off once you've reached the top."

When there is no clarity about the Tao itself, the Tao does not function. There must first be an elimination of the causes and reasons of passion, so extraneous thoughts can be swept away. The first task then is establishing the foundation for the work of self-refinement.

此道之不行由於道之不明也. 初功在寂滅情緣. 掃除雜念. 除雜念是第一着築基煉已之功也.

Translator's Commentary
If you don't know what something is, how can you find its function? The word "Tao" to most people is just a meaningless and fanciful term. It has no function or basis for use within their lives. The Tao is where you originally came from and where you will return. Many cultivators, like my teacher, used the method of asking themselves while in meditation, "What did I look like before my mother was born?" The question has no answer in a rational sense. It is simply a means to draw the mind blank

Refining the Elixir

about attachment to self, others, and a life—to be selfless. Within that question is a great doubt about the reality of a self, others, and a life.

Eradicating all emotions and becoming "selfless" is very difficult to undertake. Basically, in Taoist terms, it means eradicating the negative effects of happiness, sorrow, anger, anxiety, fear, grief, and love/lust—the Seven Emotions (Seven Negative Qi), or even better translated as the Seven Passions (七情, Qi Qing). Everyone experiences these seven emotional aspects on an almost daily basis and normally they do us very little harm, so eradicating them doesn't mean one feels no more emotions ever. Rather, what should be eradicated are the extreme and negative conditions of these emotions. When we become extremely joyful about something, for instance, we can cry with extreme happiness and this crying can lead to extreme sadness when we lose what we were so happy about. Extreme anger will sap all the energy from us and we become listless and exhausted. Extreme fear can cause anxiety and perplexities, so much so that we can't control our actions. Extreme love may cause us to be possessive, jealous, hateful, controlling, or suspicious. Extreme hate turns into complete ignorance because we become blinded to what is right and just. Extreme lust causes our minds to become scattered and

Upper Verses on the Great Process

confused and we can lose self-control and the ability to function in our daily life.

Taoists have no problem with expressing emotions, as long as they are felt in moderation and don't become extreme. Emotions can be very positive responses to certain situations. For example, it is good to express joy at the birth of a child. It is good to express unhappiness and discontent over some atrocity. Fear protects us from many things, like putting our hands in fire and forcing us to be cautious. Loving others is a wonderful experience of being human and it brings out compassion in us. Hatred can actually lead to understanding because hatred basically comes from something wrong with the self, not others. Lust can even be a wonderful expression of love, provided it is with someone you love and with whom you can express it physically. There is a huge difference between people who simply crave sex so much that they have no conscience about what they do and with whom, as opposed to people who are lustful with those they love and who reciprocate their feelings.

Taoists do not believe sex is bad or even harmful to cultivation provided it is approached with moderation and clarity. As in the layperson's precept in Buddhism, which states, "I vow not to commit sexual misconduct," this does not say "never have sex." Taoists and Buddhists alike are

Refining the Elixir

saying don't have sex that creates bad karma. Rape, sexual abuse, child abuse, and so on only create bad karma, and these acts of misconduct interfere with the happiness and freedom of others. Taoists see sex as a natural and healthy act as long as it doesn't become a condition of extreme lust. When we treat emotions like a passion or obsession they are harmful, but if expressed in a moderate fashion with clarity, they can actually help us in our spiritual cultivation.

The idea of establishing a foundation for self-refinement begins with making sure none of the Seven Emotions are out of harmony. If any one of them becomes extreme or negative, it will prevent any progress in cultivation. Many people think that self-refinement and restoration simply means protecting the heart from attachment and stopping the flow of sexual secretions. This is not true. Self-refinement and restoration are about cutting off anger and dullness. When we sit (or do any other practice of self-cultivation) on a regular basis, there will be periods in which you will tell yourself you can't practice because you have too many other things to do, and so the mind conjures up this erroneous anger about practicing interfering with your activities. Dullness also plays a strong role in preventing us from refining and restoring ourselves. This happens when we say we are too tired to

Upper Verses on the Great Process

practice, that we worked too hard, and just don't have the energy for it. Yet, we will plop ourselves down on the couch and watch television for two hours or more. Both anger and dullness keep us from cultivating. What most beginning cultivators forget is that the simple act of sitting will, over time, end both of these obstacles. There really isn't that much work or effort involved in refinement and restoration. It is purely a question of just disciplining ourselves to practice a little bit every day and gradually we start thinking that practice is more relaxing and peaceful than television.

Once a person removes the [mundane] mind, the Heavenly Mind returns. Once a person cleanses desires, the Heavenly principles will be constantly preserved.
人心既除．則天心來復．人欲既淨．則天理常存．

Translator's Commentary
The first line of the *Yin Convergence Scripture* reads, "Contemplate the Tao of Heaven and maintain the activities of Heaven. Then all is done." Zhang Sanfeng is expressing the same idea here. When we stop rationalizing everything that comes into our mind, the mind become clearer and empty of extraneous thoughts. A clear mind is a bright mind, a bright mind produces a strong spirit, and a strong spirit will return to its essence, the Tao.

Refining the Elixir

A very important word is being used here: "desire." In Chinese, there are two terms for desire and both are pronounced "yu." When reading Taoist texts you have to know which of these ideograms is being used.

One form of *yu* (慾) uses the radical xin (心) for "mind" as its main radical. This character means "lust," "covet," and "passion" and is the negative, extreme meaning of sensual desires. It also refers to the Six Sense Desires. The other character for *yu* (欲) is the same, but without the radical xin. It means "to wish for" or "long for." In this text, Zhang Sanfeng chooses to use this character for yu (欲), as does Lao Zi in the *Scripture on Tao and Virtue*. The "desire" being referred to here is the desire associated with the rational mind. Negative desire can be seen as comprising greed, anger, and ignorance—which are based on an attached sense of self. Positive desires are charity, compassion, and wisdom—the selfless desires. Negative desires of an attached self have to be cleansed away, and when cleansed, the principles of the Heavenly Mind will be with you always. This is like people who believe they can think their way into experiencing and understanding Tao. Because they are clever and want to know it, somehow their rational mind will figure it all out. In truth, it is the empty, or selfless, mind that is clear, and a clear mind can

Upper Verses on the Great Process

perceive the Heavenly Mind and allow Heavenly principles to enter.

If Zhang Sanfeng had used the other character for desire, this whole verse would read much differently, because cleansing the mind of extreme desires, like those of the Six Sense Desires and Seven Emotions, would not create the conditions for the Heavenly Mind. There would still be a self. Yes, the Seven Emotions need to be regulated and not allowed to become extreme, and this is true of the desire for wanting the Heavenly Mind, as the more something is sought, the further away it becomes.

There is an old Buddhist meditation analogy that can help make this clear. When looking at a glass of dirty water, if the glass is constantly being agitated, the debris keeps spinning about inside the glass. The debris causes the water in the glass to be murky and unclear. If we take away the agitation (negative desires), the debris will gradually sink to the bottom of the glass and leave the remaining water crystal clear. This is just like the mind—so agitated and murky we cannot see our clear Heavenly Mind. When we control and cleanse ourselves of negative desires, both the extreme negative kinds and the desire for spiritual attainment, it is like letting the debris sink and making our mind bright and clear. Desires are still there, but they are sitting on the bottom of the glass

Refining the Elixir

like the debris, and the difference now is that you are not agitating them any longer. The key, then, is not to want attainment and to equally not to not-want attainment. Just be tranquil. Don't let anything disturb your mind. This is the true meaning of being without desire, or desire*less*. You have desires, we all do, but we can't allow them to stir or agitate the mind, especially when sitting in contemplation. Just be mindful of the method and then all will be done. Gradually, desires and emotions will not turn you or control your actions, but you will turn and control them.

Each day let there first be a time of tranquility so the body and mind have a fixed peacefulness, and the qi and breath are harmonious and even. Begin by slightly closing the two eyes like hanging curtains, and contemplate to illuminate the area below the heart and above the genitals to a space between them, about 1.3 inches inward. Do not forcefully put your attention upon it nor depart your attention from it. Keep mindful of it, yet do not fixate your attention upon it. When the never-ending flow of thoughts subsides, and only when the spirit is present, is it called "correct mindfulness." When in a state of mindfulness, the qi will be lively and natural.

每日先靜一時．待身心都安定了．氣息都和平了．
始將雙目微閉．垂簾觀照．心下腎上．
一寸三分之間．不卽不離．勿忘勿助．萬念俱泯．

Upper Verses on the Great Process

一靈獨存．謂之正念斯時也．於此念中．
活活潑潑．於彼氣中．

Translator's Commentary
This all goes to what was discussed in the last verse. The important point here is the idea of not forcefully putting your attention on the Elixir Field and equally not departing from it, keeping mindful of it, but avoiding fixating on it. This is the key to correct mindfulness.

Regarding raising or drawing out [the breath], do not put pressure on the heart above by inhaling too high. When exhaling, do not allow it to sink too low by putting pressure on the genitals. One opening and one closing is one [breath] coming in and one going out. Practice this for one or two weeks until the kidneys and genitals gradually and naturally begin to produce heat and feel as though steam is rising from them and the qi in the Elixir Field feels hot. At this point, the breath will naturally regulate itself and the qi also will naturally refine itself.

悠悠揚揚．呼之至上．上不衝心．吸之至下．
下不衝腎．一闔一闢一來一往．行之一七二七．
自然漸漸兩腎大蒸．丹天氣暖．息不用調而自調．
氣不用煉而自煉．

Refining the Elixir

Translator's Commentary
At the point of having correct mindfulness, the qi will appear and begin moving about the body. Again, you cannot force the qi to appear or move. It will happen naturally when the endless chatter in your brain subsides and the spirit is present. All that needs to be done is to take some time each day to sit and let the body and mind be tranquil and peaceful. When we do this, the breath will gradually settle and be gentle, then the qi will appear. Most of us want to force it, however, so we get anxious about it and exaggerate our breathing by bringing in so much air that pressure is put on the heart, or we exhale so completely that the genitals are affected. The breath only need be focused into the Dan Tian, and once the breath is in the Elixir Field, the whole body will breathe. This is just like an infant who has no mental intention to breathe correctly, so the breathing is just natural. If you watch an infant breathe, you will immediately see the breath is focused in the lower abdomen, not the lungs, and the whole body is breathing. Even the fingertips move subtly with each inhalation and exhalation.

This verse of the text is also revealing that this method of mindfulness is the Fire Process because it is the heat of qi that is being experienced, and as the text states it "feels like steam" rising in the body, the vapors of the heat below in the abdomen. It also reveals that

Upper Verses on the Great Process

the breath and qi will regulate and refine themselves, provided you maintain correct mindfulness. There are numerous texts and commentaries that actually go too far in explaining this Fire Process. It is better to just sit and let the breath and qi take care of themselves, as Zhang Sanfeng advises.

When the qi and breath have naturally united in the upper, middle, and lower [Elixir Fields], they neither go out nor come in, they neither arrive nor depart. This is called, "Embryonic Breathing," "Spiritual Breathing," the "True Bellows," the "True Cauldron and Furnace," "Returning to the Source and Restoring Life," the "Gate of the Mysterious Female," and the "Root of Heaven and Earth."

氣息既和. 自然於上中下. 不出不入. 無來無去.
是為胎息. 是為神息. 是為眞橐籥. 眞鼎爐.
是為歸根復命. 是為玄牝之門. 天地之根.

Translator's Commentary
All these terms mean the same thing. Once the qi follows the breath, it will naturally operate and open the three Elixir Fields. Your breathing will become natural and will naturally function of its own accord. The reason for this, in part, is because of the combined breath and qi generating heat, which the three Dan Tian then absorb.

Once this occurs, it's as if your breath completely takes over by itself. In meditation this can sometimes

Refining the Elixir

frighten the sitter. Once the breath and qi unite, the consciousness you felt about breathing, your awareness of the breath itself, disappears. It feels as if the physical functions of breathing disappear and you feel something else internally operating the breath. A typical response to this is being jolted back into conscious breathing because you panic from the thought that you are no longer breathing. Actually, this is exactly the way you breathed when you were in your mother's womb. Since an infant is inside a sack filled with water, he or she is breathing via True Breath from the Elixir Field.

At this time, the qi reaches a stage that resembles a budding flower or an embryo at first conception. This True Qi then naturally circulates and moves like steam. From the Tail Gateway [尾露, Wei Lu] it penetrates up the spine to the Muddy Pellet [泥丸, Ni Wan], then down through the nasal passages into the Twelve Storied Pagoda [重樓, Zhong Lou, the esophagus] and into the Crimson Palace [絳宮, Jiang Gong, heart region], where it then drops directly into the lower Elixir Field. This is the initial stage of mobilizing the River Cart [河車, He Che]. However, this is only the qi arriving, as it has not yet united with the spirit [shen]. Therefore, it's not actually the true mobilization of the elixir, so pay no attention to this.

氣到此時. 如花方蕊. 如胎方胞. 自然眞氣
薰蒸營衛. 由尾露穿夾脊. 升上泥丸下鵲橋.

Upper Verses on the Great Process

過重樓．至絳宮．而樓於中丹田．是為河車初動．
但氣至而神未全．非眞動也．不可理他．

Translator's Commentary
This is an important section as it shows there is a transition happening between the Fire Process and the Water Stage. The Fire Process is about the sensations of heat and steam, and the Water Stage is about the sensations of the elixir, a fluid.

I just keep my gaze very subtly fixated as though guarding the Central Palace [中宮, Zhong Gong], naturally [sensing] the limitless root-power of life. This is called, "Nourishing those of Yin E."[33] Practicing this for one or two months, the Spirit becomes increasingly more tranquil. Being tranquil for long periods during sitting, the Vital Energy will accumulate. This practice is called, "Spirit creating Vital Energy, and Vital Energy creating Spirit."

我只微微凝照．守於中宮．自然無盡生機．
所謂養鄞鄂者此也．行之一月二月．我神益靜．
靜久則氣益生．此為神生氣．氣生神之功也．

---

[33] *Yin E* (鄞鄂) literally translates as the provinces of Zhejiang and Hubei, which in Zhang Sanfeng's time was Central China, so the idea of *guarding the Central Palace* in the body is like guarding the central location of the country.

165

Refining the Elixir

Translator's Commentary
Once you sense the heat and movement of qi moving up and down through the meridians, just keep being mindful and observing it (watching over it). Do not force it, try to manipulate it, or advance it.

Just practice mindfulness. It is this mindfulness and allowing the qi to accumulate of its own natural accord that will cause the spirit to create and refine the qi, and likewise the qi to start refining the spirit.

Supposing you practice for one hundred or perhaps more than a hundred days, the Essence [jing] and Spirit [shen] will increase constantly and the True Vital Energy [qi] will gradually reach full potential. The Great Process will produce abundant heat, and the blood circulation will be good. Naturally Water and Fire will have intercourse, and Heaven and Earth will assemble and harmonize. The Spirit will feel fluid, and the Vital Energy unrestrained. Shortly afterward when the True Vital Energy congeals, it will feel like a whirlwind spontaneously moving upwards through the hundred pulses of your body. This is the true movement of the River Cart.

或百日. 或百除日. 精神益長. 眞氣漸充.
溫溫大候. 血水有除. 自然坎離交媾.
乾坤會合. 神融氣暢. 一霎時間. 眞氣混合.
一陣回風上衝百脈. 是為河車眞動.

Upper Verses on the Great Process

Translator's Commentary

Practicing for one hundred days is called "One Hundred Days of Spiritual Work" (百日神功, Bai Ri Shen Gong), and "One Hundred Days of Setting Up the Foundation," (百日築基, Bai Ri Zhu Ji).

The cultivator is now fully into the Water Stage because the spirit is beginning to feel fluid, and there will be sensations of waves of qi throughout the body, hence the idea that the movement is like a River Cart or Waterwheel.

The terms Water (坎, Kan), Fire (離, Li), Heaven (乾, Qian), and Earth (坤, Kun) are used here, as in most Taoist alchemical texts, to represent the idea that Water (精, jing/essence) and Fire (氣, qi/vital energy) have congealed together to form the elixir, and the mind (shen/Heaven) and body (jing/Earth) have harmonized. All this creates the sensation of thunder and wind rushing through the entire body. You feel it in your blood and in your muscles, and everything feels more alive than you can remember.

The River Cart is much more than the idea of what people commonly think of as just the Dumai and Renmai meridian channels in the body. Like the experience of the Free Circulation of Qi, where the heat and qi spread throughout the body causing an increase in blood circulation, the next stage is feeling the qi moving within meridians. These are all

Refining the Elixir

aspects of the Fire Process, which are caused by the qi energy. In the Water Stage, there's a similar experience of feeling like wind and fluid (waves) are rushing throughout the entire body. This is caused by the spirit (shen) energy, which then sets up the conditions for the elixir to flow through the meridians previously opened by the qi. The River Cart, then, relates to both experiences in the Fire and Water stages.

During this process a point of spiritual light will be perceived in the Elixir Field. This is what is called, "the dark pearl in the water's bottom," or "a yellow bud sprouting up through the soil." It is at this point when the one yang arrives and returns, appearing like a hazy red sun when first ascending through the morning mist and reflecting through the fog on the ocean, very obscure yet visible. This then is the "Lead Fire" being created within you.

中間若有一點靈光．覺在丹田．是為水底玄珠．土內黃芽．爾時一陽來復．恍如紅日初升．照於滄海之內．如霧如烟．若隱若見．則鉛火生焉．

Translator's Commentary

The *"dark pearl in the water's bottom"* is a reference to the teachings from the *Jade Tablet Decrees on Nature and Life* and the *Yellow Court Scripture*. The *"yellow bud sprouting up through the soil"* is a reference from the *Secret of the Golden Flower* and

Upper Verses on the Great Process

the *Yellow Court Scripture.* When you see this hazy reddish light emanating from the Elixir Field, it means the True Essence and True Breath have come together, hence the term *"Lead Fire."*

To unite Heaven, Earth, Water, and Fire, you must quiet the Spirit so it is absolutely tranquil and empty even of emptiness, allowing no interruptions or severance in your practice until you bring everything together as one solid whole. This is called, "Mating the Five Activities."

方其乾坤坎離未交. 虛無寂滅. 神凝於中.
功無間斷. 打成一團. 是為五行合配.

Translator's Commentary
The Five Activities are consciousness energy (Metal), regenerative energy (Wood), vital energy (Fire), spirit energy (Water), and primordial energy (Earth). When reaching a state of absolute tranquility these five energies, or activities, mate together and become one. Actually, the text points out that this state of *"Mating the Five Activities"* is about the mating of the five consciousnesses of the sense organs, because this also occurs as a result of entering absolute tranquility, returning the light, and reverting the hearing inwards. The senses of sight, sound, smell, taste, and touch each have a consciousness. These consciousnesses overlap or, better said, fuse together within absolute tranquility.

Refining the Elixir

The eyes can smell, sounds can taste, touch can see, tastes can hear, and so on.

When Water (jing) and Fire (qi) intermingle, attention must be paid in assuring the cultivation of two processes:

1) The River Cart will begin to circulate in reverse—up the spine and down the front of the body—and during this you must obtain the medicines (or energies) of four distinct intervals: the Bai Hui (top of the head), Bright Palace (solar plexus), Hui Yin (perineum), and Double Barrier (middle of the back).

2) The spirit must be retained internally so the light of the elixir will not depart.

At this point there will be a congealing or crystallization of the vitality of the yang element (congealed jing and qi) within the center (Dan Tian). This will remain stored while all residual desires subside and habitual emotions are stilled, and yet it will have actual appearance and form. When you get to this stage, the breath will constantly stay within the womb. You must incubate this both inside and out with constant and continuous practice of what is called the "Ten-Month Effort."

This is where the real work of cultivating and refining the elixir becomes difficult. It is also where most cultivators fail and give up. Because it is here

Upper Verses on the Great Process

where there must be a constant vigil of sorts for a ten-month period—like a hen brooding on her eggs for ten months straight. Most cultivators, will have to repeat this process of the Ten-Month Effort many times. The reason it is so difficult is because you must first wait for the reversing of the River Cart to occur. In analogy this is like waiting for the tide to go out, but in this case the tide only goes out every year or so. Likewise, you must be ready for this Ten-Month Effort, and preparing for it is no small matter. It requires an absolutely quiet and stress-free environment.

Back in the 1930s there was a man named Yinshizi who wrote a wonderful book about meditation (see page 93). His book is based entirely on his experiences in meditation and how he went about ensuring he had both the time and environment in which to cultivate. He wrote that he worked hard, saved his money, and when he felt his family could be provided for, he rented a small apartment in Beijing. He spent his days sitting and refining the elixir without disturbance and so became a very accomplished cultivator. In China his book has become a classic of sorts and he has become very popular.

Yinshizi's idea of shutting himself off from the world was by no means novel. This is what Taoist hermits had been doing for centuries. What made

Refining the Elixir

him different was that he accomplished all this within the confines of a very busy city, Beijing, not in some remote mountain region.

No matter the location, the important thing is to have a ten-month period without disturbance so you can sit when the need arises, and not have to deal with any worldly concerns. Otherwise, it is doomed to fail. To become accomplished in the Fire Process, the need to separate from the world is not that important. Much can be accomplished in this stage without such total dedication, but the Water Stage is an entirely different matter and usually a cultivator needs to make several attempts before mastering it.

Upon arriving at the point when Water and Fire mutually enjoin, the second process is undertaken. The River Cart will then accordingly begin turning. With the fourth process, the medicine is obtained. The Spirit dwells internally, and the elixir is bright and does not depart. This is called "The Great Heavenly Circuit," and "The Great Restoration of the Active Nine Revolutions." At this time, the Essence will reach the highest point of Yang, and will be fixed and connected to the Center. This is the time of concealment when desires are cleansed and the emotions are settled, yet there is image and there is form to it, and attaining an Earthly position. The breath advances from the embryo so the internal and external are warmed and

Upper Verses on the Great Process

nourished instantly without any lack. This is also called "The Ten Month's Work."

至若水火相交．二候採取．河車逆轉．
四候得藥．神居於內．丹光不離．謂之大周天．
謂之行九轉大還也．此時一點至陽之精．
凝結於中．隱藏於欲淨情寂之時．而有象有形．
到此地位．息住於胎．內外溫養．頃刻無差．
又謂之十月功夫也．

Translator's Commentary

When the True Essence (Water) is joined with the True Breath (Fire), the River Cart will then begin its ascent and descent along the spine and down the front of the body. Zhang describes two events in the process, but he skips mentioning the third process and moves directly on to the fourth. The third process is the Nine Revolutions required to form the drop of Yang Spirit, and then the medicine of immortality is obtained. Actually, he does mention the Nine Revolutions when he separates the ideas of the *Great Heavenly Circuit* and *The Great Restoration of the Active Nine Revolutions*. The reason he did this is because the Great Heavenly Circuit is about cleansing and opening all the subtle meridians in the body, from the legs up through the upper body. The Great Restoration of the Active Nine Revolutions is about the circulation of the elixir through the Control Vessel (Dumai) and Function

Refining the Elixir

Vessel (Renmai) nine times to produce the drop of Yang Spirit.

In the introduction I talked about True Breath coming from within the Elixir Field, and here Zhang states the same thing with slightly different semantics, saying "the breath advances from the embryo." He further states, "the internal and external will be warmed and nourished instantly without any lack." This is a reference to the ideal Taoist stage of "living off wind and dew," where *wind* is qi (vital energy) and *dew* is jing (essence).

When Zhang says, "Water and Fire mutually enjoin," he is stating that when True Essence and True Breath come together this will then warm and nourish the body, both internally and externally, and that cultivators will have no more need for the coarse uses of food and clothing to nourish and warm themselves.

The statement about "The Ten Month's Work" is really not ten months, as Zhang clearly explained above. The ten-month work is just a metaphor used in the regenerative analogy of internal alchemy, as early Taoists counted a female's pregnancy from the moment of conception through the gestation period, which is actually ten months, not nine. So "ten months" here basically means the time it takes to form the spiritual embryo and produce the spiritual child.

Upper Verses on the Great Process

Cultivators can take all this from the material worldview of an Earthly (physiological) position, or from the Heavenly (psychological) perception. You can take this verse as literally meaning ten months, or it could be ten seconds, ten minutes, ten days, ten weeks, ten years, or as my teacher Master Liang said to me, "maybe ten lifetimes."

Lower Verses on the Great Process for Refining the Elixir

煉丹大候說下

The training of tranquility occurs in each interval of time. Even within a quarter hour there is transmuting refined Essence into Vital Energy and transmuting refined Vital Energy into Spirit, and the work of taking the refined Spirit to restore it back into the Void. This process is not just in the ten months, it is also within one hour, one day, one month, or one year. When you sit down with your legs crossed, close your eyes to become aware of your Spirit and to quiet the mind and regulate your breathing. This then is the work of transmuting the refined Essence into Vital Energy.

夫靜功在一刻．一刻之中．亦有煉精化氣．
煉氣化神．煉神還虛之功．夫在內不獨十月然也．
卽一時一日．一月一年．皆然坐下．閉目存神．
使心靜息調．卽是煉精化氣之功也．

Translator's Commentary

Simply put, Zhang is saying that whenever you sit down to meditate you are effectively practicing all four stages of Setting Up the Foundation. It is not a question of trying to design a long-term practice schedule spread out over a ten-month period. Rather,

Refining the Elixir

by simply practicing meditation to attain tranquility, your Essence, Vital Energy, and Spirit are all being transmuted in a cyclic manner. However, this verse is also assuming that the cultivators reading it have already refined their Essence. For those people, he is saying that training tranquility by sitting, focusing on the Spirit (in the lower Elixir Field), quieting the mind, and regulating the breathing is the stage of "transmuting refined Essence into Vital Energy."

Return the light to reflect the illumination by fixing the Spirit in the Elixir Cavern [lower Elixir Field], and so cause the True Breath to come forth. Be centered internally. There is movement in ultimate tranquility, and in ultimate movement there is tranquility. This is the limitless root-power of Heaven. This is the work of transmuting refined Vital Energy into Spirit. This is the way to gather the True Breath at the source, where yin and yang return to intermingle and each undergo change. Naturally, the wind becomes calm and the waves are stilled. At this time, I maintain correct mindfulness and bring it to rest in the Elixir Field. This is "tightly sealing up the firing process."

迴光返照. 凝神丹穴. 使眞息往來. 內中靜極而動.
動極而靜. 無限天機. 卽是煉氣化神之功也.
如此眞氣朝元. 陰陽反復. 交媾一番.
自然風恬浪靜. 我於此時. 將正念止丹田.
卽是封固火候.

Lower Verses on the Great Process

Translator's Commentary

Here Zhang explains that the process for *Returning the Light* is just simply focusing our mind on the Elixir Field, and this will aid in bringing forth our True Breath. Movement and tranquility have the same source, Tao. The Tao is constantly changing (movement) and constantly still (tranquility), and from ultimate movement and tranquility we can gain insight into the root-power of Heaven. Root-power (機, Ji) is a term meaning "the very power and source of Heaven's and Nature's organic functionality and processes." *Ji* carries the meanings of "mechanism," "organic," or "modus operandi," so Zhang is stating that since Heaven models itself on the Tao, movement and tranquility are what bring function (root-power) to Heaven. As the *Clarity and Tranquility of the Constant Scripture* states, "Heaven moves and the Earth is tranquil." This is to say, "yang moves and yin is tranquil," and as the text then relates, the yin and yang come together in the Elixir Field where they intermingle and undergo change. This is the Ultimate Movement and Ultimate Tranquility to which Zhang is referring. The wind (breath) and the waves (thoughts) are calmed and stilled, so breath moves, yet the mind is tranquil.

Zhang then relates that all one need do is maintain correct mindfulness of the Elixir Field by

Refining the Elixir

"tightly sealing up the firing process." This means the mind is completely focused on the Elixir Field with no wandering thoughts or disturbances, and from this the "firing process" can be experienced. The firing process is analogous to setting the fire beneath the furnace to heat the refined Essence and Vital Energy within the cauldron. Simply put, the warmed breath coming from the Elixir Field will give movement to the heated Essence and Vital Energy.

Be it a year, month, or day, practice these three stages continually, and this is not a matter of entering a garden alone for ten months. It is said, "In performing this process even for a quarter hour, there is a quarter hour Heavenly Circuit, so it is with an hour, a day, a month, or a year, each has its own Heavenly Circuit."

年月日時．久久行此三部．功夫不但入圜十月也．
故曰．運之一刻．有一刻之周天．
運之一時一日一月一年．
即有一時一日一月一年之周天也．

Translator's Commentary
Three stages refers to refining Essence, Vital Energy, and Spirit, and Zhang makes the point that there's no need to go into a long-term hermitage to do so. Again, he is emphasizing that these three stages can be done for fifteen minutes, an hour, a day, a

Lower Verses on the Great Process

month, or a year because within any time frame a person can work on experiencing the Heavenly Circuit.

Therefore, in a quarter hour, the first half of that interval is the "warming" and "Advancing the Fire," "full moon" and "first quarter of the moon," and "the dawn of *Beginning Difficulties*" and "spring and summer." The second half of the cycle is "cooling" and "Withdrawing the Convergence," "end of the lunar cycle" and "last quarter of the moon," and "the evening of *Youthful Folly*" or "autumn and winter." In a two-hour interval, there are four quarter-hour divisions in both the first and second half of the interval. The same is true of a day, month, or year.

然一刻中．上半刻為溫．為進火．為望．為上弦．
為朝屯．為春夏．下半刻為涼．為退符．為晦．
為下弦．為暮蒙．為秋冬．一時則有上四刻．
下四刻之分．即一日一月一年皆同．

Translator's Commentary

The idea here is that no matter what time frame a cultivator decides on for practice, the first half will be devoted to the Fire Process, producing heat and advancing the Vital Energy. The second half will be devoted to the Water Stage, condensing and cooling the Essence.

The use of the terms *Beginning Difficulties* and *Youthful Folly* are the titles of the third and fourth

Refining the Elixir

hexagrams in the *Book of Changes*. *Beginning Difficulties,* ䷂, is comprised of the trigrams Thunder (below) and Water (above) and represents the origination and appearance of all things—thus the dawn and the sun rising. *Youthful Folly,* ䷃, is comprised of the trigrams Water (below) and Mountain (above) and represents the development and concealment of all things—thus the evening and the moon appearing.

Regarding *advancing fire* and *withdrawing the convergence,* these are alternate ways of saying, Advancing Yang Fire (進陽火, Jin Yang Huo) and Withdrawing the Yin Convergence (退陰符, Tui Yin Fu). These are specialized terms for the process of the Lesser Heavenly Circuit, which involves reversing the flow of the elixir up the spine with the method of using thirty-six breaths, and descending the flow of the elixir on the front of the body with twenty-four breaths. See *Three Barriers on the Front, Three Barriers on the Back* (pp. 110–113).

This is called "Gathering the Five Forces of Yin and Yang." So even within a quarter hour's practice you undergo the breathing process of one entire year. At this time you can be truly empty and tranquil. Continue on for one or even two years, even up to ten years, or a hundred years, and you will eventually break through to the Void and merge

Lower Verses on the Great Process

with the Ultimate Void. This is the practice for "Returning the Refined Spirit to the Void."

此之謂攢簇陰陽五行. 一刻之功夫. 奪一年之氣候也. 到此乃是眞空眞靜. 或一二年至十年百年. 打破空虛與太虛同體. 此為煉神還虛之功也.

Translator's Commentary
The Five Forces are the Five Activities of Earth, Metal, Water, Wood, and Fire along with their Yin and Yang aspects, and these can be seen in the Ten Heavenly Stems as used in Chinese astrology. Here is a brief summary of the stems and their meanings on nature and internal alchemy:

Jia (甲) is Yang Wood and is likened to forests and trees in nature. **Yi** (乙) is Yin Wood, likened to small plants and flowers. In internal alchemy, Yang and Yin Wood represent the correlations associated with True Mercury (Heavenly Spirit, Hun) the celestial animal Green Dragon, Inner Nature, the liver, the color green, and the easterly direction.

Bing (丙) is Yang Fire and is likened to the sun. **Ding** (丁) is Yin Fire and likened to fires and flames. Yang and Yin Fire represent the correlations associated with the Cinnabar (Before Heaven Qi), the celestial animal Vermillion Bird, Original Spirit, the heart, the color red, and the southerly direction.

Wu (戊) is Yang Earth and is likened to boulders and rocks. **Ji** (己) is Yin Earth and is

Refining the Elixir

likened to soil and farmed fields. Yang and Yin Earth represent the correlations associated with the Elixir, the celestial Cauldron (where all four celestial animals converge), Mind-Intention, the spleen, the color yellow, and the central position.

Geng (庚) is Yang Metal and is likened to steel and swords. **Xin** (辛) is Yin Metal, likened to gold and silver. Yang and Yin Metal represent the correlations associated with True Lead, the celestial animal White Tiger, emotions (Earthly Spirit, Po), the lungs, the color white, and the westerly direction.

Ren (壬) is Yang Water, likened to rivers and oceans. **Gui** (癸) is Yin Water, likened to rain and dew. Yang and Yin Water represent the correlations associated with Original Essence (Before Heaven Jing), the celestial animal Black Tortoise (or Dark Warrior), the kidneys, the color black, and the northernly direction.

When all Five Forces are refined and united, Returning Spirit to the Void can occur.

Before the ten-month effort is fully complete you must watch over the infant consistently and constantly. Be it ten steps, a hundred steps, one thousand miles, or ten thousand miles the spirit will gradually seek to leave. Do not let it wander out without some sort of restraint, otherwise it will become lost and unable to return.

Lower Verses on the Great Process

前功十月既滿．須時時照顧嬰兒．十步百步神．
千里萬里．以漸而出．倘或放縱不禁．
必致迷而不返．

Translator's Commentary
In this section of the text Zhang provides a warning to those who successfully create the spiritual infant. They must not allow the spirit to leave their body and wander about, unless it is monitored by an accomplished teacher. There are numerous stories of such occurrences in Taoism. In one tale, for example, an accomplished adept decides to let his spirit out and go visit his ailing mother, but he does not return immediately. He stays for three days and then returns. While he was away his fellow cultivators thought he had died, so they buried his body. He then had to find another body from a recently deceased person, but it was deformed so he had to live out his days in pain.

The *Classic on Immortality* [仙經, Xian Jing] states, "The Spirit must merge with Vital Energy to become an embryo. The Vital Energy must return to the Spirit to congeal into an elixir." This is called, "One droplet descending into the Yellow Court."

仙經曰．神入氣成胎．氣歸神結丹．
所謂一點落黃庭是也．

Refining the Elixir

> **Translator's Commentary**
> When the Spirit is completely directed into the Elixir Field, a spiritual embryo is formed within it. When the Vital Energy returns to the Spirit, they congeal together. In essence, they are the same. The embryo is the elixir, and the elixir is the embryo. Think of it this way, when a sperm cell attaches itself to a fertile egg, it is an embryo. The sperm cell and fertile egg are likewise the elixir, as they congeal together. The "one droplet" is the Yang Spirit and results from this merging and congealing of Spirit and Vital Energy. The Yellow Court is the womb of the embryo and future spiritual child.

People who have few extraneous thoughts can obtain the elixir quickly, but those who are inundated with extraneous thoughts are slow to obtain the elixir. The method is simple and quite easy.

但人雜念少者得丹早雜念多者得丹遲．此法簡易．

> **Translator's Commentary**
> This verse is very clear and straightforward. Those who have trouble stopping all the extraneous, false, and wandering thoughts in their mind will find obtaining the elixir difficult and slow. Those who can settle their minds, find it easy. For anyone taking up the practice of meditation, no matter the tradition or goal, two obstacles must be overcome:

Lower Verses on the Great Process

confusion and dullness. Confusion is the result of too much thinking, and dullness is a result of lack of energy and focus. Those who have very active lives suffer from confusion, while inactive people suffer dullness.

The difficulty lies in not putting forth the effort. If you practice consistently over a long time, you will most certainly acquire the spiritual penetration skills of "entering metal and going through stone," "entering water and walking through fire," and "comprehending Heaven and penetrating the Earth."

奈人不肯勇猛耳. 若能恆久行持. 必然透金實石. 入水蹈火. 通天達地.

Translator's Commentary
Zhang believed that anyone seeking to attain tranquility and refine the elixir must first keep in mind these three simple ideas:

First, it does no good to toil the body with long periods of meditation until the body is prepared to handle it comfortably. You should begin with what Zhang called the "Quarter-Hour Method," learning how to sit quietly for just fifteen minutes. Then if you enter a state of tranquility, you will naturally sit for hours unaware of the time. He saw no point in forcing yourself to sit for long periods because it's

Refining the Elixir

all a matter of the mind and body naturally entering tranquility and allowing it to happen.

Second, follow the three stages of practice described below, while first being concerned with the breath and posture. It is extremely important to just be mindful of the Dan Tian, as this will allow the breath to become naturally low. Do not force the breath to be deep and long. If you do, the breath will become pensive and erratic. Just let the breath be what it is and it will naturally sink into the lower Elixir Field. Inhale and exhale through the nose only. Also, constantly pay attention to your posture. Make sure your back is straight, but not rigid. Keep your head level with the eyes slightly open, allowing a hairline of light through. Make every effort to keep both knees touching your sitting mat. Rest your hands in your lap. Keep the head slightly suspended upward as if by a thread. The breath should be natural, not so full or forced that the inhalation puts pressure on the heart, nor the exhalation so low that it affects the genitals. Focus solely on the lower abdomen. The breath should not just push the front of the stomach outward, rather the whole abdomen should expand and contract like a bellows. When inhaling, sense as much of an expansion on the lower spine as you do on the front of the abdomen, and when exhaling, the lower spine and front of the abdomen will contract equally as

Lower Verses on the Great Process

well. When an inhalation occurs, the anal muscles contract. When exhaling, they expand—opening and closing constantly with each complete breath. Hold the tip of the tongue against the roof of the mouth. Lower the eyelids so that just a fine line of light can enter. Sink the shoulders, hollow the chest, and slightly raise the back with the spine held upright. Position the legs in full-lotus, half-lotus, or in the immortal posture.[34]

Third, being sincere in repeating the methods and staying mindful when doing so are the only secrets of success. Life brings about many changes, but a cultivator should always be mindful that success depends on his or her ability to be changeless within change. This means that you do not allow conditions to distract you, rather you remain changeless within those distractions. Always find time to practice, keep repeating the methods, and you will experience benefits from it.

The following *Three Stages of Cultivating the Elixir* is an easy progression of how Zhang Sanfeng thought a cultivator should begin. Normally, it isn't the case that one could just follow this procedure and attain the elixir. Rather, the process is repeated until the cultivator no longer needs to do the First

---

[34] See *Clarity & Tranquility: A Guide for Daoist Meditation* (Valley Spirit Arts, 2015).

Refining the Elixir

Stage, or Second Stage, or eventually even the Third Stage.

Note that the lengths of time and numbering of the methods differs from the treatise text. One reason is that the number 9 and multiples of nine, as used here for the number of days in a stage, are considered ultimate Yang numbers. Many Taoists feel it is more auspicious to cultivate according to such numbered designations. Likewise, the difference in listing nine months here instead of ten has to do with the Yang numbering, and also Zhang alternates between nine and ten months in his various works.

Three Stages of Cultivating the Elixir
First Stage: Preparing the Cauldron (制备鼎, Zhi Bei Ding)

Refining Jing to Transmute into Qi
(Relaxing the abdomen and letting the breath sink low)

This is an eighteen-day beginning period of just sitting, standing, and walking meditation. Your only concern should be ridding the mind of emotional distractions and wandering thoughts. Pay attention to the workings of the breath, but only in the sense of just being mindful of what it is doing and following along with it.

Lower Verses on the Great Process

Second Stage: Forming the Pearl (成形珠, Cheng Xing Zhu)
Refining Qi to Transmute into Spirit
(Opening the Elixir Field in the lower abdomen)

In this ninety-nine-day stage, you concentrate on the lower abdomen until you see a light or bright pearl being formed in the Dan Tian. If you experience a vibration in the lower abdomen or a sensation of heat, both are excellent signs of progress.

Third Stage: The River Cart (河車, He Che)
Refining Spirit to Return to the Void
(Mobilizing the breath and sending qi up the spine)

During this nine-month stage, you observe the pearl ascend the spine to the Bai Hui (or Ni Wan) cavity on top of the head, where it then descends through the Upper Dan Tian (Third Eye), the nasal passage and esophagus, and into the Bright Palace (Middle Dan Tian), where you then wait for it to drop into the Lower Dan Tian.

Even if you feel you aren't being successful in any of the three stages—eighteen days, ninety-nine days, or nine months—go through the entire practice. Most students will continue these three cycles of practice many times in their lives, and this certainly doesn't mean progress isn't being made. Within this method, you will begin to experience

Refining the Elixir

sensations of qi and your spirit will become brighter and stronger. The destination is not always as fruitful as the treasures you may find along the Way. Also, if you remain mindful of each moment along the path, the destination will become easier to achieve. Being mindful is the key.

Repeatedly practice on top of more practice. Be willing to work to amass the great medicine of the spiritual elixir until the marvelous spiritual body can fly in broad daylight directly out from your private dwelling. How would this affect either the shallowness or deepness of my merit and virtue? Supposing I dismiss furthering my cultivation of the spiritual elixir, deciding instead to just turn my back on it and soar up and away with my Yang Spirit. When I return to my body, I would only see a pile of dust from my old bones. It would be better to fly very high during broad daylight and just remain in peace for countless ages in perfect harmony with the universe.

再行積行．累功服煉神丹大藥．必然形神俱妙．白晝飛昇．全家拔宅．此又在功德之淺深如何耳設或不服神丹．只顧陽神沖舉．同視舊骸一堆塵土．夫亦白日羽翰萬刼長存．可與宇宙同泰者矣．

Translator's Commentary

This last verse of the text speaks about the creation of a spirit body that can fly away into the empyrean after having achieved the highest goals of internal alchemy. What Zhang Sanfeng is questioning here is why anyone would want to return to his or her body? He wonders why they don't just live peacefully and in harmony for countless ages. He also questions how flying, whether in spirit or bodily form, can be of any use to one's merit and virtue, asking whether it makes it any deeper or even more shallow. It appears from his summation, that it is meritorious to achieve such a skill, but there is no virtue in practicing going in and out of the body. Rather, he surmises, it is far better to remain in peace in the Tao forever.

Verses on Seated Meditation
打 坐 歌
Da Zuo Ge

Those beginning the practice of contemplative absorption should direct each inhalation and exhalation into the Mysterious Pass. Delicately and continuously harmonize the breathing, simmering one yin and one yang within the cauldron.

初打坐. 學參禪. 這個消息 在玄關.
祕祕綿綿調呼吸. 一陰一陽鼎內煎.

Translator's Commentary
To early Taoists the term "meditation" (思, si) did not have quite the same meaning or purpose as with the term "Tranquil Sitting" (靜坐, Jing Zuo). Meditation just meant the act of quietly thinking or contemplating something. Tranquil Sitting, or as it is called in the Dragon Gate sect of Taoism "Sitting and Forgetting" (坐忘, Zuo Wang), went far beyond the processes of just quietly thinking.

Tranquility to a Taoist meant absolute stillness and purity of mind—no thoughts, not even thoughts of not thinking could enter the mind. The mind becoming so still there could be no sense or awareness of the perfect stillness being experienced. Tranquility to a Taoist meant total absorption into the perfect light of emptiness. In the *Secret of the Golden Flower,* it states, "Emptiness is not empty, it is full of light." This total absorption into absolute tranquility is where the term "contemplative absorption" (參禪, tan chan) originated, and was incorporated by Chan Buddhists. So, there's an enormous difference, especially to a Taoist, when the terms meditation or Tranquil Sitting are used. In the West we generically apply the term meditation to anyone who sits down and remains quiet for a few minutes to those advanced cultivators who actually enter tranquility or samadhi (三昧, San Mei, in Chinese).

Samadhi is a Buddhist Sanskrit term meaning "complete abstract contemplative absorption," being identical with the definition of the Taoist term of "clarity and tranquility." The experiences and processes of tranquility and samadhi are not the same as those normally associated with the more mundane experiences of meditation.

The *Mysterious Pass* is a qi cavity residing between the eyes and back into the brain about one inch, and is what the text refers to as the "cauldron." Each inhalation and exhalation should be felt and visualized in this cavity, and, as the text instructs, with a delicate and continuous rhythm to "harmonize the breathing."

"Simmering one yin and one yang within the cauldron" means to allow the exhalation (yin) and the inhalation (yang) to generate heat within it.

This first verse of the treatise is actually the gist of the entire text because just sitting in this manner

Verses on Seated Meditation

(of contemplative absorption) will stimulate and begin developing the qi.

When seated in a meditation posture, first seek to calm your mind by breathing into your lower Elixir Field (Dan Tian). This is not a forceful action, rather it is purely a matter of drawing your attention down into the Elixir Field.

When Taoists say, "abide by the Dan Tian," it means all your mind attention is drawn to the lower abdomen. The breath will follow naturally. Qi follows the mind; the mind does not follow the qi —so don't attempt to force the breath low. Just keep your mind on the Elixir Field and the breath will naturally follow to where you are putting your attention.

Your entire abdomen should feel the breath expanding like a bellows. It is not a matter of feeling the front of your stomach pushing out—this is only a half breath. You should feel the breath expanding onto your lower back and sides of the abdomen as well. If you want the qi to move up your spine then you have to feel the breath there as well. Breath and qi are one in the same thing. If you just feel the front of your stomach pushing out, you will never feel the qi ascending the spine—so pay attention to feeling the breath expanding on your lower spine as well as in the front of your abdomen. It is through

Refining the Elixir

this type of "Bellows Breathing" that qi can be stimulated to mobilize up the spine.

Only breathe through your nose.

It is best to sit so that the left heel is pressed into the genitals (to prevent dissipation of jing and qi), and so the right leg and foot are attached and laid in front of the left thigh. Likewise make sure both knees are attached to the floor or sitting mat.

The right hand should grasp the left thumb, and position the hands in front of the Dan Tian so that the back of the left hand is facing out and encompassing the back of the right hand. This hand position is called the "Tai Ji Knot."

Keep the head slightly suspended upward so the bottom of the chin is perfectly level. When suspending the head, think of the area that used to be your soft spot as a baby. Feel it being suspended upward as if by a thread. Doing so will awaken your spirit and keep you from feeling dullness during meditation.

Keep the spine erect, but not rigid. This means to straighten up your spine but then internally hollow your chest (which will automatically raise your back).

Keep your tongue on the roof of your mouth so to stimulate the saliva and keep the throat moist.

Lower your eyelids so that just a faint area of light can be seen.

Verses on Seated Meditation

Three excellent signs of progress occur when you begin to feel a great deal of heat in the lower abdomen, you feel a strong vibration in your lower abdomen, and/or the spine begins sweating profusely during meditation.

When you can sit for one hour without disturbance in your mind and body you are ready to begin the Great Process of internal alchemy.

The above instructions are for creating the conditions of true tranquility and developing heat (qi) in the Dan Tian. Without some experience and skill of these two effects (tranquility and qi) you cannot form the elixir, so please pay attention to first sitting and getting the breath to naturally sink into the Elixir Field and to be capable of sitting undisturbed (no mental agitation or dullness of mind) for one hour.

Granted, you need not perfect these conditions immediately, but once you have accomplished some skill and gained enough experience from sitting and developing your qi, then you can move on to directing your attention into the Mysterious Pass, as Zhang advises in the first verse.

The secret here is not to lose the sensation of the breath in the Lower Elixir Field, but to feel like the breath is connected and affecting the Upper Elixir Field simultaneously. When the lower abdomen expands and contracts, sense the Mysterious Pass

Refining the Elixir

open and close in rhythm with it. This must be done delicately. The mind must be perfectly calm and you should feel no physical strain or uneasiness. Your breath should be gentle and easy. Let it all occur naturally.

Two excellent signs of progress may occur in this practice:

1) Your entire mind is filled with light. As the *Secret of the Golden Flower* states, "The Void is not empty. It is full of light."

2) You feel a throbbing and/or heat sensation in the Mysterious Pass during meditation.

Awaken your nature to perpetuate your destiny. Do not carelessly tend the strength of the fire. When closing your eyes guard the origin of life by contemplating the mind. Both the clarity and purity of non-action are the root source. Within one hundred days you will see the responses fulfilled.

性要悟. 命要傳. 休將火候當等閒.
閉目觀心守本命. 清淨無為是根源.
百日內. 見應驗.

Translator's Commentary

Everyone's destiny is to be an immortal, but to realize it you must awaken your true nature. Awakening your true nature is to see and experience yourself as being one with the Tao.

Verses on Seated Meditation

The *strength of the fire* is the breath and qi within your lower abdomen, so the text warns to be mindful of constantly abiding by your breath in the lower abdomen. The origin of your life is your shen (spirit). The gate to this origin resides in the Mysterious Pass, so by concentrating on this cavity you are in essence guarding it. The line, "Both the clarity and purity of non-action are the root source" is basically saying that tranquility is the cause for realizing your true nature.

After one hundred days of continuous and concentrated effort of "contemplative absorption" you will experience the response of forming the elixir, and the process of attaining immortality will become abundantly clear.

If you can maintain a daily disciplined effort at meditating in this manner for one hundred continuous days, you will have set up the conditions for the elixir to begin forming. In essence, by adhering to the above regimes you will have started to stimulate the qi in the lower Dan Tian and will have begun opening up the Mysterious Pass. These are the prerequisites for acquiring the Golden Elixir.

Within the region of the kidneys there is first an upward movement followed by a reverting back motion. The region of the liver acts as a go-between. Thus, a perfect circle

Refining the Elixir

around the infant and young girl [lungs] is formed. Her beauty is never exhausted.

坎中一點往上翻. 黃婆其間為媒妁.
嬰兒奼女兩團圓. 美不盡.

Translator's Commentary
This paragraph is basically describing the Lesser Heavenly Circuit, but more in reference to how it creates a circle about the interior spirits (the "infant" and "young girl") associated with the lungs.

This is a reference to both sensing and internally seeing the qi rising upward to the area of the kidneys, to the liver, and back down to the Dan Tian. This process, called "Circulating the Qi in the Lower Elixir Field," includes the lower Dan Tian, the Hui Yin (perineum), the kidneys, the lower lungs (diaphragmatic muscles), and the front of the stomach.

Within this area of the lower Elixir Field you must visualize a beautiful young girl sitting. Her robe is purple and her hair is long and black. She represents the jing (regenerative force) that is stored and accumulated in the kidneys. Until you can sufficiently visualize and sense this young girl, you will not have sufficient qi and jing to cause the ascent of the elixir. Most cultivators only accomplish getting qi to rise upward into the Bai Hui (top of the head), but this is not the elixir and

Verses on Seated Meditation

the effects are much different when it is the elixir rising upward, as opposed to just the heat of the qi. Until you fully accumulate jing and qi in the lower field, you cannot form the elixir.

To all this I respond. The qi of the entire body, upper and lower, can soar into the Heavens. Who knows the ebb and flow of the Tao? The ignorant cannot speak of it. They are only dreaming.

對誰言．渾神上下氣沖天．這個消息誰知道．
啞子做夢不能言．

Translator's Commentary
Upper and *lower* are references to the qi of the Hun (Heavenly Spirit) and Po (Earthly Spirit). When these unite and the qi is sufficient, your spirit bodies can soar about the Heavens.

The *ebb and flow of the Tao* cannot be predicted or made to conform to one's will. The Tao is "naturally just so," and those who think they can define the ebb and flow (the movement and actions) of the Tao are ignorant and still exist in an illusionary state.

In the Chinese, this verse is more of a chiding remark than an instruction. As mentioned, when you only feel your qi rising into the heavens (the head), you are not experiencing the true elixir. This is just making use of Fire, not Water, so the

Refining the Elixir

ignorant cultivator is only dreaming of attaining the Tao and immortality.

Quickly set to work gathering of the Before Heaven within the places of the Three Gates, so the efficacious medicine will pass through directly from the Dan Tian up to the Bai Hui on top of the head and then descend through the Zhong Lou [esophagus], whereupon it will enter the Zhong Yuan [lower Dan Tian]. Acquiring the True Lead and Mercury takes Fire and Water, but if there is no Wu and Ji the elixir cannot be accomplished.

急下手．採先天．靈藥一點透三關．
丹田直上泥丸頂．降下重樓入中元．
水火既濟眞鉛汞．若非戊己不成丹．

Translator's Commentary

The Before Heaven Qi is what you inherited at birth from your parents. It's your natural qi level and disposition. Gathering it in the Three Barriers (三關, San Guan, three Elixir Fields) means to do the cultivation work of accumulating the Before Heaven Qi in them. When mobilized, the *efficacious medicine* is then your After Heaven Qi.

All this talk about *Lead* and *Mercury*, *Fire* and *Water*, *Wu* and *Ji* are simply referring to the qi and jing.

The gathering of the Before Heaven is also a reference to your primordial jing and qi, and you must ensure that the elixir is placed within the Three Gates. How is this accomplished? First, you must learn to circulate the jing and qi within the lower gate (Dan Tian), then the middle gate (Bright Palace), and then the upper gate (Mysterious Pass). The lower Elixir Field area is most important, however, for that is where you cultivate the jing (in the kidneys) and the qi (in the Dan Tian). The mixture of jing and qi (elixir) is also referred to as the "efficacious medicine."

"True Lead" and "Mercury" are yet another way of saying jing and qi, but to acquire them takes both "Fire" (breath/qi) and "Water" (sexual secretions/saliva/blood). In other words, through abdominal breathing and directing of the breath/qi, you cultivate the mobilization of qi. Through absorbing sexual secretions, stimulating saliva production, and increasing blood circulation, you cultivate the integration of jing with the qi.

The reference to the combined term of "wu and ji" represents the element of Earth, and it's meant to be interpreted as a dual compound, not separately. It's also not a reference to time (late night and early morning) as many translators have rendered them. Actually, wu and ji are considered an "earthly dual combination" and so must be considered as an indicator of using your Po spirit (Earthly, jing) to stimulate and mobilize your Hun spirit (Heavenly,

Refining the Elixir

shen). Hence, the idea is that without making use of (Earthly) sexual energy and (Heavenly) spiritual energy in dual combination, the elixir can never be formed. These two aspects must be united and cultivated together if there is any chance of forming the True Elixir.

When the mind seeks its own death, the will is strengthened. Three thousand dazzling lights completely brighten the spirit. Without casting a shadow, the Golden Rooster [金雞, Jin Ji] beneath a tree cries out. The Red Lotus [紅蓮, Hong Lian, tongue] appears in the depth of the night, and the One Yang arrives at the Winter Solstice [冬至, Han Zhi] to return to its origin.

心要死. 命要堅. 神光照耀遍三千.
無影樹下金雞叫. 半夜三更現紅蓮.
冬至一陽來復始.

Translator's Commentary

The mind being spoken of here is the rational thinking mind, the mind that's forced to think in terms of opposites. When this mind dies, you can then perceive the "One," or Tao. When the Tao is perceived, the will is strengthened. Nothing under Heaven and Earth is beyond this will's influence.

Until you experience these thousands of tiny lamps swaying about inside the brain, your spirit has not fully awakened. It is one of the most joyous

Verses on Seated Meditation

sensations a human being can experience, but for these lights to appear you must be in a state of complete detachment of the mind. This is the mind seeking its own death.

Once while meditating and staring upward, I saw a bird flying high in the sky. The bird was hundreds of feet up in the air. I could see it circling about, but simultaneously I heard it flying with my eyes as well, and I remember thinking that this was the perfection of sound. This is not easy to explain. It's as difficult and mysterious as a Golden Rooster standing and casting no shadow, but whose cries can be heard. The term "Golden Rooster" in Taoism is a synonym for the "Original Spirit" (Yuan Shen).

When completely detached from the mind, the consciousnesses of sight, sound, smell, taste, and touch can all intermix. The ears can see, the eyes can touch, and so on. This is how I heard a bird fly with my eyes. It took me many weeks to listen to music again because nothing compared to the perfection of how that bird sounded.

When the mind dies, the tongue will naturally ascend to the roof of the mouth (a position of midnight) and one drop of Yang Shen (pure Yang Elixir) will attach itself to the Dan Tian (the position sometimes referred to as the Winter Solstice), and so returns to its origin to produce the immortal fetus.

Refining the Elixir

Becoming an immortal is just like a female becoming pregnant. There is little difference between a physical pregnancy and a spiritual one. The mind dying is just like the ejaculation of a male and orgasm of the female in which the entire mind becomes totally focused. The circulating of qi is no different than the sperm working its way toward the female egg. The drop of Yang Shen is just like the one sperm that completes the journey and attaches itself to the fertile egg, only here it is the Dan Tian. The processes are very similar, as are the processes of nurturing the immortal fetus into an immortal spirit that can leave the body. It is all the same.

This verse of the treatise could be interpreted more accurately in the following way:

It is only during the sensation of orgasm that both the body and mind experience the effects of dying. This is the only prolonged experience when all the senses unite and the body freezes, being similar to death. This experience, if used correctly, will strengthen the shen (spirit), and from it the thousands of dazzling lights can be internally viewed inside the brain.

A *golden rooster beneath a tree crying out* is a metaphor for the erection experienced during meditation. The tree is the body, so the image is of a man in meditation whose qi enters the penis causing an erection. The "crying out" is referring to the urges the man feels during this experience.

The *red lotus* (tongue) must be placed on the roof of the mouth, meaning it is placed in the position of midnight (twelve o'clock).

The *one yang* is referring to the one drop of Yang Shen (pure spirit) that arrives back into the Dan Tian (the origin) or in the verse terminology, the Winter Solstice (Earth, the lower abdomen).

With the sounding of thunder, Heaven trembles. The dragons are summoned, and the tigers are joyous. All the immortals cry out unreservedly with joy.
霹靂一聲震動天. 龍又叫. 虎又歡.
仙藥齊鳴非等閒.

Translator's Commentary
This is one of the most interesting and unique verses of any Taoist work, as it is can be interpreted on many different levels. On the alchemical level, it means that when you internally hear the sound of thunder coming from your lower abdomen, your spirit is awakened and the Yang (dragon) and Yin (tiger) have transmuted into forming the elixir. The immortals cry out with joy because a new spiritual fetus has been conceived, and they become ecstatic over the promise of a new arrival in their realm.

Refining the Elixir

In Buddhism, it is said that when an earthquake occurs and no human being is killed by it, someone has just attained enlightenment. Also, within meditation when the lower abdomen quakes (a vibration is felt and a loud bang is heard in the mind), the cultivator has just gotten rid of the bad karma that prevented him or her from attaining enlightenment. When this happens all sorts of spiritual beings rejoice.

Even on a much more mundane level, Taoists have long believed that when thunder shakes the skies it is because the dragons have been summoned to bring rain. The rain makes the tigers happy because it cools off the Earth and provides all the plant growth and food they need.

One year in Indonesia, the government wouldn't allow the Chinese temples to perform dragon dances in the streets during their New Year celebrations, claiming it was too disruptive. The result was that the dragons became irritated and rain deluged the country with widespread flooding ensuing. Because of the flooding, numerous sightings occurred of tigers leaving the mountains and forests in search of food, hence causing a lot of fear in the towns and villages. The situation became so severe that the government insisted the dragon dances be performed again. Two days after the dances took place, the skies cleared, the flooding

Verses on Seated Meditation

ceased, and the tigers returned to the forests and mountains. Never underestimate the force and influence of dragons and tigers.

The sound of thunder is a loud clapping noise heard internally in the head (Heaven). This is the first sign of becoming an immortal, or in Buddhism it indicates that enough bad karma has been removed to ensure enlightenment. When this happens, dragons (Yang/male energies) and tigers (Yin/female energies) are all in perfect harmony. Hence, other immortals can now see the formation of a new immortal. This is much like the joy we humans experience when we know of the coming birth of a child.

Vague and obscure, hold onto being and non-being. Within the midst of this there is limitless creation. It is a mystery within the abstruse and abstruseness within a mystery.

恍恍惚惚存有無. 無窮造化在其間. 妙妙中玄.

Translator's Commentary
This is paraphrased from the *Scripture on Tao and Virtue*. It would be too lengthy to begin an adequate explanation here, but in brief it is saying that the Tao is vague and obscure—meaning, you can't really point at it and say, "There it is." Well, actually you can, but no one except an enlightened being or

Refining the Elixir

immortal would have any idea of what you were pointing at.

This, for example, would be like an average person seeing a blackboard with some long and complex astrophysical computation upon it. He or she could recognize it as a mathematical equation, but couldn't tell you anything specific about it, what any of the symbols meant, or what branch of mathematics it was from. Only astrophysicists could look at it and immediately see and understand it as one thing, the entire equation having one conclusion.

The Tao is similar in this respect. Common people can look at nature or into the heavens and tell you what they see—trees, water, birds, sun, moon, stars, and so forth, all parts and aspects of the Tao. What they can't see is what connects these things or what the source is for all of it—meaning, they can't really see the Tao in it. They may see the parts, but not the whole. When Taoists talk about entering the Great Void, they are describing on one level the wholeness of everything because all the parts have become one. Not two, but one. Within this oneness, there are no parts. It is just one thing, Tao. Tao is everything and yet no-thing simultaneously.

In the *Clarity and Tranquility of the Constant Scripture,* it states, "The Tao is void of even voidness." In other words, "It is empty even of emptiness." It's impossible for the human rational mind to contemplate the idea of emptiness being void of its own emptiness. Try it. Think of emptiness, and then attempt to understand that emptiness is even empty of itself.

For this reason, I never agreed with some translators who assume the Tao is but an idea of God non-personified. Many religions claim that God exists in everything and is omnipresent. This is true of the Tao as well, and Taoists would agree with the comparison if only these religions related that God would be empty of even being God—no God within God itself—but this would contradict every religion's conception and ideal of a *God on High,* an omnipresent figure.

Taoism has a God, the Jade Emperor, and his omnipresence and power are identical to the concepts of God in Middle Eastern cultures and India, but Taoists also understand that the Jade Emperor is just one aspect of Tao, a part of Tao, not the Tao itself.

Western religions say that human beings were made in the image of God, but, again, Taoists would say that humanity is only one part of Tao—not an image of the Tao nor even important to the Tao. Tao doesn't need us to represent its image no more than the Tao needs the Jade Emperor to represent it. The Tao is imageless and therefore creates nothing in its image. The Tao is formless and formless of even non-formlessness. The Tao is empty and empty of even emptiness. The Tao is imageless and imageless of even non-imagelessness. A Taoist would never think he was made in the image of Tao.

Philosophizing about the Tao in this way is pointless. The Tao isn't about answers, nor even questions. Taoists seek perfect tranquility in all their doings. What do questions and answers have to do with tranquility? Philosophies and religions bring disturbances, keeping a person preoccupied with questions about reality, and in the case of religions, often creating guilt and obstacles to self-cultivation.

The Taoist meditation practice of Zuo Wang is about sitting and forgetting. Forgetting is good. It is wonderful to forget everything, even your name—to be just like an infant in a perfect state of being in the moment.

If I have disturbances, if I have guilt and obstacles, I can't forget because I am constantly remembering and worrying. Sitting and forgetting is Taoism at its best. Some may argue that Taoism is a philosophy, but if so, it's about subtraction and getting rid of things, rather than adding theories to your life and trying to figure out reality.

If you hold on to the existence of things (有, you) and the non-existence of things (無有, wu you), you will understand that all creation comes

Verses on Seated Meditation

from it. Much like a womb through which its emptiness gives life, so it is with the Tao, which appears empty, yet everything comes from it. This then is the mystery within a mystery.

Regarding meditation, you must hold onto your very being while experiencing emptiness. Within it you will discover that your mind is limitless creation. It is the Tao. Discovering this on an empirical basis, not just theoretical, is to see the absolute abstruseness of the mysterious Tao.

Many great immortals and enlightened beings all go through a period of not wanting to teach others, seeking to be alone and not speaking of their realization to which this verse is referring. They don't believe anyone will understand it. Unless someone actually realizes (or breaks through the rational mind's veil of vagueness and obscurity) that existence and non-existence are identical, that the material and spiritual are identical, that mind and Tao are identical, the experience of realizing the Tao, or Returning to the Source, can neither be believed nor accepted. So they simply keep quiet.

Then there comes a point when they do speak, because their matured wisdom and compassion leads them to do it. Just as Lao Zi said, "He who knows does not speak. Those who speak do not know," but then he went on to write five thousand characters attempting to explain the Tao and its

Refining the Elixir

power, De (virtue). This is called a "mystic's paradox."

Like an infant you won't really be able to discern much as things seem real and unreal at the same time. Everything seems magical and spiritual, and the tendency is to read into everything. This is why the text says, "to hold onto being and non-being." Too many cultivators create false interpretations of themselves and of events during this stage. Just know that life, immortality, and all events are really just mysteries. Mysteries you cannot understand, so it is best not to try. Buddha advised disciples not to engage the mind in metaphysics, or have discussions about beginnings and endings, or trying to discern the meaning of life. These are all the erroneous illusions with which many philosophers injure and distract themselves. The point is to keep cultivating and not be distracted by events and mental perceptions.

The River Cart circulates and transports, passing through the Three Barriers. Heaven and Earth prosper when they unite to give birth to the Ten Thousand Things. Day by day ingest the sweet dew, which has the taste of honey.

河車搬運過三關天地交泰萬物生.
日飲甘露似蜜甜.

Verses on Seated Meditation

Translator's Commentary

The *River Cart* is the Lesser Heavenly Circuit of qi through the Dumai and Renmai meridians of the body. The qi in these meridians pass through the *Three Barriers* (Dan Tians) in the lower abdomen, the heart region, and within the brain.

Heaven (a reference to Yang qi) and *Earth* (a reference to Yin qi) unite and give birth to the immortal fetus, which when mature can produce ten thousand transformational spirit bodies.

The *sweet dew* is the refined saliva, which will taste like sweet honey. In Taoism the statement of "immortals live off the wind and dew" is stating that they survive simply by ingesting their own breath (qi) and saliva.

This verse is just affirming the idea to keep cultivating. Allow the elixir to circulate through the Three Barriers repeatedly, as this is the process of forming your spiritual fetus. The sweet dew is the saliva, but because of your cultivation the saliva has thickened and turned very sweet.

Now, as to the actual length of time one needs to keep doing this is really an individual matter. Some may practice their entire life and never achieve true immortality, while others may only practice for a short while before doing so. This is more a matter of one's Before Heaven Root-Power; meaning, we are all born with greater and lesser

Refining the Elixir

abilities and propensities for immortality. This is not to say that those who achieve slowly are any less wise, or those who achieve quickly are greater spiritual beings. Some of the greatest Taoist writers, cultivators, and sages never achieved immortality. The important thing is that they understood the true process and meaning of immortality.

Immortals are Buddhas; Buddhas are immortal. The one nature of the bright circle is not two things, just as the Three Philosophies were originally one family.
仙是佛．佛仙．一性圓明不二般．三教原來是一家．

Translator's Commentary
There was a lot of debate in early China about who was higher on the spiritual ladder, Buddhas or immortals. This is a pointless debate, as it is only the terminology that creates such distinctions. Buddha himself talked about his eight hundred lifetimes as the Patient Immortal. He also said that we are all Buddhas. So the statement is correct, immortals and Buddhas are the same. Buddha was an immortal, and immortals are Buddhas.

This verse also shows that Zhang Sanfeng, like most Taoists of his time, believed that all three teachings of Taoism, Confucianism, and Buddhism were of one family and origin. Early Taoists incorporated aspects of all three philosophies into

Verses on Seated Meditation

their teachings. For example, in the Complete Reality Sect of Taoism, monks and nuns were well-versed in the *Heart* and *Diamond Sutras,* as well as adhering to the beliefs of the Guan Yin cult of the Buddhist Pure Land teachings and *The Doctrine of the Mean* from Confucianism. Buddhism also borrowed much from Taoism. Chan (Zen) Buddhism is actually more influenced by Taoist meditation practices than the original meditation schools of India. During the Song dynasty, the neo-Confucians produced many works that are obviously more Taoist in tone than Confucian. The *bright circle* that shines around all spiritual beings, their halo as it were, is the same whether you are an accomplished Buddhist, Taoist, or Confucianist. Spiritual attainment is spiritual attainment no matter the philosophy. Spiritual nature is the same in all of us. If a proclaimed Taoist denounced a Confucian or Buddhist simply because he or she doesn't believe or adhere to Confucian and Buddhist teachings (even if such adherents had spiritual attainments), then that Taoist would be forever mired in delusion about the Tao.

Hunger results in taking food to eat; weariness results in closing the eyes. Burn incense in offering, bow, and practice meditation. This is how to know the Great Tao that sits right before your eyes.

Refining the Elixir

飢則喫飯困則眠．假燒香．拜參禪．
豈知大道在目前．

Translator's Commentary
How sad it is that we live for our stomachs. How sad it is we seek to constantly rest. When we overeat, the jing is damaged. When we toil the body too much, the shen is damaged. Do not concern yourself with eating delicious food or eating a lot. Eat enough to satisfy your hunger and don't eat again until you have defecated. Do not bring yourself to the point of weariness. Work just enough so you feel joyful about it.

Light a piece of incense, bow to the spirits and your teacher, and then sit in meditation. The Tao is right there, but you cannot see it if you worry over food or become worn out. Everything is naturally just so and this is how you should treat your life and practice.

Each school of Taoism has its own ritual method for lighting incense and offering it, each school has its own deportments for bowing, and each school has its own specific method for sitting in meditation (more properly, its own way of Tranquil Sitting). Knowledgeable Taoists can recognize what sect of Taoism people belong to by observing how they light incense, bow, and practice meditation, but no matter the sect all Taoists understand that it is within these three functions that a person can know the Great Tao.

Lighting and offering incense is an act of reverence and charity, bowing is an act of humility and compassion, and sitting in meditation is an act of clarity and wisdom. Reverence, humility, and clarity are the three staples of Taoist cultivation because they lead to non-contention, non-interference, and non-conformity. When we are truly reverent we do not contend, when we are truly humble we do not interfere, and when we have true clarity we do not conform. To be non-contentious, to be non-interfering, and to be non-conforming are the ideals of a true Taoist according to the teachings of Lao Zi.

To be charitable, compassionate, and to attain wisdom is the ideal of a true Buddhist. In Buddhism it is taught that through charity and compassion wisdom can be attained. In Taoism it is the same idea, that through non-contention and non-interference the state of non-conformity can be attained. Non-conformity in Taoism is identical to the Buddhist ideal of "not being turned by conditions." To a Taoist, conformity is the biggest obstacle and hindrance for attaining the Tao. If you are a conformist than you are just a common person influenced by all that is around you, and everything will distract you from cultivating. To be a non-conformist doesn't mean being a rebel against society or others (that would be contending), rather it means to not allow outside conditions to turn you away from your practice.

We can all think of times when it was easy to do something else other than practice, but the best example of not letting conditions turn you comes from a story of one of Master Liang's teachers, Xiong Yanghe (熊養和), who during an earthquake continued sitting in meditation while all his students ran for cover, including Master Liang. When my teacher asked Master Xiong later why he didn't run for cover, he responded, "Why should I let an earthquake disturb me? Maybe if I ran for cover I would be running right into harm's way. Better I just sit and not let the earthquake turn me from my tranquility."

If you can keep an earthquake from turning you, think how much easier it would be to prevent friends and society from distracting you.

To paraphrase what Zhang Sanfeng is ultimately getting at in this verse, "Eat only when you are hungry and sleep only when you are tired, then you will be able to light incense, bow, and meditate without disturbance so you can see the Great Tao right before your eyes."

Verses on Seated Meditation

To just be vegetarian for one's deceased parents is wrong. This is to be really confused, and only vastly robs the body of the Vermilion Man. Simple-minded men erroneously think this is the way to the Western Paradise. It is as if they were blinded by their own sweat or walking by night deep within the mountains.

昏迷喫齋錯過了. 一失人身萬劫難.
愚迷忘想西天路. 瞎漢夜走入深山.

Translator's Commentary
In Buddhism there's a practice of not eating meat to acquire merit for one's parents, eradicating some of their bad karma so they may be admitted into the Pure Land (Western Paradise) of Amitabha Buddha. Taoists like Zhang Sanfeng believed such types of ascetic practices only serve to injure the heart organ, the Vermilion Man, or other spirits within the body. Zhang, of course, wasn't implying that it's wrong to be vegetarian, but he was criticizing the idea of thinking that one can affect another person's fate through such self-denial.

Taoism at its heart is a philosophy and practice of self-attainment, just as Chan (Zen) Buddhism is. Many religions rely on gods and/or spirits to provide them with eternal happiness, salvation, and protection. Taoism relies on self-reliance and self-cultivation, so practices that toil the heart of the person adhering to them weaken the interior spirits

Refining the Elixir

and thereby hurt the body, and if you harm the body, your cultivation is thereby obstructed.

Heaven's root-power is so abstruse, yet it leaves nothing undone. The hidden springs of Heaven's plan are not to be revealed lest it bring upon a mountain of retribution. With the Four Proper Principles, set forth your will on absorption. Breaking through the Mysterious Pass so the subtle mystery can be penetrated.

天機妙．非等閒．洩漏天機罪如山．四正理．
着意參．打破玄關妙通玄．

Translator's Commentary

Heaven's root-power accomplishes everything because its root-power is the Tao. The *hidden springs of Heaven's plan,* in part, refers to the spiritual penetration skills of an immortal who can clearly see the fates and destinies (events and outcomes) of people's lives. However, to reveal this to others brings about great retribution to the immortal. In Buddhism, it's said that when cultivators acquire the ability to heal others, they must be very careful because they may be obstructing a person's natural need to undergo their karmic retribution. Immortals, likewise, have to let mortals find their own way in life and not attempt to interfere, contend, or influence their life choices, so this part

Verses on Seated Meditation

of the text is a warning to those who do achieve immortality.

The *Four Proper Principles* have both a coarse and subtle meaning. The coarse meaning applies to meditation and includes keeping the tongue on the roof of the mouth, rolling the eyes upward inside the head to gaze upon the Mysterious Pass, tightening the anus and perineum when inhaling and relaxing it when exhaling, and keeping the mind intention in the lower abdomen. These four actions or principles are what focus the will (mind intention) upon absorption (tranquility).

The subtle meaning means having True Mind-Intention, True Water, True Fire, and True Wind. *True Mind-Intention* is the application of the four coarse principles, *True Water* makes use of Primordial Qi, *True Fire* is using the Primordial Spirit, and *True Wind* is using Embryonic Breathing.

When the Mysterious Pass (third eye) opens, the subtle mysteries of the Tao are penetrated and seen clearly, and you are at once an immortal.

Uninterrupted through the night, in the hours of Zi and Wu, and in the early morning of Mao and You pay reverence to your illuminated teacher, so you may form the elixir.

子午卯酉不斷夜. 早拜明師結成丹.

Refining the Elixir

Translator's Commentary
The hour of Zi is 11:00 p.m. to 1:00 a.m.; the hour of Wu, 11:00 a.m. to 1:00 p.m.; Mao, 5:00 to 7:00 a.m.; and You, 5:00 to 7:00 p.m.

Your *illumined teacher* lies within your self, within your upper Dan Tian (Mysterious Pass). When your illumination is experienced, the process for forming the elixir of immortality can be undertaken.

There are records of men who have acquired the True Lead and Mercury, and who gave descriptions of their long life, youthfulness, and immortality. One day of practice is one day strengthened. Guard your cultivation and lower your eyes to contemplate. In three years and Nine Revolutions the work is completed. Refine and complete the one seed of the golden azure elixir.

有人識得真鉛汞. 便是長生不老丹. 行一日. 一日堅. 莫把修行眼下觀. 三年九載功成就. 煉成一粒紫金丹.

Translator's Commentary
The *True Lead* is the "true breath/qi" and *True Mercury* is the "refined regenerative force/jing." *Nine Revolutions* means circulating the qi nine times through the Lesser Heavenly Circuit so that one drop of Yang Shen (one seed of the golden azure

Verses on Seated Meditation

elixir) can be deposited into the lower Dan Tian and so produce the immortal fetus.

Again, there is a vast difference between circulating qi through the Dumai and Renmai channels (Lesser Heavenly Circuit) and the Nine Revolutions of the elixir through these channels. In analogy, circulating qi is like blowing wind through a hose, and the Nine Revolutions is like running water through it. The sensations, experience, and outcomes are completely different. The Lesser Heavenly Circuit is relatively easy, but the Nine Revolutions can take a whole lifetime of practice and discipline, and few are able to achieve it.

The function of the Lesser Heavenly Circuit is to move qi, the energy of the breath through the two channels. The function of the Nine Revolutions is to circulate the elixir (jing and qi). After nine such circulations, a seed (one drop of Yang Shen) is developed, and after nine such revolutions the elixir is congealed enough to attach to the lower Dan Tian. If you cultivate the Lesser Heavenly Circuit, do not delude yourself into thinking that because you have experienced tingling, movement, or heat sensations of qi up the spine that this is the elixir. The elixir has a completely different set of sensations.

Likewise, even if you manage to form the elixir, there is no guarantee you will be capable of actually circulating it nine times to create the one seed—just like it doesn't mean that every time a couple has sex a pregnancy will occur.

The text says that *in three years and Nine Revolutions the work is completed,* but we must put this is context. First, how many of us can really devote three solid years to practice, every day and all day? This statement takes for granted that the reader is living high in the mountains, in a hut, with nothing else to do but practice. By the mere fact that you took the trouble to purchase and read this book implies that your situation and environment are not the same as Zhang Sanfeng's, so three years, for most of us, is not the standard.

As my teacher often said, "Life begins at seventy." The main reason he said this was because it was only after he had retired, moved beyond many desires, and had no worries about earning an income that he was able to devote so much of his time to practice.

Aside from the realities of modern society, Zhang did say that *one day of practice is one day strengthened,* which is not only true but encouraging. Do not be dismayed if you are unable to devote each and every day to practice during your early years. All of it is cumulative and not in vain. Practice as much as time allows and be comfortable with the fact that there will come a time when you can lower your eyes, cross

Verses on Seated Meditation

your legs, and practice without distraction. It is the same as saving money, where small amounts can grow into big reserves. Your practice, then, is like a savings account you can draw on and use later.

If you must know who composed these verses, it was the Taoist Qing Xu, the immortal Sanfeng.
要知此歌何人作．清虛道人三丰仙．

Translator's Commentary
Qing Xu was Zhang's previous Taoist moniker before he went to Dragon-Tiger Mountain (龍虎山, Long Hu Shan). There he named himself after the three peaks (三豐, san feng) of a mountain near where he cultivated.

Verses on the Sleeping Immortal

睡仙歌

Shui Xian Ge

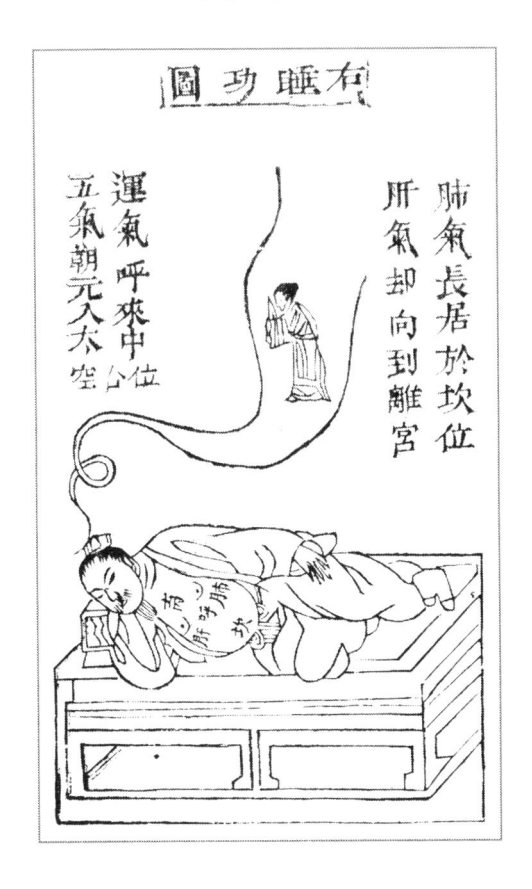

Refining the Elixir

Translator's Comment

Chen Tuan was also known as the Sleeping Immortal, so it may be that Zhang Sanfeng is referring to him. The above illustration comes from the *Book on Immortality of Ten Thousand Years* (萬壽仙書, *Wan Shou Xian Shu*). The sleeping position is called the Jade Lion Pose (玉). Other works, such as *Discourses on the Marrow of the Red Phoenix* (髓紅鳳論, *Sui Hong Feng Lun*), call it the Jade Dragon Pose (玉龍圖).

Chen Tuan is also credited with the practice of a dreaming method for internal alchemy, literally titled *Reverting the Elixir in Dream States* (夢寐還丹, *Meng Mei Huan Dan*). The method is based on making an autosuggestion and visualization right before sleep. The adept visualizes the outcome of Reverting Jing to Restore the Brain, for example, so as to experience it during sleep.

We find a similar story in Lu Dongbin's *Yellow Millet Dream* (黃梁夢, *Huang Liang Meng*). Also, within Taoism there are numerous accounts of adepts having immortal visitations during their sleep states. So, it appears that in Taoism there are practices not only for the conscious state of mind, but also for the unconscious state.

The spiritual immortal sleeps with his head high upon a stone pillow and is unaware even of what year it is.

睡神仙．石枕高臥不知年．

Translator's Commentary

In this treatise, the idea of the immortal being asleep is erroneous. It is only because he is supine and his body is so still that it appears as though he is asleep. As this treatise will demonstrate, the immortal is in a deep state of contemplative absorption. To quote from the work of Zhuang Zi, "The body is like dead wood and his mind like cold ashes"—meaning, the body is so still it appears lifeless.

Most people need very soft pillows to rest their heads upon when they sleep because of the tension

Refining the Elixir

and anxiety experienced in their daily lives. They toil and abuse their bodies so much that when they get home all they can think about is soft comfortable chairs, sofas, and beds. We may think these soft receptacles for our bodies are really beneficial, but in reality they damage us in the long term. Soft furniture only weakens our spines, hurts our joints and bones, deadens the muscles, and obstructs blood circulation in our bodies.

A long time ago when I was once visiting a family in China, I noticed that they only had wooden furniture in their reception area. The chairs and sofa just had straight wooden backs, no cushions, and were hand carved with dragons, phoenixes, and various motifs. They were beautiful, but very hard and uncomfortable, so I took it upon myself to buy the head of the family, a seventy-year-old man, a reclining chair so he could watch TV in some comfort.

The old man looked at me with a smile and said, "You truly are an American aren't you?" I looked at him curiously for a moment and he said humorously, "Are you trying to kill me? All that soft furniture will only weaken every part of this old body. Better I sit on a big stone than all that cotton wadding."

"In the West," he continued, "so many older people have arthritis and numerous musculature

Verses on the Sleeping Immortal

ailments because they constantly seek comfort everywhere. Look at Buddhist monks who never lay down to sleep, sitting in full-lotus instead, or Taoist priests who only lie upon a thin blanket to rest. They all maintain a strong and healthy spine throughout their lives. I am honored you wish to buy me such a wonderful chair, but I prefer to keep my spine upright and strong."

He was correct. In the West, we are constantly seeking comfort, and it is that comfort that eventually destroys us. The point of all this is that when we sleep upon a really soft bed, it is harder to wake up in the morning. This then leads to needing all sorts of stimulants to help us wake up—shrieking alarms, blaring radios, coffee, cigarettes, noisy televisions, and so on. We have adapted to needing to be jolted out of our sleep then stimulate ourselves, rush to work, and then wonder why we feel so exhausted at work and at the end of the day. It is interesting that almost all over Asia many people wake up and begin doing exercises like Taijiquan, qigong, and meditation to even further calm and revitalize themselves. Hence, they approach their workday feeling relaxed and refreshed, not stimulated and rushed.

The sleeping immortal here is just like a cat. A cat can lie down anywhere and sleep in complete comfort, doing so because it has no anxiety or tension in its body. Even though the sleeping immortal rests *his head high upon a stone pillow,* he finds no discomfort because his body is soft, not the stone pillow. Common people need soft pillows because their bodies are so hard and tense, but once the body is made soft and relaxed even stones are comfortable.

When I first arrived at Gold Mountain Monastery (金山寺, Jin Shan Si) in San Francisco (老金山, Lao Jin Shan, Old Gold Mountain) they gave me a room that had just a wooden plank for a bed. I had great difficulty falling asleep the first few nights because my body ached so badly. I kept collecting blankets and used my clothing to create a makeshift mattress, but even with those my body ached. After a few weeks, however, my body began to relax and the pains subsided and I could sleep comfortably without my stacks of blankets and clothes.

One of the most important aspects of self-cultivation is the discovery of your spine. This may sound odd, but it's true. Most of us go through life constantly weakening our spine and so have no awareness of what a strong and supple spine feels like. If you seek to feel qi move up your back, or as it is called in Taijiquan "adhering qi to your spine," you must first have a supple and strong spine. If

Verses on the Sleeping Immortal

not, there will simply be too many blockages along the spine for the qi to move through.

The Three Bright Ones no longer concern him. His self-nature is complete.
三光沉淪. 性自圓.

Translator's Commentary
The *Three Bright Ones* are the sun, moon, and stars. This line of the verse could alternately read, "The Sleeping Immortal is unaware of the year, the days, and the nights." Like an infant, he has no concern about space and time, and this is what makes his self-nature complete. Because all anxiety has left him, his spirit is as Zhuang Zi describes, "naturally just so."

The meaning of this verse goes beyond just the reference to the sun, moon, and stars, which are the Three Bright Ones concerning Heaven. The Three Bright Ones for the Earth are fire, water, and air. For humanity, they are jing (essence), qi (breath), and shen (spirit).

Immortals are not concerned about the sun, moon, and stars because space and time do not affect them as they do with mortals. Mortals have to calculate everything concerning space and time. We toil our spirits with concerns of what year it is, what month is it, what day it is, and what time it is.

Refining the Elixir

Immortals also transcend the elements, so they are unconcerned about the effects of fire, water, and air. "Immortals walk through fire unburned, sit in water and do not drown, and can use the air for flight."

Likewise, since their self-nature is complete, they have no need to cultivate or worry about their jing, qi, and shen.

We mortals, however, still need our calendars and watches. We need to use fire, water, and air to survive, and we have to cultivate our jing, qi, and shen.

His Vital Energy and breath return to the Mysterious Cavity, allowing his breath to be completely natural so it is neither dispersed nor disordered, and with absolute tranquility and quietude.

氣炁歸玄竅．息息任天然．莫散亂．須安恬．

Translator's Commentary
This verse is describing that when a cultivator enters into deep tranquility and quietude (silence) the qi is concentrated internally of the Mysterious Cavity (third eye). This is part of the meaning for Returning the Light, for once the qi is concentrated there, it will not disperse or be disordered (distractions will not occur).

Verses on the Sleeping Immortal

Nourishing the Mercury Child enables him to fulfill his nature. In waiting for the Lead Child, flowers appear.

養得汞兒性圓. 等待他鉛兒花現.

Translator's Commentary

This is probably the most important verse of the text because it really defines what self-cultivation is. The *Mercury Child* is an analogy for the initial Fire (qi) which brings forth our temperament (性, xing, nature), and the *Lead Child* is is an analogy of the initial Water (jing) that brings forth our emotions (情, qing). *Nourishing the Mercury Child* means to cultivate the Nine Revolutions, and awaiting the *Lead Child* means to cultivate the Seven Reversions. The term "child" is used because both the mercury and lead are not yet matured, or complete in their development. When they do mature, they are called "True Lead and True Mercury," which is the Reverted Elixir. The meaning of waiting for the *Lead Child* is that Nature cannot come forth unless the Seven Emotions[35] are kept from their extreme expressions, which damage the spirit, and we develop a non-attachment to their influences—like infants who can cry in one instant and be laughing the next because they aren't attached to their emotions.

---

35   *Seven Emotions*, or Passions (七情, Qi Qing) also refer to the Seven Earthly Spirits (七魄, Qi Po) and Seven Energies (七氣, Qi Qi).

Refining the Elixir

These different terms are all connected in that the seven can be viewed and experienced as an emotion, spirit, or energy, and unless they are regulated and controlled, the Nine Revolutions cannot occur. This is why many Taoist internal alchemy texts use the term "Nine Restorations and Seven Returns" (九環七返, Jiu Zhuan Qi Fan) to describe this crucial requisite for the formation of the elixir.

This subject of Seven Reversions is very complex as each emotion is connected to the functions of the Five Viscera (五臟, Wu Zang: heart, liver, spleen, lungs, and kidneys) and Six Bowels (六腑, Liu Fu: small intestine, gall bladder, stomach, large intestine, pericardium/blood vessels, and Triple Warmer). So any emotion becoming extreme will injure the qi and cause illness or disease. For example, the emotion of extreme happiness or love injures the heart, anger and hate injures the liver, grief injures the lungs, sorrow and depression injure the spleen, fear injures the kidneys, anxiety injures the gall bladder, and lust injures the spirit of the liver and the qi of the lungs. In turn, what affects the heart will affect the small intestine, what affects the liver affects the gall bladder, what affects the spleen affects the stomach, what affects the lungs affects the large intestine, and what affects the kidneys affects the pericardium, blood vessels, and Triple Warmer.

Verses on the Sleeping Immortal

Emotions are always at the root of any bad habit, and by simply being made aware of such extremes in our behavior we begin the process of reverting them into good habits or conducts. In my book *The Immortal,* Li Qingyun comments on the ill effects of extreme bad habits in the following statement:

Eight out of ten are injured by: Staring for too long hurts the Essence, lying down for too long hurts the Qi, sitting for too long hurts the circulation of blood, standing for too long hurts the bones, walking for too long hurts the muscles. Anger injures the liver, anxiety injures the spleen, overthinking injures the heart, too much sorrow injures the lungs, eating too much injures the stomach, fearing too much injures the kidneys, laughing too much injures the waist, talking too much injures the secretions, spitting too much injures saliva, sweating too much injures the Yang energy, tearing [of the eyes] too much injures the blood, sexual intercourse too frequently injures marrow.

Li Qingyun said that "greed, anger, and arousing affections," along with "bitter sadness" (depression) and "being vexed by hatred" (negative compulsions), are what greatly affect our lifespan and our physical and mental health. Therefore, he had many warnings:

Refining the Elixir

Greed, anger, and arousing affections are the most likely [emotions] to rob the human body and mind, and so keeping away from these are the Way of Longevity. When people embrace silence, the spirit will not be injured. Thinking less feels good, like candlelight shining in the mind. Don't get angry, and the Qi and Spirit will react smoothly. Be without worry and the mind will be calm and pure. Do not desire, and then there will be no effects of flattery and pride. Don't be stubborn, then everything will be flexible. Don't be greedy, then you can feel wealthy. Be conscientious, then why would you fear even monarchs? Lightly tasting will let you experience the sweetness of food. If the qi is stable, then the breathing pattern will naturally become thin and lingering. All that has been mentioned here is for correcting the two aspects of "greed and anger."

Keep in mind, no one can achieve immortality if the internal organs and functions are not in good order. Therefore, the underlying factor of the Seven Reversions is primarily about restoring and refining our internal organs and functions, and to do so the Seven Emotions, Seven Spirits, and Seven Qi must be regulated and controlled. The *Seven Reversions* then represent the psychological aspect of cultivation, whereas the Nine Restorations are more about the physiological aspects.

When cultivators successfully control the Seven Emotions through Seven Reversions, they not only can experience seeing flowers, but also pure white snow may appear to be falling all around them. Snow and flowers fall all about them and everything feels incredibly light. Both the flowers and snow are illusionary and there is nothing real about either of them. This is just an effect of the mind that is cleansing itself, a mind that is completely absorbed in abstract contemplation.

The meaning of this verse is very abstruse. To *nourish* the Mercury Child and Lead Child means nourishing the qi and jing, but more so it means that the Spirit and Qi (Mercury Child) has entered the Tail Gateway, kidneys, and spinal column, but the jing (Lead Child) is not yet strong enough to fully transform the marrow or complete Reverting Jing to Restore the Brain. The Lead Child is the jing (essence) and as it ascends the spine the restoration of the marrow allows it to pass through and into the brain. When this elixir (jing and qi) reach the brain, then visions of falling flowers and snow can appear.

Refining the Elixir

Guarding against erroneous actions he mobilizes the True Fire within himself by practicing the Seven Reversions, and unperturbed cultivates Nine Restorations.

無走失．有防閑．眞火候運中間．行七返．
不艱難．煉九還．

Translator's Commentary

This verse of the text requires a great deal of explanation as there are four aspects needing clarification. The first is the meaning of "Guarding against erroneous actions," then the definition of "Mobilizing the True Fire," an explanation of the "Seven Reversions," and lastly the meanings of the "Nine Restorations."

Guarding against erroneous actions

This subject is not about moralistic conduct, but rather it is about mindfulness. An erroneous action is any activity in which a person engages wherein the principles or goals of self-cultivation are not at the forefront of their thoughts and purposes. So no matter what activity cultivators might find themselves performing it is the mindfulness of that activity and their cultivation that is of paramount importance—be it washing the dishes, shopping, taking out the garbage, doing your banking, sitting in meditation, and so on—everything should be done with

Verses on the Sleeping Immortal

mindfulness. This is true "guarding against erroneous actions."

If we look at the behaviors of Taoist sages we do not always find what we might consider noble moral conduct. Zhang Sanfeng behaved very strangely, especially in public, by using foul language, urinating where he pleased, never bathing, and putting on airs of being insane. The Seven Sages of the Bamboo Grove (third century CE) gave the impression they were raging alcoholics and ranting lunatics with their practice of drinking wine and doing improvisational poetry duals. Zhuang Zi laughing and playing a drum after his wife's death surely did not fit propriety. Then the great sage Yang Zhu (楊朱, 440–360 BCE) appeared to many as a mere hedonist and epicurean. But the actions of these great Taoist sages were not exercises in mere satiation of base desires, these were actions of pure mindfulness.

Self-cultivation doesn't mean disciplining or developing just one aspect of yourself, but your entire self. Yang Zhu, for example, was most definitely not a hedonist or epicurean, at least not in how a common person would define or view these behaviors. Yang Zhu exercised non-conformity, non-interference, and non-contention with both himself and all others. Yang Zhu was very mindful of the idea that human beings and society in general are preoccupied with wanting all other human beings to conform to their way of thinking, thus interfering and contending with their true nature. Likewise, as Yang Zhu teaches, a person cannot live in the Tao by being a conformist, or if they interfere or contend with others. To do so in Yang Zhu's view is nothing more than living in false pretense.

Therefore, "guarding against erroneous actions" is to be constantly mindful about not being a conformist, guarding against interference, and about not contending with others—to live and let live—this is perfect freedom action, living in the Tao, or as my teacher once said, "If you want to be an immortal then stop acting like a common mortal."

Mobilizing the True Fire
True Fire is the heat created from the qi, but is not the qi itself. In analogy this is like saying there is a heat source, a flame from the stove, that heats a pot (abdomen) of water (blood and body fluids). When the water boils, steam is produced. The steam is symbolic of the qi in the human body. So True Fire here is referring to the heat produced in the lower abdomen, but not necessarily the qi itself.

In Taoism the term "mobilize" (yun) is a reference for actually moving, circulating, or activating the Fire and qi. Mobilizing the True Fire simply means to feel the sensations of heat in

Verses on the Sleeping Immortal

various parts of the body, and throughout the body. Meaning, first cultivators seek to feel heat in their lower abdomen, but as their cultivation progresses they can will this heat up into the spine, top of the head, and so forth. Mobilizing the qi is more a matter of moving it through meridians; i.e., the Dumai and Renmai channels up along the spine and down the front of the body respectively. It is therefore paramount and crucial for beginning cultivators to first feel heat in the lower abdomen and then seek to mobilize it with their mind-intent upward throughout the body. This then clears the way, so to speak, for mobilizing the qi when it becomes abundant and strong enough to be circulated.

So True Fire is not just the warmth of the body as one might experience from strenuous exercise or hot flashes. True Fire is felt in the lower abdomen and is generated from a cultivator constantly "Abiding by the Elixir Field" and keeping the breath below the navel.

In Taijiquan one of the initial stages is the experience of "free circulation." This is where the cultivator feels heat in the hands, tingling sensations, and increased perspiration. These are very good signs, but they aren't True Fire. Free circulation is a result of increased blood circulation that aids in moving the qi throughout the body, and this is crucial for increasing and restoring one's health. But True Fire is first felt in the lower abdomen and will remain stagnant unless the cultivator makes use of the mind-intent to mobilize it.

For commentary on the *Seven Reversions* and *Nine Restorations* see p. 241.

How regrettable it is that the tiger and dragon do battle in the Hall of War while contemplating within tranquility.
何嗟歎. 靜觀龍虎戰場戰.

Translator's Commentary
Even when a cultivator enters tranquility there is still the residual expression of yin (tiger) and yang (dragon) battling for dominance. Some might say this is the battle between good and evil in a person, but Taoism doesn't believe a person is either good or evil. Yes, people can do good things and they are capable of doing evil things, but this has nothing to do with their true nature that is beyond this duality. What Taoists do believe is that a human being is composed of yin and yang and these are in a constant state of change. When perfect tranquility is reached, both yin and yang are being transformed into one—the Tao. So like a candle that is just about to burn out it flares up before extinguishing, and this is what is meant by "the tiger and dragon do battle in the Hall of War" (the rational mind).

Verses on the Sleeping Immortal

Sometimes the battle is lost, actually most of the time it is. Some cultivators when they enter tranquility will start to shake violently, thus disturbing their tranquility. They shake because when you enter into an extreme state of yin, the yang will naturally come forth. Mostly what happens to cultivators is that when they first enter tranquility, the mind conjures up some great fear, like the sensation of thinking they are not breathing, or they are losing their very identity and existence. Then there are those who simply fall asleep because the spirit is not strong enough to pass through this stage, so dullness comes forth and off to sleep they go. These are not Sleeping Immortals, rather Sleeping Mortals.

Grasp hold of obscurity and turn over to invert the Yin and Yang.
唔把陰陽顛倒顛.

Translator's Commentary
Turn over to invert the Yin and Yang means to return to your original and primordial nature. There is an old Taoist woodblock showing Pan Ku holding a Taiji symbol. The symbol is turned so that the yang is on the left and upper side, and the yin is on the right lower side. This is the proper positioning of

Refining the Elixir

the Taiji symbol. It is just a way of symbolically demonstrating the meaning of this verse.

Grasp hold of obscurity goes to the heart of the Taoist idea of chaos, and to "grasp hold of it" means to accept it and flow with it. Taoists never believed that people should spend all their life and energy attempting to bring order to anything in nature. Nature is chaos and no one can confine it or box it up like someone putting a bird in a cage. Rather, Taoists understand that it is the grasping of obscurity that leads a person to finding the Tao. For instance, imagine yourself on a raft drifting down a river. You have two options, either drift with the current or attempt to fight it. Taoists will drift, letting the current just take them toward their destination.

Verses on the Sleeping Immortal

So the gist of this verse is that when we simply accept the chaos and obscurity of nature we are that much closer to realizing our own original nature, and this is the meaning of turning over the inverted yin and yang. In other words, until you learn to just drift with the current of life and Tao you will forever be upside down in your thinking and actions. Actually, you will only be opposing your original nature and Tao.

This verse also goes to the heart of what Lao Zi instructed, "Hold on to being and keep to non-being." This obscure statement has caused much debate among scholars and philosophers for centuries. All I want to say further about it is that a Taoist understands on a very simple level that we must simultaneously accept both our existence and non-existence, accept our reality and non-reality, and accept our permanence and impermanence. Only when we accept this, just like accepting there is a yin and yang nature and aspect to everything, can we hope to see the source, the Tao. So finding the "One" as it is often referred to isn't selecting either being or non-being as being the source, or one. It is seeing the source of the two.

As human beings we are caught in a constant interplay of dualities—right and wrong, black and white, up and down, so on and so forth. Everything we think and do is caught up in and relies on duality. So Lao Zi wisely taught acceptance of the two, not the denial of one over the other. You'll never find the Tao if you are one-sided. So to Embrace the One (抱一, Bao Yi) is not about thinking you can embrace the Tao as such, rather it is about embracing the oneness of two. This is kind of reverse thinking, or inverted thinking.

To help clarify this, I will retell an old Buddhist story.

Buddha had a favorite disciple named Ananda. Ananda was exceptional because he could remember everything he ever heard, word for word. In fact if it wasn't for Ananda there would probably be no Buddhist sutras. Ananda had an uncle who was a famous philosopher and his philosophy was based on annihilation—meaning, everything in the universe was subject to annihilation, impermanence, extinction, and so forth. Ananda's uncle didn't much like his nephew being with the Buddha and he wanted Ananda to come and be his disciple. So the uncle went to the Buddha and asked for his nephew back. Buddha then said he would gladly give Ananda back if the uncle could defeat him in a debate. The uncle agreed and Ananda looked on as the Buddha asked the uncle just this one question. "Do you believe and accept your own philosophy?" The uncle could say nothing. Why? Because if he confirmed that he did believe and accept it, he would

Verses on the Sleeping Immortal

be admitting it too was subject to annihilation and therefore not the ultimate truth of things, and if he denied he believed in his philosophy, then he would just be admitting everything he taught was untrue. So Ananda stayed with the Buddha and the uncle went home, but later he returned to study with the Buddha as well.

The reason for telling this story is to better illustrate what Lao Zi taught about not being one-sided and holding an extremist view, not even about the Tao.

Others say my own sweat has blinded me because I reject actual sleep. But I'm not sleeping, just being perfectly still.
人言我是矇瞳汗．我却眠兮猶未眠．

Translator's Commentary
When I read this verse, I think about a particular monk I had met while staying at the City of Ten Thousand Buddhas. On many levels, he was a very coarse person. He swore a lot, and was not someone you wished to cross. As time went on and I had the opportunity to know him better, I came to greatly respect him. On several occasions I witnessed him entering the dining hall for the one-meal-per-day rule. He would walk through the door, sniff the air, and grumble, "Smells like shit" and walk out

Refining the Elixir

without eating. Later I discovered he had once fasted for forty-nine days, a really incredible feat.

What impressed me most about him were his abilities concerning meditation and sleep. The rule was for monks to sleep upright in a meditation posture. In the Chan Hall we had benches that were raised off the floor about two feet, and most of us sat on these benches during the meditation sessions each morning and evening. Always at night, after the last ceremony and meditation period, we would all exit to go to our private sleeping rooms. But not this monk, he would simply sit on the Chan bench with his legs crossed, throw a blanket over his head, and there he would stay. I was never sure whether he slept or meditated. In the early morning, exactly at 3:30 a.m., we would all go back to the meditation hall for the morning ceremony and meditation period. It always amazed me that he would still be sitting perfectly upright there with the blanket over his head. When the gong would sound for the beginning of the ceremony the blanket would come flying off and he would be ready for the ceremony.

I should also mention that on several occasions during the night when I had to visit the bathroom next to the Chan Hall I would peek inside and see him just sitting in perfect repose with his tattered blanket strewn over his head, and never did I see him moving.

Verses on the Sleeping Immortal

One time I asked him if he ever really got any sleep? He said, "One hour of meditation is the same as four hours of sleep, so actually I get way too much sleep." This is why this line of the text always reminds me of him. He didn't actually reject sleep, he was just being perfectly still.

In contrast, I had to use a Chan chair, a bench with a wooden back and a rope to fasten around my chest to prevent me from falling over at night. I can't count the number of times I woke up on the floor when not using the rope, or the number of lumps upon my head. Even during Chan sessions (those pesky periods when there would be twenty hours a day of meditation for twenty-one days or longer), many of us laypeople learned how to appear to be meditating but were actually sleeping. There was a running joke that if you did it right, you could get in a good eight hours of shuteye. This was a joke, mostly, because between the hourly bell ringing out the signal of a meditation period ending and beginning and the monk who quietly would sneak up on you and hit the incense board across your shoulders if he heard you snoring or saw you wobbling in your posture, there was no such thing as real sleep.

Whether leaning upon a rock, sitting upright in a meditation posture, or laying down in the Jade Lion Pose, it is not a question of sleep. It is purely a

Refining the Elixir

matter of entering perfect stillness. In Taoism, sitting upright in a meditation posture to sleep is rarely practiced. There were monks and nuns within the early formation of the Complete Reality Sect headed by Wang Chongyang who did emulate their Chan Buddhist counterparts by never laying down to sleep. But the more common practice was to sleep in either the Jade Lion Pose or to lie upon a rested right arm and lean upon something during sleep. The steadfast rule was to sleep upon the right side, not the left. Sleeping on the left side of the body can constrict the heart and cause disturbances during sleep, such as bad dreams and bodily movements—but the main prohibition against it is that it can cause heart problems from the pressure put upon the heart by a person's body weight.

You must practice and study. Cultivate until all is complete so the True blends with the Chan. This is the true embryo.
學就了. 眞參禪. 養成了. 眞胎元.

Translator's Commentary
The *True* is the Tao and *Chan* (Zen) is the experience of it. In this verse it also states that a cultivator must *practice and study*. After reading and studying any book on cultivation, even this one for example, you must continue to study. Albert Einstein was quoted as saying, "Practice without

Verses on the Sleeping Immortal

theory is blind, and theory without practice is sterile." All cultivators should pay attention to this statement.

Just practicing is not enough, as the theories behind the practice are of equal importance, so don't rely purely on what you are taught. Study the works of the old masters and glean as much insight as you can. If you reach the higher states of internal alchemy, you must be able to discern the experiences you encounter. Without study this would be well-nigh impossible.

The Sleeping Dragon once rose up and ascended into Heaven. This is the Jellyfish Method. Whose method is this?

臥龍一起便升天. 此蜇法. 是誰傳.

Translator's Commentary

The *Sleeping Dragon* is Zhang Guo Lao (張果老), one of the Eight Immortals. His origin is unknown, but he lived as a hermit. Legends say he rode a white donkey and could cover great distances in just one day. He also rode the donkey backward because, as he claimed, "it was better to see where one had been then to worry about where one was going."

When he stopped to rest on his travels he could fold up his donkey into a piece of paper and keep it

Refining the Elixir

in his hat. When he wished to ride the donkey, all he needed to do was unfold the paper, spray spittle from his mouth over it, and the donkey would reappear. Zhang Guo Lao lived during the Tang dynasty and was invited to the imperial court, but he never responded. Later during the reign of Ming Huang, he was again summoned, but this time he simply laid down and died. His disciples buried him but said later that when they checked his coffin, it was empty.

In drawings of Zhang Guo Lao he is depicted seated and riding backward on his donkey and holding a wooden fish (ritual drum), a musical instrument that was used as both a drum and castanets.

Verses on the Sleeping Immortal

Recently, scientists have proven that the Turritopsis nutricula species of jellyfish is biologically capable of immortality. This jellyfish can revert to its earlier polyp stage, effectively restarting its lifecycle and reversing the aging process. Calling this transmission the *Jellyfish Method* is fascinating because it not only shows that Taoists equated jellyfish with immortality centuries ago, but that they knew this long before modern scientists discovered the ability of the Turritopsis nutricula species.

Dwelling in the mountains I just naturally use my bent arm as a pillow. There is such joy being in the midst of having the acquaintance of no one.
曲肱而枕自尼山. 樂在其中無人譜.

Translator's Commentary
What a beautiful and poetic image this paints. How wonderful it would feel to be sitting in the mountains, reclining upon some big rock with a bent arm to rest the head upon, and the best part is not having to deal with, talk to, or even see anyone. Best to say no more about this verse, lest the image it so wonderfully creates is spoiled.

Five dragons dance and fly about in the deep vastness.
五龍飛躍出深潭.

Refining the Elixir

Translator's Commentary
The *Five Dragons* are the Five Elements sublimated into the Tao. Metal, Fire, Wood, Water, and Earth no longer have an effect upon immortals, who can then dance freely about the deep vastness of the Great Void.

Heaven bequeathed these methods through transmitting the Southern Map. The Southern Map is but one pulse, but who is able to follow this? The Dirty Taoist, Zhang Sanfeng.
天將此法傳圖南．圖南一脈能繼．
邋遢道人張三丰．

Translator's Commentary
The *Southern Map* is a reference to the River Map and Lo Script from which the *Book of Changes* developed. Here again is an obscure reference to the correlation of the processes of internal alchemy having been created within the workings of the *Book of Changes*. The statement about it being "one pulse," means internal alchemy is just one thing, one teaching, one process, despite the numerous methods and writings on the subject, as they are all talking about one thing, "obtaining the Tao." The one pulse is another way of expressing the Taoist adage, "It is not two, just the One."

See the History of Zhang Sanfeng section for an explanation on why he was called "Dirty Zhang."

Ancestor Lu's One Hundred Character Tablet

註呂祖百字碑

Zhu Lu Zu Bai Zi Bei

諸張三峰仙祖

Commentary by Immortal Ancestor Zhang Sanfeng (Zhang Zi)

Lu Zi's Text[36]

Nourish the qi. Guard against false speech.

養氣忘言守.

Zhang Zi's Commentary[37]

Cultivators must first practice nourishing their qi. The method for nourishing the qi is to forget words and Guard the One.[38] Forgetting words, the qi will not disperse; Guarding the One, the spirit will not leave. The secret is called, "Seal the tongue in tranquility, and retain the spirit by embracing it."

---

36 *Lu Dongbin* (呂洞賓) was born in 796 CE during the Tang dynasty. He was a Chinese scholar, poet, and cultivator who was elevated to immortal status. Revered by Taoists, Lu, or as he's called in this work "Lu Zi" (Master or Philosopher Lu), is one of the most widely known of the Eight Immortals (八仙, Ba Xian) and is normally considered the leader. Lu is a historical figure, mentioned in the official history book, *History of Song*. Lu is one of the earliest masters of the internal alchemy tradition, and is usually accepted as the author of the *Secret of the Golden Flower*. He is depicted in art as being dressed as a scholar and he often bears a sword upon his back that dispels evil spirits.

37 *Zhang Zi* is Zhang Sanfeng. Herein referred to as Master or Philosopher Zhang.

38 *Guarding the One* (守一, Shou Yi) is another term for Embracing the One (Bao Yi), literally "to guard," or "embrace," the Original Spirit, but here the notion is meant more as "to abide by the Elixir Field" within the lower abdomen.

Refining the Elixir

養氣忘言守．凡修行者先須養氣．養氣之法．
在乎忘言守一．忘言則氣不散．守一則神不出．
訣曰緘舌靜．抱神定．

Lu Zi's Text
Surrender the mind to active non-doing.
降心為不為．

Zhang Zi's Commentary
The minds of common men move and drift endlessly. If cultivators seek to enter tranquility it is important to subdue the two eyes. The eyes are like a gateway to the mind. It is essential they are lowered like window screens to prevent distractions from entering. With each and every situation use the mind like a sword. Regard all worldly affairs as having no benefit whatsoever to you, then distractions and cravings will vanish without attempting to rid yourself of attachments.

  The secret is to direct the eyes to gaze upon the nose, and through the nose, gaze upon the navel. Align the upper and lower, and keep the mind and breath unified. Then draw the mind-intention to the Mysterious Pass and you will overcome all thoughts and anxieties.

凡人之心動盪不已．修行人．心欲入靜．
貴乎制伏兩眼．眼者心之門戶須要垂簾塞兌．
一切事體．以心為劍想世事無益 於我．火烈頓除．
莫去貪著．訣云以眼視鼻以鼻視臍上下相顧．
心息相依．著意玄關．便可降伏思慮．

Ancestor Lu's One Hundred Character Tablet

Lu Zi's Text
In movement and tranquility know the Original Ancestor.
動靜知宗祖.

Zhang Zi's Commentary
Movement and tranquility are just one yin and one yang, and the Original Ancestor[39] is the place where the body is born. Cultivators must know that prior to the birth of their father and mother there is the Mysterious Female.[40]

This is the place where the upper and lower parts of the body, the Heavenly and Earthly, the Eight Diagrams, the Five Activities, and the Four Images of one's being all gather together. This is also the place prior to Heaven and Earth where they are not yet separated, and is the one point of your perfected spiritual light, this then is the Supreme Ultimate.[41]

Below the heart and above the genitals, internally this is where never-ending thoughts arise and dwell, just like in the head. But this is the Original Ancestor and through movement and tranquility, it can harmonize the True Breath, and this naturally brings about the principle of True Origination.

---

39   *Original Ancestor* (元祖, Yuan Zu) is a term for the Elixir Field.

40   *Mysterious Female* (玄牝, Xuan Pin). This term comes from chapter 6 of the *Tao De Jing:* "The valley spirit never dies. It is called the mysterious female. The door of the mysterious female is the root of Heaven and Earth. Being continuous, it appears to exist. Yet in use it is inexhaustible."

41   *Supreme Ultimate* (太極, Tai Ji).

Refining the Elixir

Because when communicating with exhaling the Root of Heaven, and communicating with inhaling the Root of Earth, this then is the gateway and meaning of the *Creativity of Heaven* (乾, Qian), and this then is the gateway and meaning of the *Receptivity of Earth* (坤, Kun).[42]

Exhaling is associated with the humming of a dragon rising into the clouds; inhaling is associated with the hissing sound of a tiger living on the wind. With each gate, each breakthrough, each movement, and with each tranquil moment, your mind will not move. Allow the True Breath to come and go continuously, as though it seeks existence. Meaning, breathe until you achieve breath without breathing, and become one with it. Then the spirit will be solidly retained and the elixir can be produced.

動靜知宗祖：動靜者一陰一陽也．宗祖者．
生身之處也．修行人．當知父母未生之前．
即玄牝也．一身上下乾坤八卦五行四象聚會之處．
乃天地未判之先．一點靈光而成．即太極也．
心之下．腎之上．彷彿之內．念頭無息．所起之處．
即是宗祖所謂動靜者．調和氣．安理真元也．
蓋呼接天根．吸接地根．即闔戶之謂坤．
闢戶之謂乾呼則 龍吟雲起．吸則虎嘯風生．
一闔一闢．一動一靜．貴乎心意不動．
任其 真息往來．綿綿若存．調息至無息之息．
打成一片．斯神可凝．丹可就 矣．

---

[42] *Creativity of Heaven* is image #1 ☰ and *Receptivity of Earth* is #2 ☷ in the *Book of Changes*. This is a cryptic way of saying the movement of the River Cart.

Ancestor Lu's One Hundred Character Tablet

Lu Zi's Text
With no affairs, what else is there to seek?
無事更尋誰.

Zhang Zi's Commentary
If you can nourish the qi, forget words, subdue the body and mind, return the spirit to the Qi Cavern,[43] focus the mind-intention on the center of the circle, the Yi Qi[44] will merge and issue forth like steam.

This is all just like a hen brooding on her eggs or a dragon nurturing a pearl. Keep the mind constantly on the present, without leaving it for even a moment, and then in the course of time when the effort becomes so abstruse there will naturally appear a pearl the size of a piece of fine rice. Bright, it will shine like the sun, and this spot will then transform into Original Spirit, and the spiritual illumination will be unfathomable. Thus, this is so.

若能養氣忘言守. 降伏身心. 神穴. 意注規中.
混融一如雞抱卵如龍養珠. 念茲在茲.
須臾不離日久工深. 自然現出黍米之珠.
光耀如日. 點化元神. 靈明莫測. 即此是也.

---

[43] *Qi Cavern* (氣穴, Qi Xue) is another term for the Elixir Field.

[44] *Yi Qi* (一氣) translates as the "One Breath," and is also another term referring to the True Breath.

Refining the Elixir

Lu Zi's Text
The True and Constant responds to all living things, so in responding to others it is essential not to become confused.

真常須應物. 應物要不迷.

Zhang Zi's Commentary
The Way of the Tao is through the True and Constant.[45] It is easy to become scattered and confused when responding to situations. Therefore, when coming into contact with people remain unconfused by the dust of what occurs. When not responding to others, be empty, silent, and vacant. But when others come to you and it is necessary to respond, then let it all pass when it is past. Be bright, intuitive, upright, and magnanimous and you will not become confused. There will then be clarity and tranquility of your True Nature, and the Original Spirit will congeal.

It is said the secret is to pay attention to everything, and to errors of non-doing that may fall into vacuity.

此道乃真常之道. 以應事易於昏迷.
故接物不可迷於塵事若不應接. 則空寂虛無.
須要來則應之. 事去不留. 光明正大. 乃是不迷.
真性清靜元神凝結. 訣曰. 著意頭頭錯.
無為又落空.

---

[45] The *True and Constant* (眞常, Zhen Chang) is the everlasting or infinite truth of the Constant Tao.

Ancestor Lu's One Hundred Character Tablet

Lu Zi's Text

When unconfused, your Nature is naturally fixed, and when your Nature is naturally fixed the qi will naturally return.

不迷性自住．性住氣自回．

Zhang Zi's Commentary

The nature of common people is fiery, like the fires of pleasure, anger, sorrow, and joy. Loving, hating, liking, and disliking, constantly changing their behaviors and attitudes, they're so inconsistent. Any sort of stimulation causes them to give rise to illusion and vain fantasies. It is so difficult to bring tranquility to their nature.

It is absolutely necessary that anger be restrained, to cause the Fire to descend; true lessening of these emotions causes Water to ascend. Physical stillness is called "Refining the Jing" and refining the jing causes "the tiger to hiss," the Original Spirit will then be strong and congealed. Mental stillness is called "Refining the Qi" and refining the qi causes "the dragon to sing." The Original Spirit will then be preserved and guarded. Unmoved thought is called "Refining the Spirit" and refining the spirit causes the two qi to intertwine and the Three Origins to merge. The original qi can then naturally return.

The Three Origins are jing, qi, and shen; the two qi are yin and yang. When cultivators respond to others without confusion the Original Spirit can naturally return and the original nature will naturally come to rest. When your Nature comes to rest, the Before Heaven Qi will then naturally return

Refining the Elixir

to be within your body. How then could it be difficult for "returning life and returning to the root?"

The secret is said to be "return the light and return the illumination within to the very presence of the mind," so that inner thoughts are not expressed externally and external thoughts are not expressed internally.

凡人性烈如火．喜怒哀樂．愛惡欲憎．
變態無常．但有觸動．便生妄想．難以靜性．
必要有真懲忿則火降．真寡欲則水昇．
身不動名曰煉精．煉精則虎嘯．元神凝固．
心不動名曰煉氣．煉氣則龍吟．元氣存守．
念不動名曰煉神．煉神則二氣交．三元混．
元氣自回矣．三元者精氣神也．二氣者陰陽也．
修行人應物不迷則元神自歸本性自住矣．
性住則身中先天之氣自回．復命歸根．有何難哉．
訣曰回光返照．一心中存．內想不出．外想不入．

Lu Zi's Text
When the qi returns, the elixir naturally forms. Kan [Water] and Li [Fire] mate within the gourd.

氣回丹自結．壺中配坎離．

Zhang Zi's Commentary
When cultivators do not confuse their Nature with the dust of affairs, the qi will naturally return. They can thereby see the two qi ascending and descending within their bodies, and the

Ancestor Lu's One Hundred Character Tablet

yin and yang mate within the Cauldron of the Elixir.[46] Suddenly they will be fully aware of a threadlike hot qi rising up from the genitals, ascending into the Heart Palace.[47] Emotions then return to Nature, just like a husband and wife mating, acting all doting and intoxicated.[48]

The two qi and generative forces form the substance of the elixir, and Fire and Water combine within the Qi Cavern. This cycle goes on ceaselessly, so that the spirit motivates the qi and the qi maintains the body. There is then no more need for the various arts of natural long-life.

The secret is said to be the Three Treasures—ears, eyes, and mouth—close them off and do not allow them to advance their intercourse with things.[49] True Beings dive deep into the abyss and just float about, and always keep within the center

---

[46] *Cauldron of the Elixir* (丹鼎, Dan Ding) is yet another term for the Elixir Field.

[47] *Heart Palace* (心府, Xin Fu) is the solar plexus or Middle Elixir Field.

[48] With the qi rising up from the genitals into the Heart Palace, cultivators will experience intense emotions and feelings of bliss. Hence, the analogy of a man and woman doting over each other and being intoxicated.

[49] The jing is preserved or dissipated through the ears. Hence the need for *Reverting the Hearing Inwards*. The shen is preserved or dissipated through the eyes. Hence the need for *Returning the Light*. The qi is preserved or dissipated through the mouth. Hence the need for *Guarding the Speech*.

Refining the Elixir

of the circle. Doing so until the qi in the Elixir Field is full and the Jade Spoon[50] is formed.

修人．性不迷塵事則自回．將見降中宮．
陰陽配合於丹鼎．忽腎中一縷熱．上沖心府．
情來歸性．如夫婦配合．如癡如醉．二氣絪縕．
結成丹質而穴中水火相交．循環不已．
則神馭留形．不必雜術自長生訣曰．耳目口三寶．
閉塞勿發通．真人潛深淵．浮游守規中．
直至丹田氣滿．結成刀圭也．

Lu Zi's Text

Yin and yang then arise, completely inverting and overturning until changing into one sound of thunder.

陰陽生反覆．普化一聲雷．

Zhang Zi's Commentary

When both the effort and skill arrive at the point of inverting, the spirit will not run off to the outside and the qi will not seep out. The spirit returns to the Qi Cavern, and Kan [Water] and Li [Fire] will have already mixed. Further increase your efforts

---

50　*Jade Spoon* (刀圭, Tao Gui) was an ancient jade spoon spatula/knife-like utensil used for measuring medicinal powders. The outer edge and tip were sharp and the center concave. In the *Master of Embracing Simplicity* (fourth scroll on the "Golden Elixir"), the term Tao Gui is used various times regarding instructions for taking a prescription for immortality—i.e., "take one 'Jade Spoon' of the medicine for one hundred days and you will become immortal." Zhang Sanfeng here uses the analogy of the Elixir Field as being symbolic of this Jade Spoon, which measures and holds the refined elixir.

Ancestor Lu's One Hundred Character Tablet

and courage to advance these essences until reaching the stage of ultimate of emptiness; hold on to the trueness of tranquility. Then the body will be tranquil within the Darkness of the Center,[51] and the mind will find clarity in the Country of Nothing Whatsoever.

The True Breath will then naturally cease, the one hundred pulses will naturally stop, the sun and moon will halt, and the North Star will not move. At the Supreme Ultimate, stillness will then give rise to movement. The production of yang comes from Kun [Earth] in the southwest, and Kun is then the abdomen. This is also called, "The Winding River."

Suddenly a point of spiritual light, like the size of a large grain of rice, is the indicator the medicine is producing. A blazing brightness will then pass through the two kidneys like hot boiling liquid, and the bladder will feel like it is on fire within the abdomen. Within the abdomen there will be sounds like a roaring wind and pealing thunder. This is from the image of *Returning*,[52] and is when the Root of Heaven manifests.

When the Root of Heaven appears, it then fixes the mastery of the mind, which aids the spirit, resulting in the qi becoming like fire applied to metal and moves upwards, boring through the coccyx [wei lu]. Lightly mobilize it, and

---

[51] *Darkness of the Center* is the Void. The *Country of Nothing Whatsoever* is the Void of even Voidness.

[52] *Returning* is image #24 ䷗ in the *Book of Changes*.

Refining the Elixir

silently raise it as though one perfect ball of qi, and it will rumble just like thunder. Raise it upwards to the Ni Wan where it will swiftly spread throughout the entire body. This then is the Heavenly Wind, and the image of *Pairing*.[53]

From the Moon Cave [54] and arriving at the Sealed Hall[55] between the eyebrows, where the original light leaks out, then at the Supreme Ultimate, movement gives birth to yin, which transforms into spiritual water like a sweet dew. Internally there is a grain of rice like a pearl, and it descends and settles within the Yellow Court.[56]

In silence I then meet with the spiritual mercury within and form the sage-like body. Activating the Heavenly Circuit[57]

---

[53] *Pairing* is image #44 ☰ in the *Book of Changes*. In *Returning*, image #24 ☷, the trigram Earth is topmost and in image #44, Heaven is topmost. In image #24 the trigram Thunder is below and in image #44, Wind is below. Heaven and Earth here represent the upper Elixir Field (Heaven) and the lower Elixir Field (Earth). Thunder represents the inception of the elixir, and Wind the movement of the elixir. In brief, these two images represent the root of the elixir and the movement of it.

[54] Moon Cave (月窟, Yue Ku) is the Hundred Gatherings Cavity (Bai Hui Xue).

[55] Sealed Hall (印堂, Yin Tang) is the Third Eye or upper Elixir Field.

[56] Yellow Court (黃庭, Huang Ting) is the lower Elixir Field.

[57] Heavenly Circuit (天周, Zhou Tian) is the circulation of qi through the extraordinary or subtle meridians up the spine and then down the front of the body, Dumai and Renmai.

Ancestor Lu's One Hundred Character Tablet

to advance the Fire in one cycle. Cook and refine so the elixir will naturally congeal.

功夫到此神不外馳．氣不外洩神歸穴．坎離已交．愈加猛烈精進．致虛之極．守靜之篤．身靜於杳冥之中．心澄於無何有之鄉．則真息自住百脈自停日月停景．璇璣不行太極靜而生動．陽產於西南之坤．坤即腹也．又名曲江．忽然一點靈光．如黍米之大．即藥生消息也．赫然光透．兩腎如湯煎．膀胱如火灸．腹中如烈風之吼腹內如震雷之聲 即復卦天根現也．天根現．即固心王．以神助之．則其如火逼金上行．穿過尾閭．輕輕運默默舉．一團和氣．如雷之震．上升泥丸．周身踴躍．即天風姤卦也．由月窟．至印堂．眉中漏出元光即 太極動而生陰化成神水甘露．內有黍米之珠．落在黃庭之中．點我離中靈汞結成聖相之體．行周天火候一度．烹之煉之．丹自結矣．

Lu Zi's Text

From the highest peak white clouds gather and the sweet dew flows like wine from the Central Mountain.

白雲朝頂上．甘露酒須彌．

Zhang Zi's Commentary

When reaching this point the medicine has been obtained. The two qi mix together and form the Jade Spoon. The passes and apertures open and circulate. Fire descends and Water ascends, and this one qi flows and circulates. From within the

Refining the Elixir

Supreme Ultimate it moves the Root of Heaven and passes through the Mysterious Valley Pass,[58] ascending twenty-four times up through the sections of the vertebra until it reaches Heavenly Valley Pass.[59]

In the Moon Cave, yin is then born, fragrant, sweet, and delicious. It then descends down the Chung Lou without cease and without rest. This is called, "Sweet Dew Cleansing the Central Mountain."[60]

The secret meaning of this is when the mouth is filled with sweet dew, follow it with your eyes and using the mind-intention, follow it down to the Cauldron of the Elixir[61] where the Original Qi can be congealed and nourished.

到此地位．藥即得矣．二氣結刀圭．關竅開通．
火降水升．一周流從太極中．動天根．
過玄谷關．升二十四椎 骨節．至天谷關．
月窟陰生．香甜美味．降下重樓．無休無息．
名曰甘露洒須彌．訣曰．甘露滿口．以目送之．
以意迎之．送下丹釜．凝結元氣以養之．

---

[58] *Mysterious Valley Pass* (玄谷關, Xuan Gu Guan) is the area between the Hui Yin (perineum) and the Wei Lu (coccyx).

[59] *Heavenly Valley Pass* (天谷關, Tian Gu Guan) is the area between the Jade Pillow (Yu Chen) and Hundred Gatherings (Bai Hui).

[60] *Central Mountain* (須彌, Xu Mi) is an abbreviation for Mount Sumeru (Buddhist term), the highest peak of the Himalayas.

[61] *Cauldron of the Elixir* (丹釜, Dan Fu) is another term for the Elixir Field.

Ancestor Lu's One Hundred Character Tablet

Lu Zi's Text
Having imbibed the wine of long-life you wander freely about the remote regions. Who can know of this?
自飲長生酒．逍遙誰得知．

Zhang Zi's Commentary
When reaching this stage of nourishing the qi, the joints of the bones are already open. The Spiritual Water continuously flows and circulates above and below, coming and going without cease time and time again. This then is the "wine of long-life."

The secret meaning is that the flowing pearl is forced down to nourish the spiritual root and nature. Those who cultivate this know the unknowable.

養氣到此．骨節已開．神水不住．上下周流．
往來不息．時時吞咽謂之長生酒．訣曰．
流珠灌養靈根性．修行之人知不知．

Lu Zi's Text
Sit and listen to the string-less song, until completely understanding the root-powers of creation and transformation.
坐聽無線曲．明通造化機．

Zhang Zi's Commentary
When the work and skill arrives you will hear the sounds of the immortals' music, and the tones of their drums and bells. The

Refining the Elixir

Five Qi[62] all gather together at the origin, and the Three Flowers[63] assemble upon the peak. This is all just like the appearance of a crow coming to roost.[64] The mind field is open and bright, knowledge and wisdom naturally arise, and there is a clear understanding of the writings in the Three Teachings.[65]

Former lives and original roots[66] will be realized, and foreknowledge of what will be good fortune and misfortune in the future. It's as if the great Earth, and all the mountains and

---

[62] *Five Qi* (五氣, Wu Qi) are the Five Sense consciousnesses of seeing, hearing, smelling, tasting, and touching. Each of these senses has an organ and a function, but they also have a consciousness. When the cultivator departs from the distractions of the organ and function, only the consciousnesses remain and they fuse, becoming one. The Five Qi is also a reference in Dao Yin practices as the energies of Essence (精, Jing), Spirit (神, Shen), Heavenly Spirit (魂, Hun), Earthly Spirit (魄, Po), and Mind-Intent (意, Yi).

[63] The *Three Flowers* (三花, San Hua) are the three Hun Spirits coming together in the head (peak) and so the three components of immortality are reverted.

[64] *A crow coming to roost* is a reference to attaining Pure Yang Spirit. Sometimes this is called the *Three Legged Crow in the sun*.

[65] The *Three Teachings* are Buddhism, Confucianism, and Taoism.

[66] *Original roots* means the original causes of experiences.

Ancestor Lu's One Hundred Character Tablet

rivers, exist within the palms of your hands, you're able to see ten thousand miles, and obtain the Six Penetrations.[67]

This then is the Real, and I practiced the Real until having attained the limit.

However, suppose these are all just empty words, so that future students make errors [in their cultivation]. I must then receive punishment from Heaven, possibly even banishment,

---

67   *Six Spiritual Penetrations* (六通, Liu Tong):
    1) Spiritual Foot Penetration (神足通, Shen Zu Tong), also called *Proving the Realm of Spiritual Wisdom*. Never leaving footprints, and the spirit can transverse to any of the Three Realms (Form Realm, Formless Realm, and Void Realm) at will.
    2) Celestial Eye Penetration (天眼通, Tian Yan Tong), also called *Celestial Wisdom Eye*. See directly into the Heavenly Realms, and also all six ways a spirit is born into life and dies (womb born, egg born, moisture born, transformation born, thought born, and thoughtless born).
    3) Celestial Ear Penetration (天耳通, Tian Er Tong), also called *Celestial Wisdom Ear*. Clearly hear the wisdom of spiritual worthies speaking the Tao. Also, hearing immortal beings directly in Heaven.
    4) Other's Mind Penetration (他心通, Ta Xin Tong), also called *Wisdom of Other's Thoughts*. Knowing the thoughts of others and the root causes of another person's actions.
    5) Predestination Penetration (宿命通, Su Ming Tong), also called *Wisdom of Preordaining All Events*. Knowing what teaching each person needs and has affinities with.
    6) Ending All Outflows Penetration (漏盡通, Lou Jin Tong), also called *Wisdom of Ending All Outflows*. Having no more distractions or confusion regarding the reality of any of the Three Realms, and no longer trapped by the causations and conditions of life and death.

Refining the Elixir

and never be able again to acquire a teacher. Yet keep in mind these matters are the most difficult to understand.[68]

功夫到此. 耳聽仙樂之音. 又有鐘鼓之韻.
五氣朝元. 三花聚頂. 如晚鴉來棲之狀.
心田開朗. 智慧自生. 明通三教經書.
悟前生根本. 豫知未來休咎. 大地山河如在掌中.
目視萬里. 已得六通之妙. 此乃實有也.
吾行實到此際. 若有虛言. 以誤後學. 天必誅之.
遇之不行. 罪遭天譴. 非與師遇. 此事難知.

Lu Zi's Text

These twenty verses in their entirety are truly a stairway into Heaven.

都來二十局. 端的上天梯.

Zhang Zi's Commentary

Self-nourishment of the qi and forgetting words is the highest of these twenty verses, but all are Ancestor Lu's true and

---

[68] Zhang Sanfeng is stating that what he says is true and real. If it were not, he would be responsible for the errors that future cultivators make from having read his words, and then he would be punished by Heaven. Heaven could also banish him so that he could never achieve immortality, nor could he ever have again find the good fortune of meeting a teacher who could show him the way of immortality. He is stating that he would not dare transmit false teachings or words, but he concludes by stating that these matters of how Heaven would react is too difficult to predict, so he is only guessing as to what the retribution would be. It could be worse when punishing false teachers of the Tao.

Ancestor Lu's One Hundred Character Tablet

correct secret words. The effort must not be a half measure, as this will only bring about falseness. There are cultivation procedures in order to reach the highest Heavens, and to achieve awakening through these secrets and commentary. You cannot forget to practice and it is wrong to dissipate, yet do not proclaim you are a bad person, otherwise you will only accomplish turning Heaven away from you. Take good care of yourself and follow the practices, so you will be able to go up to the Tower of Heaven.[69]

自養忘言．至此二十局．皆是呂祖真正口訣．
工夫無半點虛偽．乃修行上天之階梯．
得悟此訣與註者．可急行之．勿妄漏洩．
勿示匪人．以遭天譴．珍重奉行．克登天闕．

---

[69] *Tower of Heaven* (丹釜, Tian Xue) literally means the "look out tower over the front gate of Heaven where all can be seen in both Heaven and on Earth.

History of Zhang Sanfeng

張 三 豐 之 史

Zhang San Feng Zhi Shi

Probably no figure in ancient Taoist lore is as enigmatic and difficult to trace as Zhang Sanfeng. No historical data can prove the assertion that he created what has become popularly known as Taijiquan, or that he ever wrote anything concerning Taoism or Taijiquan. However, there are figures in Chinese history during the Song dynasty matching some of the criteria of this popular immortal, but nothing so substantial and evident enough to actually pinpoint him. Despite the lack of historical evidence of his person, there still exists an abundance of Taoist texts attributed to him, and in consideration of the numerous written legends about this Taoist immortal, there's also no reason to not affirm him as Taoist lore has presented him. In fact, he represents in many ways the Taoist ideal of the elusive rogue, hermit, cloud wandering immortal envisioned in so much of Chinese literature and folklore.

The Creation of Taijiquan
Legend has it that Zhang's first realization of Taijiquan came after seeing a bird and snake fighting. The story runs that Zhang was meditating in his hut on Wu Dang Mountain (無當山, Wu Dang Shan) when he heard a bird attacking a snake. He watched intently as the snake yielded and counterattacked all the movements of the bird. If the bird tried to seize the tail of the snake, the snake struck back with its head. If its head was attacked, the snake countered with its tail. Likewise, if the snake's body was attacked, both the head and tail countered the bird. Zhang thought this

Refining the Elixir

was really clever and so believed that instead of utilizing the hard and unyielding movements in Shaolin Kung Fu (少林功夫), the martial art of Taijiquan should focus on yielding and softness, incorporating the pliable aspects of the Snake style; the light, nimble, and changeable movements of Dragon; the intently focused, agile, and powerful traits of Tiger; the exacting, calm, and expansive energy of the Crane; and the light, nimble, and concealed traits of the Leopard.

As to internal alchemy and Taijiquan, another story tells of a discovery Zhang made while dwelling in his famous meditation hut on Wu Dang Mountain. This story relates that late one evening he went outside to practice his Taijiquan. When he began repeating the movements of *Step Back and Chase the Monkey Away,* he found that when he kept his buttocks opened and relaxed, his qi would rise up his spine and into his brain[70]—so he kept practicing this method night after night until he finally achieved immortality. It is this story that elevated Taijiquan from being just a method for health and self-defense into a working method of internal alchemy.

How Zhang actually created Taijiquan, beyond the insights he experienced while watching the bird and snake, is unclear, but it's believed he had known or learned Shaolin Kung Fu earlier in his life, specifically the Five Animal exercises of the Tiger, Dragon, Snake, Leopard, and

---

[70] In Taoist internal alchemy practices this is identical with the process of Reverting Jing into the Brain.

History of Zhang Sanfeng

Crane. It is surmised that he took the principles of the Dragon and Snake forms (which is highly probable because many of the names of Taijiquan postures coincide exactly with many Shaolin Kung Fu posture names) and thus added *Book of Changes* (易經, *Yi Jing*) theories on yin and yang and the Taoist breathing techniques of Leading and Guiding (導引, Tao Yin). In essence, he created a physical form of expression of Taoist philosophy, or Taoist philosophy in motion, or possibly better said he created moving internal alchemy.

Over many years of studying the teachings attributed to Zhang Sanfeng, it has become vividly clear that the actual historical evidence of this Taoist immortal is for the most part unimportant, as it is the myths of Zhang that are so inspiring to all cultivating Taoists. Hence, to accept his existence is not nearly as important as accepting and applying the teachings attributed to him.

Legends of Zhang Sanfeng
Two versions tell of when and where Zhang Sanfeng was born. The first says that he was born in Liaoning province (northeastern China) in 1247 CE, and the second says that he was born in the same year, but within the region of Dragon-Tiger Mountain in Jiangxi province (southeastern China). Legends say he mounted a dragon and ascended into an immortal paradise in the year 1417, living to the venerable age of 170. Again, some records say he passed away in 1471 on Wu Dang Mountain and others claim it was on Dragon-

Refining the Elixir

Tiger Mountain. The accounts of Zhang's birthplace, his dwellings, and death appear to be altered depending on whether the sources tend more towards the Wu Dang Mountain martial art lineages or those of the Dragon-Tiger Mountain internal alchemy lineages. The martial art contingent seems to focus a great deal on his spending most of his life in northern China and on Wu Dang Mountain, whereas the internal alchemists seem to accentuate his life mostly in southern China, especially the two areas of Ge Hong and Dragon-Tiger Mountains. Truthfully, little information substantiates either account.

His birth name was Quan Yi, and he used the aliases of Jun Shi, Jun Bao, and Yu Xu Zi during the first part of his life, and later used the other sobriquets of Qing Xu, Zhang Tong, Xuan Xuan, Xuan Hua, and Zhang Sanfeng. This elusive immortal called "Three Peaks," a name Zhang is said to have chosen for himself while cultivating on Ge Hong Mountain (葛洪山),[71] or, as other accounts tell, on Southern End Mountain (終南山, Zhong Nan Shan) or Precious Chicken Mountain (寶雞山, Bao Ji Shan), where he saw three high peaks and so thought it a fitting name for himself.

According to legend, Zhang's life spanned three dynasties, beginning near the end of the Song dynasty,

---

[71] This is presently known as the Lou Fu Mountains (羅浮山) in Guangdong province. It is sometimes called Ge Hong Mountain because it is where the famous Taoist scholar and alchemist Ge Hong (283–343 CE) lived and cultivated. Today, it is a national park and has many memorials and temples dedicated to Ge Hong.

History of Zhang Sanfeng

extending through the entire Yuan, and ending in the early Ming. Probably the best research done on the existence and history of Zhang Sanfeng can be found in Anna Seidel's chapter "A Taoist Immortal of the Ming Dynasty: Chang Sanfeng" in *Self and Society in Ming Thought*.[72] In this work, Seidel presents a great deal of information on the possible existence of a Taoist priest named Zhang (under several assumed names) during the Ming dynasty, but could not prove conclusively if a figure named Zhang Sanfeng actually invented Taijiquan or wrote any discourses on Taoist philosophy and internal alchemy. Despite the efforts made here to render a reasonable history of Zhang, please refer to Anna Seidel's material, as it is a far more authoritative work.

Legendary history claims that Zhang in his early years was a county magistrate in the northeastern province of Liaoning, but quit his position in mid-life and left his family to become a Taoist priest. Zhang Sanfeng claimed to have been initiated as a Taoist priest by Xuan Du (玄獨), but this name could also simply mean "a mysterious stranger or hermit," and for whatever reason Zhang chose not to reveal his identity or background. In any event, Xuan Du transmitted the meanings of *The Treatise on Understanding Reality* by Zhang Boduan.[73] Therefore, in being given the

---

[72] *Self and Society in Ming Thought,* edited by W. T. Barry (Columbia University Press, 1970).

[73] *The Treatise on Understanding Reality* (悟眞篇, *Wu Zhen Pian*) by Zhang Boduan (張伯端, 987–1082 CE).

Refining the Elixir

Taoist surname of Zhang, he would have to have been initiated into either the Southern Complete Reality Sect (全真南派, Quan Zhen Pai) attributed to Liu Haichan (劉海禪), or, more likely, the Azure Yang Sect (紫陽派, Zi Yang Pai) founded by Liu's disciple Zhang Boduan.

It's also noted that Zhang Sanfeng had a close but short relationship with the Northern Quan Zhen Sect at White Cloud Monastery (白雲觀, Bai Yun Guan) in Beijing, as it is recorded he befriended three master monks there. Zhang Sanfeng was later considered a patron immortal of White Cloud Monastery and so a statue and shrine was erected in his honor.

In 1325, when Zhang was seventy-eight years old, it is said he met a Taoist immortal hermit by the name of Fire Dragon Immortal (火龍仙, Huo Long Xian) on Ge Hong Mountain who taught him the internal alchemy methods for becoming an immortal and/or actually gave him the formula for producing the pill of immortality, as well as teaching him acupuncture. It was at this time he changed his name to Xuan Hua. The Fire Dragon Immortal claimed to be a disciple of Wang Zhe (王嚞), founder of the Northern Sect of Quan Zhen, and this may have been the reason for his connection with the priests at White Cloud Monastery in Beijing. Four years later, the Fire Dragon Immortal told Zhang he should leave and go find another auspicious and sacred place to practice, as Ge Hong Mountain would not be the place he would attain his immortality. This is when Zhang entered the Wu Dang

History of Zhang Sanfeng

Mountains and decided this was the appropriate place to forge his immortality, and he did so for nine years before accomplishing his goal.

Zhang then undertook the tradition of what Taoists call "cloud wandering," traveling throughout the sacred mountains of China such as Hua Shan (華山) in Shaanxi province and Heng Shan (恆山) in Hunan province.

In 1385 the emperor Tai Zu (太祖) ordered Zhang to take an official post, so he escaped and went into hermitage in the mountain regions of Yunnan province until 1399—the year when Hui Zong (惠宗) became emperor and the former emperor Tai Zu's command would have been rendered invalid. It was this year that Zhang reportedly reappeared in his birthplace on Dragon-Tiger Mountain and lived out his years until his immortal ascension in 1417.

During the years prior to 1399, Zhang traveled a great deal, spending most of his time helping others, especially farmers. He would collect medicines to heal them and give them instructions on the Tao. The tales of his benevolence are numerous, and it was all these deeds that endeared him to the populace and eventually gained him the notice of emperors.

Zhang had been a cloud wanderer for most of his life and his whereabouts were often uncertain. Other cloud wandering Taoists who happened upon him said he was a true Hermit Immortal (隱仙, Yin Xian), and many claimed to have witnessed his spiritual skill of performing

Refining the Elixir

physical flight and never leaving footprints where he walked. Whether in the hottest of summers or coldest of winters he would only wear one garment and sandals. When walking through snowy areas, the snow would melt beneath his feet, and at times he would simply sleep in the snow. This was all evidence of his cultivated qi. Likewise, when he climbed mountains it was if he flew up the inclines with great agility, lightness, and nimbleness, never showing signs of exhaustion or exertion. Disciples commented that when he felt the need, he could flap the sleeves of his robe and simply disappear. When Zhang ate, he consumed large quantities of food, but then sometimes would only eat every few days, and other times forego eating altogether for a couple months at a time. His mannerisms were very casual and free from restraint, and he had the temperament and presence of an immortal.

Nothing in the purported historical accounts about Zhang Sanfeng are ever mediocre, even his supposed death in 1303. The story tells that Zhang passed away while staying at Golden Terrace Monastery (金臺寺, Jin Tai Si) in western Shensi. He had announced his pending departure and gave his followers final instructions. A few days passed in preparation of the funeral and when the day arrived to place him in his grave and his casket was about to be lowered into the ground, they all heard a knocking coming from within the casket. Opening it, they found a smiling Zhang come back to life.

History of Zhang Sanfeng

In the legends describing Zhang's appearance, they all say he was very tall, with some reports claiming seven feet. He was well built with the resemblance of a tortoise and had a crane-shaped back, very long ears, and round, piercing eyes. His beard was black, long, very thick and bristly. In Chinese woodblock prints, he is normally depicted as wearing a Taoist cassock with a palm-bark rain cape, a wide-brimmed bamboo hat, straw sandals, and carrying a sword and gourd. Other images show him in a seated meditation posture, with one such statue erected in his honor at Wu Dang Mountain. In other cases he is shown simply standing holding only a fly whisk.

Teachings of Zhang Sanfeng
Zhang maintained five practices of cultivation:
   1) Performing sword movements in moonlight because this would "enliven the spirit" (增神, zeng shen).
   2) Practicing Taijiquan in the dark of night because it "increased essence" (益精, yi jing).
   3) Climbing a mountain on windy nights because it "broadened qi" (長氣, zhang qi).
   4) Studying and reading scriptures on rainy nights because it "illuminated the mind" (明心, ming xin).
   5) Sitting in meditation at midnight because it would bring "clarity to one's nature" (見性, jian xing).
   Zhang said these five practices were the essence of his Taoist cultivation.

Refining the Elixir

The perspective in the Ming dynasty about the Three Religions (Buddhism, Taoism, and Confucianism) was that they all came from the same origin, and Zhang Sanfeng shared this general view of his contemporaries. He maintained that the Three Religions had the same intent—that is, to cultivate one's original nature and to bring benefit and order to the world. Whether one spoke of Lao Zi, Buddha, or Confucius, the basic premise was the same and, therefore, Buddhism and Confucianism could be classified as aspects of Taoist teaching. In the Ming dynasty, as well as in the previous Song dynasty, Taoists were known to study aspects of Buddhism and Confucianism, and vice versa. In Zhang Sanfeng's *Discourses on the Great Tao* (大道論, *Da Tao Lun*), he explains: "Confucians try to practice the Tao of society to bring order and benefit to the world. Buddhists seek to realize the Tao to awaken and bring salvation to the world. While Taoist immortals simply preserve the Tao to transform all of humanity."

Zhang saw all three teachings as useful and part of the process for awakening one's "Original Nature" (元性, Yuan Xing). His overriding view was that the cultivation of Tao meant the study and practice of three entrances for attaining immortality: "Awakening the Spiritual Nature," "Nourishing-Life," and "Harmonizing the Yin and Yang."[74] He also considered that the three entrances had to be rooted

---

[74] These three methods of cultivation are also referred to as the Three Gateways of Taoist Philosophical Arts, Nourishing-Life Arts, and Joining Vital-Energies Arts, respectively.

in the cultivation of merit and virtue,[75] as these are the very essence of attaining the Tao, while the cultivation of the elixir of immortality is the application of the Tao. Both are necessary components for attaining immortality.

As Zhang, and all legitimate Taoist schools of internal alchemy, express, unless students are willing to change their mortal temperament and conduct through the measures of accumulating merit and virtue, the methods of internal alchemy meditation will have very limited results. In other words, it is a student's merit and virtue that is the foundation and catalyst, the very essence, for attaining the Tao. No one can enter the Tao without merit and virtue. As the *Scripture on Tao and Virtue* confirms, "the Tao honors and accepts only the good."

Internal alchemy (cultivating and forming the elixir of immortality) is thereby the application by which a person can fully realize the Tao. Both "attaining the Tao" and "realization of the Tao" are the two necessary components for achieving immortality. In Taoism, this is summed up in the characters 得 (de) and 悟 (wu), "attain" and "realize." As stated in the last verse of the *Clarity and Tranquility of the Constant Scripture*, "Attain and realize the Tao," and it is these two distinct purposes and functions to which Zhang is

---

75 *Gong De* (功德), "cultivating merit and virtue," is the main practice of the Accumulating Virtue School. The main text for this teaching is the *Tai Shang Gan Ying Pian* (太上感應篇). See *Actions & Retributions: A Taoist Treatise on Attaining Spiritual Virtue, Longevity, and Immortality (Attributed to Lao Zi)* by Stuart Alve Olson (Valley Spirit Arts, 2015).

Refining the Elixir

referring. "Attaining the Tao" means the cultivator has found the correct Tao and so practices it to attain merit and virtue, and "Realizing the Tao" is the successful transformation into immortality produced from the practices and one's merit and virtue.

This means no accomplished teacher or immortal could ever teach anyone true internal alchemy who has not first cultivated his or her merit and virtue, as an ill-tempered and ill-mannered person is simply not worthy of receiving the treasures of the Tao and immortality. The spirits of such people are simply too clouded and perplexed, hence they create their own obstacles for not attaining and realizing the Tao. In the end, a person's inability to attain and realize the Tao is not from the lack of a teacher's instruction or the quality of a teaching, rather it's more about such persons not perceiving the cultivation of merit and virtue as necessary, and thinking only the application and method of internal alchemy is important.

The Ming Emperors and Zhang Sanfeng

In 1385 of the Ming dynasty, the emperor Tai Zu sent envoys throughout the Taoist sacred mountain areas to search for Zhang, but to no avail. During the years 1403 through 1425, the emperor Cheng Zu (成祖) repeatedly sent his imperial officials and envoys to locate him in several known mountain regions where Zhang cultivated, but time and again the envoys would be told they had just missed him or had the wrong location (and for eight years the

History of Zhang Sanfeng

imperials were unaware of his ascension in the year 1417). Zhang's disciples would always forewarn him of the approaching imperial officials so he could quickly escape and go into hiding until their departure. The emperor Cheng Zu had hoped to convince Zhang to serve as an official in his royal court. Even though the emperor could not locate Zhang, he still, out of honor and respect for him, helped to make Zhang's prophecy for Wu Dang Mountain becoming a sacred place come true. This prophecy is one of the more popular stories attached to Zhang. After he built his meditation hut on Wu Dang Mountain, he placed all the unused wood, bushes, and rubble into a pile and predicted to his disciples that this mound of debris will one day flourish and become a famous monastery. It was Cheng Zu who had a large Taoist temple constructed on the mountain in 1420.

After Zhang's disappearance, later reports began circulating that claimed he took on the persona of being a crazy beggar so as not to be recognized by the imperials searching for him, and to ensure his anonymity among the populace. When visiting a village, he would smear mud and dirt over his face and body, openly urinate in public, shout profanities at people, reek of bad odors from never bathing, and would on occasion appear belligerently drunk. All of this behavior earned him the moniker "Dirty Zhang."

Despite all of Zhang's efforts to maintain anonymity during his life, in 1459 the emperor Ying Zong (英宗) canonized him with the honorific title "Perfect Manifestation

Refining the Elixir

of Pervasive Subtlety." In 1486, the emperor Xian Zong (憲宗) granted him the title "Brilliant and Lofty Perfect Immortal." In 1623, Emperor Xi Zong (熹宗) announced Zhang Sanfeng had descended unto the temple altar on Wu Dang Mountain, visibly manifesting his spirit to everyone there, and so offered him the title "The Perfected Flying Dragon Sovereign Who Bestows Salvation, Promotes Benevolence, and Benefits the World." All the emperors of the Ming dynasty admired and bestowed honors upon Zhang Sanfeng, which served to further propagate his legend and also create a surge of Taoist believers in him. Since then, Zhang's life and immortality has undergone many revisions while his legendary status has steadily grown. Even into the Qing dynasty, stories still circulated about Taoist searchers meeting Zhang Sanfeng and being taught the Taoist arts of immortality from him.

Written Records of Zhang Sanfeng

If Zhang had been a county magistrate in Liaoning province it would have meant he was well educated and would have most probably entered the Civil Examinations as a young man. If this were true, then indeed he would have had the literary skills to write at least some of the texts attributed to him. He was also said to have had a photographic memory as he could remember by heart whatever books he read, and was very skilled in writing poems and discourses. The more popular and present

History of Zhang Sanfeng

Chinese texts that have been circulated bearing his name include:
- *Zhang Sanfeng's Secret Arts for Refining the Elixir* (張三豐太極煉丹秘訣, *Zhang San Feng Tai Ji Lian Dan Bi Jue*).
- *Zhang Sanfeng Essays on the Essentials of the Great Tao* (張三豐大道指要, *Zhang San Feng Da Tao Zhi Yao*).
- *Collections on the Sect of Zhang Sanfeng Taoist Arts* (張三豐道術滙宗, *Zhang San Feng Tao Shu Hui Zong*).
- *Collections on the Sect of Zhang Sanfeng Martial Arts* (張三豐武術滙宗, *Zhang San Feng Wu Shu Hui Tsung*).

All these texts, however, are basically excerpted and annotated reprints of Li Xiyue's (李西月) work. Published in 1844, *The Complete Book of Zhang Sanfeng* (張三豐全書, *Zhang Sanfeng Quan Shu*) is a compilation of preserved sections from the Taoist Canon (道藏, Tao Zang) dedicated to the teachings of Zhang Sanfeng.

Anna Seidel mentions in her research on Zhang Sanfeng that a sixteenth-century work titled *A Record of Evidences of Worthy Persons in China's Dynasties* (國朝獻徵錄, *Guo Chao Xian Zheng Lu*) discusses what was known and believed about Zhang Sanfeng in the Ming dynasty, but it provides the same inconclusive conclusions as have the researches of present-day scholars.

In the end, there are numerous references to this person Zhang Sanfeng throughout the Song, Yuan, and Ming dynasties, yet none of these references pinpoint exactly who he was. The curious aspect to all this is that Zhang Sanfeng received a great deal of imperial attention, the Taoist hierarchy likewise conferred great honors upon him and have propagated his teachings, people throughout China have left behind numerous accounts of encounters with this man, and yet with all this as reference, no real evidence exists of who he was, only of what he taught and what he represented, and all of it is based on the assumption that the person called Zhang Sanfeng is the same person under various other names. Even without concrete, verifiable proof connecting all the stories of him, it would be wrong not to accept the existence of Zhang Sanfeng, as it is highly improbable that a myth of this grand a scale could have been so widely accepted or existed for so long. Hence, to consider Zhang as just a myth equally means we must form the conclusion that all these emperors and imperial officials, all the learned and cultivated Taoists, and many reputable citizens who believed and claimed the existence of Zhang were all just simple-minded fools.

Disciples of Zhang Sanfeng
Interestingly enough, tracing the works and students descending from Zhang is far easier than actually tracing him personally, yet there is no conclusive evidence showing his post-lineage (shown below) to be completely accurate. It is recorded, however, that Zhang Sanfeng had a disciple named Wang Zong (王宗). The disciple Wang Zong has long been confused with the later fifth-generation disciple Wang Zongyue (王宗岳). Obviously, this confusion

History of Zhang Sanfeng

stemmed from the similarities in their names, but Zhang couldn't have taught Wang Zongyue as some have professed for the simple reason that Wang Zongyue lived in the mid-1600s, over two hundred years after Zhang's passing.

The following list concerns Zhang Sanfeng's descendent-lineage disciples and should not be confused with the Seven Disciples of the Wu Dang Sect, whom Zhang supposedly taught as well.

1) Wang Zong[76] from Shensi province taught Chen Zhoutong (陳州同) from Wenzhou.

2) Chen Zhoutong then taught Zhang Songxi (張松溪) from Haiyan.

3) Zhang Songxi then taught Ye Jimei (葉繼美) from Siming.

4) Ye Jimei taught Wang Zongyue[77] from Shanyou.

5) Wang Zongyue taught Jiang Fa (蔣發) from Hebei.

---

[76] Wang Zong wrote a commentary on the *Yin Convergence Scripture* that dates back to the mid-1400s.

[77] Wang Zongyue is the attributed author of two major Taijiquan works: *The Taijiquan Classic* and *The Mental Elucidation of the Kinetic Thirteen Operations*. He also supposedly wrote a book called, *Yin Fu Spear*. Again, because Wang Zong wrote a commentary on the *Yin Convergence Scripture* and Wong Zongyue wrote a book on *Yin Convergence Spear* (陰符槍, *Yin Fu Qiang*), some people assumed they were the same person.

Refining the Elixir

6) Jiang Fa, in turn, taught Chen Wangting, (陳王廷, 1590?) from Honan, founder of the Chen Style of Taijiquan.

7) Chen Wangting taught his family members, and finally Chen Zhangxing (陳長興, 1771 to 1853), the fifth generation Chen family master taught Yang Luchan (陽露禪, 1799 to 1872), who later created his own family style of Yang Taijiquan.

In 1399, differing accounts claim that Zhang returned to either Dragon-Tiger Mountain or to Wu Dang Mountain, accompanied by his two disciples Wang Zong (王宗) and Chen Zhoutong (陳州同). The Wu Dang claim appears less credible because it says that he returned to live in the temple the emperor Cheng Zu constructed in his honor, but the temple wasn't built until 1420, three years after Zhang's supposed passing. At some point in this period, seven other disciples descended upon him, and Zhang taught all of them the secrets of immortality and Taijiquan before he mounted a dragon. These students came to be known as "The Seven Disciples of the Wu Dang Sect" (武當派七子, Wu Dang Pai Qi Zi), and are recorded as:

Song Yuanqiao (宋遠橋)
Zhang Songxi (張松溪)
Zhang Cuishan (張翠山)
Mo Gusheng (莫谷聲)
Yu Daiyan (俞岱岩)

History of Zhang Sanfeng

Yu Lianzhou (俞蓮舟)
Yin Liheng (殷利亨)

Dating the Text of *Refining the Elixir Treatise*
In the publication of *The Complete Book of Zhang Sanfeng*, Li Xiyue states that the contents of his work were taken from the Taoist Canon. The fourth compilation of the Taoist Canon was produced in the Ming dynasty in the year 1444. Without access to the Ming dynasty edition, it is uncertain whether or not Zhang's treatise was included.

Yet, in 1845 at White Cloud Monastery in Beijing, missing pieces of the canon were replaced. It could be assumed that it was during this reconstruction of the canon that the works of Zhang Sanfeng were placed, but this could only be true if the publication date of Li Xiyue (1844) is wrong or if he had access to the Taoist Canon before White Cloud Monastery completed their publication. If the treatise was in the Ming dynasty edition, however, then it could very well have been the work of Zhang Sanfeng or even one of his early disciples, such as Wong Zong or Chen Zhoutong.

Conclusion
The legends surrounding the figure of Zhang Sanfeng are bountiful, and ever so mystical and empyreal, like swirling mists drifting about the mountain regions he inhabited. In the person of Zhang Sanfeng, we find several men being presented—from Dirty Zhang, to a reclusive immortal hermit, to a benevolent healer, a par excellence martial artist,

Refining the Elixir

an internal alchemist, a meditation master, and a deified sovereign of the Tao. Which is the true Zhang Sanfeng?

It's easy to assume that the legends surrounding Zhang are simply mythic history, yet within the mythical is always an element of truth. The myths of Zhang Sanfeng may in the end prove to be based on some factual incident or event, or of followers of his who chose to lend his name to the legend, or maybe he was just a shadowy enough figure in the Taoist pantheon that he could be given credit for all the various writings other teachers wished to have gain prominence by attributing him as the author.

Whatever the case may be, and maybe it is all of them, the Taoist immortal Zhang Sanfeng is engraved in China's stone of antiquity forever, and perhaps this is his true immortality.

Suggested Reading

The following books are highly recommended to those interested in pursuing a practice and deep understanding of internal alchemy. Some of the authors have multiple publications and the reader might want to examine their other works as well. Please check out Stuart Alve Olson's other publications in the About the Translator section and visit the Sanctuary of Tao's website (sanctuaryoftao.org) for more information on Taoism and internal alchemy.

- *Alchemy, Medicine and Religion in the China of A.D. 320: The Nei P'ien of Ko Hung (Pao-p'u Tzu),* translated by James R. Ware (M.I.T. Press, 1966).

- *Cultivating the Tao: Taosim and Internal Alchemy* by Liu Yiming. The *Xiuzhen houbian* (ca. 1798), translated by Fabrizio Pregadio (Golden Elixir Press, 2013).

- *Foundations of Internal Alchemy: The Taoist Practice of Neidan* by Wang Mu, translated by Fabrizio Pregadio (Golden Elixir Press, 2011).

- *Taoist Yoga: Alchemy and Immortality* by Lu K'uan Yu (Rider & Co., 1970).

- *The Method of Holding the Three Ones: A Taoist Manual of Meditation of the Fourth Century A.D.* by Poul Anderson (Curzon, 1995).

Refining the Elixir

- *The Secret of the Golden Flower: A Chinese Book of Life,* translated by Richard Wilhelm with a commentary by C.G. Jung (Harvest/HBJ Books, 1931).

- *The Story of Han Xiangzi: The Alchemical Adventures of a Daoist Immortal* by Yang Erzeng, translated by Philip Clart (University of Washington Press, 2007).

- *The World Upside Down: Essays on Taoist Internal Alchemy* by Isabelle Robinet, translated by Fabrizio Pregadio (Golden Elixir Press, 2011).

- *The Yellow Emperor's Classic of Internal Medicine,* translated by Ilza Veith (University of California Press, 1972).

- *To Live As Long As Heaven and Earth: A Translation and Study of Ge Hong's Traditions of Divine Transcendents* by Robert Ford Campany (University of California Press, 2002).

- *Understanding Reality: A Taoist Alchemical Classic* by Chang Po-tuan with a Concise Commentary by Liu I-ming, translated from the Chinese by Thomas Cleary (University of Hawaii Press, 1987).

About the Translator

Stuart Alve Olson, longtime protégé of Master T.T. Liang (1900–2002), is a teacher, translator, and writer on Taoist philosophy, health, and internal arts. Since his early twenties, he has studied and practiced Taoism and Chinese Buddhism.

As of 2015, Stuart has published more than twenty books, many of which now appear in several foreign-language editions.

Biography

On Christmas Day, 1979, Stuart took Triple Refuge with Chan Master Hsuan Hua, receiving the disciple name Kuo Ao. In 1981, he participated in the meditation sessions and sutra lectures given by Dainin Katagiri Roshi at the Minnesota Center for Zen Meditation. In late 1981, he began living with Master T.T. Liang, studying Taijiquan, Taoism, Praying Mantis kung fu, and Chinese language under his tutelage.

In the spring of 1982 through 1984, Stuart undertook a two-year Buddhist bowing pilgrimage, "Nine Steps, One Bow." Traveling along state and county roads during the spring, summer, and autumn months, starting from the Minnesota Zen Meditation Center in Minneapolis and ending at the border of Nebraska. During the winter

Refining the Elixir

months he stayed at Master Liang's home and bowed in his garage.

After Stuart's pilgrimage, he returned to Liang's home to continue studying with him. He and Master Liang then started traveling throughout the United States teaching Taijiquan to numerous groups, and continued to do so for nearly a decade.

In 1986, Stuart published his first four books on Taijiquan—*Wind Sweeps Away the Plum Blossoms, Cultivating the Ch'i, T'ai Chi Sword, Sabre & Staff,* and *Imagination Becomes Reality.*

In 1987, Stuart made his first of several trips to China, Taiwan, and Hong Kong. On subsequent trips, he studied massage in Taipei and taught Taijiquan in Taiwan and Hong Kong.

In 1989, he and Master Liang moved to Los Angeles, where Stuart studied Chinese language and continued his Taijiquan studies.

In early 1992, Stuart made his first trip to Indonesia, where he was able to briefly study with the kung fu and healing master Oei Kung Wei. He also taught Taijiquan there to many large groups.

In 1993, he organized the Institute of Internal Arts in St. Paul, Minnesota, and brought Master Liang back from California to teach there.

In 2005, Stuart was prominently featured in the British Taijiquan documentary *Embracing the Tiger.*

About the Translator

In 2006, he formed Valley Spirit Arts with his longtime student Patrick Gross in Phoenix, Arizona.

In 2010, he began teaching for the Sanctuary of Tao and writing for its blog and newsletter.

In 2012, Stuart received the IMOS Journal Reader's Choice Award for "Best Author on Qigong."

Taoism Books

- *Actions & Retributions: A Taoist Treatise on Attaining Spiritual Virtue, Longevity, and Immortality,* Attributed to Lao Zi (Valley Spirit Arts, 2015).

- *Being Daoist: The Way of Drifting with the Current, Revised Edition* (Valley Spirit Arts, 2014).

- *Book of Sun and Moon (I Ching),* volumes I and II (Valley Spirit Arts, 2014).

- *Clarity & Tranquility: A Guide for Daoist Meditation* (Valley Spirit Arts, 2015).

- *Daoist Sexual Arts: A Guide for Attaining Health, Youthfulness, Vitality, and Awakening the Spirit* (Valley Spirit Arts, 2015).

- *Qigong Teachings of a Taoist Immortal: The Eight Essential Exercises of Master Li Ching-Yun* (Healing Arts Press, 2002).

- *Tao of No Stress: Three Simple Paths* (Healing Arts Press, 2002).

Refining the Elixir

- *Taoist Chanting & Recitation: At-Home Cultivator's Practice Guide* (Valley Spirit Arts, 2015).
- *The Immortal: True Accounts of the 250-Year-Old Man, Li Qingyun* by Yang Sen (Valley Spirit Arts, 2014).
- *The Jade Emperor's Mind Seal Classic: The Taoist Guide to Health, Longevity, and Immortality* (Inner Traditions, 2003).

Taijiquan Books
Chen Kung Series
- *Tai Ji Qi: Fundamentals of Qigong, Meditation, and Internal Alchemy,* vol. 1 (Valley Spirit Arts, 2013).
- *Tai Ji Jin: Discourses on Intrinsic Energies for Mastery of Self-Defense Skills,* vol. 2 (Valley Spirit Arts, 2013).
- *Tai Ji Tui Shou: Mastering the Eight Styles and Four Skills of Sensing Hands,* vol. 4 (Valley Spirit Arts, 2014).
- *Tai Ji Bing Shu: Discourses on the Taijiquan Weapon Arts of Sword, Saber, and Staff,* vol. 6 (Valley Spirit Arts, 2014).

Forthcoming Books in Chen Kung Series
- *Tai Ji Quan: Practice and Applications of the 105-Posture Solo Form,* vol. 3.
- *Tai Ji San Shou & Da Lu: Mastering the Two-Person Application Skills,* vol. 5.
- *Tai Ji Wen: The Principles and Theories for Mastering Taijiquan,* vol. 7.

About the Translator

- *Imagination Becomes Reality: 150-Posture Taijiquan of Master T.T. Liang* (Valley Spirit Arts, 2011).
- *Steal My Art: The Life and Times of Tai Chi Master T.T. Liang* (North Atlantic Books, 2002).
- *T'ai Chi According to the I Ching—Embodying the Principles of the Book of Changes* (Healing Arts Press, 2002).
- *T'ai Chi for Kids: Move with the Animals,* illustrated by Gregory Crawford (Bear Cub Books, 2001).
- *Tai Ji Quan Treatise: Attributed to the Song Dynasty Daoist Priest Zhang Sanfeng,* Daoist Immortal Three Peaks Zhang Series (Valley Spirit Arts, 2011).
- *The Wind Sweeps Away the Plum Blossoms: Yang Style Taijiquan Staff and Spear Techniques* (Valley Spirit Arts, 2011).

Kung Fu Books
- *The Complete Guide to Northern Praying Mantis Kung Fu* (Blue Snake Books, 2010).
- *The Eighteen Lohan Skills: Traditional Shaolin Temple Kung Fu Training Methods* (Valley Spirit Arts, 2015).

Refining the Elixir

CD and Downloadable Audio Recordings

- *Book of Tao and Virtue Contemplation Meditations* (CD and MP3 versions). Features Stuart Alve Olson's translation and narration of Lao Zi's *Tao De Jing* as it appears in the book *Taoist Chanting and Recitation*. The background music is by Deni Gendron, a longtime student of Stuart's. The two tracks comprise the *Book of Tao* (chapters 1 thru 37) and the *Book of Virtue* (chapters 38 thru 81). Each track can be used in separate meditation sessions that run about 40 minutes.

- *Setting Up the Foundation* (Instructional Recordings). Includes instructions on the different breathing techniques used for stimulating the qi for completion of the Lesser Heavenly Circuit. Details on understanding the stages of Three in Front, Three on the Back; 36 and 24 Breaths; and Realizing the Dan Tian are given.

- *Yellow Court Scripture* (Course Recordings). The information in these 70 audio recordings is simply not attainable anywhere else. Recorded from online classes that Stuart conducted with a student over a year and a half, this commentary on the *Yellow Court Scripture* touches on Taoist philosophy, meditation, Internal Alchemy, medical qigong, and the spirit world like no other Taoist material provides.

About the Translator

DVDs

- **Chen Kung Series DVDs:** *Taiji Qigong, Taiji Sensing Hands,* and *Taiji Sword, Saber & Staff* (Valley Spirit Arts, 2013–15).
- *Eight Brocades Seated Qigong Exercises* (Valley Spirit Arts, 2012). Companion DVD to the book *Qigong Teachings of a Taoist Immortal.*
- *Healing Tigress Exercises* (Valley Spirit Arts, 2011).
- *Li Qingyun's Eight Brocades* (Valley Spirit Arts, 2014). Companion DVD to the book *The Immortal.*
- *Master T.T. Liang's 150-Posture Yang Style T'ai Chi Ch'uan Form* (Valley Spirit Arts, 2014).
- *Master T.T. Liang Taijiquan Demonstrations* (Valley Spirit Arts, 2014).
- *Tai Ji Quan Self-Defense Instructional Program* (3-DVD Set) (Valley Spirit Arts, 2011).
- *Tiger's Waist: Daoist Qigong Restoration* (Valley Spirit Arts, 2009).
- *Wind & Dew* (Valley Spirit Arts, 2012). This version of Wind & Dew was designed to work in conjunction with the Eight Brocades DVD (also the Li Qingyun version). All three DVDs also work with the teachings in the Setting Up the Foundation Audio Recordings.

Visit the Shop at Valley Spirit Arts for more information: www.valleyspiritarts.com/shop/

About the Publisher

Valley Spirit Arts offers books and DVDs on Taoism, Taijiquan, and meditation practices primarily from author Stuart Alve Olson, longtime student of Master T.T. Liang and translator of many Taoist related works.

Its website provides teachings on meditation and Internal Alchemy, Taijiquan, Qigong, and Kung Fu through workshops, private and group classes, and online courses and consulting.

For more information as well as updates on Stuart Alve Olson's upcoming projects and events, please visit: www.valleyspiritarts.com.

About the Sanctuary of Tao

The Sanctuary of Tao is a nonprofit organization dedicated to the sharing of Taoist philosophy and practices through online resources, yearly meditation retreats, and community educational programs. The underlying mission of the Sanctuary of Tao is to bring greater health, longevity, and contentment to its members and everyone it serves.

Please visit www.sanctuaryoftao.org for more information about the organization and its programs.

Made in the USA
Middletown, DE
16 April 2016